Equine Science and Management

EQUINE SCIENCE

AgriScience and Technology Series

Jasper S. Lee, Ph.D.
Series Editor

Interstate Publishers, Inc.
Danville, Illinois

AND MANAGEMENT

Dr. Jerry D. Gibson

Western Regional Agricultural Education Coordinator
North Carolina State University

EQUINE SCIENCE AND MANAGEMENT

Copyright © 1999 by
Interstate Publishers, Inc.

All Rights Reserved / Printed in U.S.A.

Library of Congress Catalog No. 98-73736

ISBN 0-8134-3147-6

1 2 3 4 5 6 7 8 9 10   04 03 02 01 00 99

Order from

Interstate Publishers, Inc.

510 North Vermilion Street
P.O. Box 50
Danville, IL 61834-0050

Phone: (800) 843-4774
Fax. (217) 446-9706
Email: info-ipp@IPPINC.com
World Wide Web: http://www.IPPINC.com

PREFACE

- Equine Science is becoming a very popular subject in schools.
- Textbooks in this subject are either too "deep" or too "abstract."
- This textbook is based on a curriculum analysis that determined the content of this book. The competencies and objectives are based on needs as determined by a core group of professions in the fields of equine science, education, research, child development, agribusiness, and employability.
- This textbook fulfills the needs of students, teachers, and other individuals in the field of equine science.

Equine Science and Management was written with students, teachers, parents, college professors, and employers support and approval. The book looks at the history of horses and the value they had to people in the past. It then moves into the present and how the horse industry impacts the economy. Unit Two moves into the science of horses, including anatomy and physiology, nutrition, pasture management, health management, and reproduction and genetics. Unit Three looks at the business of horses, including safety, facilities and equipment, and a chapter on the economics of horses. Unit Four deals with people and horses. Recreational horses are discussed by identifying the breeds including the origin and characteristics. Specialty horses, such as miniature and draft horses, and the business that surrounds them is introduced. One of the most exciting chapters is the one on equine careers. Specific careers and the steps in making the right career decisions, along with preparation, are reviewed. Equitation is the chapter I most enjoyed writing because I love to ride horses. Many topics, such as the steps of preparing for a ride, safety, and cooling horses. Finally, a chapter on leadership and how individuals can get involved with organizations that affect the horse industry.

This book is very contemporary. The objectives, terms, and illustrations in each chapter make learning about horses fun. The questions and discovery section at the end of each chapter will make this book user friendly to everyone.

ABOUT THE AUTHOR

The author of Equine Science and Management is Jerry D. Gibson. Dr. Gibson is a member of the Faculty at North Carolina State University and serves as Associate Graduate Faculty and Regional Agricultural Education Coordinator. He earned his B.S. in animal science from Virginia Polytechnic Institute and State University. He earned the M.S., C.A.G.S., and the Doctorate of Education from Virginia Polytechnic Institute and State University in Agricultural Education. The author has experience with all animals, but horses have always been a big part of his life.

Dedicated to *my wife, Elizabeth, and my daughter, Hayleigh,* who put daily sunshine into my life. Also to *my father,* who taught me the love of horses.

ACKNOWLEDGMENTS

The author of *Equine Science and Management* would like to show appreciation to the many people that made this book possible. These individuals helped the author see different perspectives of the horse industry as well as the unique way students learn. This team made the book become a reality for the many students interested in horses.

Information was provided from a wide source of individuals. To everyone that helped produce this book, thank you! Although everyone cannot be acknowledged, here are a few key individuals that contributed.

I would like to express my appreciation to—

- My wife, Elizabeth, who's patience and support made this book possible
- My three year old daughter, Hayleigh, who will read this book one day and ask many questions
- My colleagues in the Agriculture and Extension Education Department at North Carolina State University for their support and contributions
- The Animal Science Department at North Carolina State University for their expertise and support to this book
- Dr. Jasper Lee for his support and for his friendship
- Interstate Publishers for the opportunity to write this textbook

Additionally, thank you, to these individuals who provided invaluable information throughout the writing of this book—

- Mr. Carroll Parker, agriculture teacher, Brevard High, North Carolina
- Mr. Harvey Franklin, agriculture teacher, Madison High, North Carolina

- Mr. Chuck Michel, agriculture teacher, Madison High, North Carolina
- Mr. Arlen Johnson, agriculture teacher, East Randolph High, North Carolina
- Mr. Larry Daniels, agriculture teacher, Sampson County, North Carolina
- Mr. Tony Sedberry, agriculture teacher, East Montgomery High, North Carolina
- Mr. Mike Yoder, Equine Instructor, NC State University
- Dr. Robert Mowrey, Equine Specialist, NC State University
- Mr. David McGlothin, Harris Farms, Coalinga, California
- Mr. Robert Moss, agriculture teacher, Tazewell High, Virginia
- Dr. Melissa Hower-Moritz, Equine Science Department, University of Minnesota, Crookston
- Dr. Arden Huff, Equine Specialist (retired) Virginia Tech
- Mr. Kyle Sanders, agriculture teacher, Harrisburg, Arkansas
- American Quarter Horse Association, Amarillo, Texas
- American Morgan Horse Association, Shelburne, Vermont
- American Saddlebred Horse Association, Lexington, Kentucky
- American Paint Horse Association, Fort Worth, Texas
- American Donkey and Mule Society, Inc., Denton, Texas
- American Shire Association, Adel, Iowa
- American Miniature Horse Association, Columbus, Ohio
- Tennessee Walking Hose Breeders' and Exhibitors' Association, Lewisburg, Tennessee
- Southwest Spanish Mustang Association, Finley, Oklahoma
- United States Trotting Association, Columbus, Ohio
- The Jockey Club, New York, New York
- Lucky Three Ranch, Loveland, Colorado
- Veterinary Medical Center, Texas A&M University
- National FFA Organization, Indianapolis, Indiana

And finally, to my father, who passed away while I was writing this book. He taught me the love of horses!

CONTENTS

Preface v
Acknowledgments vii

UNIT ONE —
HORSES AND TODAY'S SOCIETY

Chapter 1   History and Development of
            the Horse Industry 1
Chapter 2   Equine Science Industry and Technology 15

UNIT TWO —
PRINCIPLES OF EQUINE SCIENCE

Chapter 3   Biology of the Horse 25
Chapter 4   Nutrition. 47
Chapter 5   Pasture Management 69
Chapter 6   Health Management 79
Chapter 7   Reproduction 103

UNIT THREE —
THE BUSINESS OF HORSES

Chapter 8   Facilities and Equipment. 119
Chapter 9   Safe Management and Handling. 133
Chapter 10   The Economics of Horses 151
Chapter 11   Recreational Horses 161

Chapter 12	Specialty Horses and Related Species	181
Chapter 13	Careers in Equine Science	193
Chapter 14	The Horse Racing Industry	209
Chapter 15	Equitation	221
Chapter 16	Citizenship, Leadership, and Organizations	235

APPENDIXES

Appendix A	Useful Web Sites for Having Fun with Horses	245
Appendix B	Names and Addresses of Selected Horse Breeding Associations and Other Organizations	247
Appendix C	Care of the Mare and Foal	251
Appendix D	Gestation Table	256
Appendix E	Using Body Measurements to Estimate Weight	257
Appendix F	Common Weight Conversions and Equivalents Used in Equine Science	258
Appendix G	Common Volume Measures Used in Equine Science	259
Appendix H	Weight Measures Commonly Used in Equine Science	260

Glossary 261
Bibliography 275
Index 277

1

HISTORY AND DEVELOPMENT OF THE HORSE INDUSTRY

Horses have been part of human life for hundreds of years. They have served many purposes. Horses have provided power for transportation and to pull plows, hay-making equipment, and other implements. Horses have been used for recreation, including pleasure riding and showing. Billions of dollars are spent each year on racing, showing, and hauling horses and on the necessary feed and equipment.

Horses are important in many ways. We use terms associated with the horse industry without thinking of their origin. The term "horsepower" is used with engines. The uses of horses your family owns today differ from the ways horses were used by your parents or grandparents when they were in school. Learning about horses is fun and exciting regardless of your area of interest.

1-1. Horses are part of today's society. These young people enjoy a daily ride.

OBJECTIVES

This chapter examines the history and development of the horse industry. The objectives of this chapter are as follows:

1. Describe the types of horses based on use
2. Explain major developments in the history of horse production
3. Discuss how the horse got to North America

TERMS

agribusiness
breeding horse
draft horse
Eohippus
equine
Equus
evolution
Merychippus
Mesohippus
Parahippus
pleasure horse
Pliohippus
specialty horse
work horse

EQUINE KNOWLEDGE

Today's horse can be traced to an animal that had four toes and was the size of a dog.

History and Development of the Horse Industry

1-2. Horses in separate paddocks.

TYPES OF HORSES

The horse industry is a growing, dynamic area. It includes the major uses of horses: pleasure riding, show horses, work horses, breeding horses, and specialty horses. The businesses around the production of horses, such as feeding, health, equipment, training, and marketing, are also in the horse industry.

Horses are animals that are owned by many different people for many different reasons. They are sometimes called *equine* and are kept in many different environments from large farms with paddocks, pasture, and assorted barns to backyard pasture lots and small barns. Horses can be kept with

1-3. FFA and 4-H members riding pleasure horses.

Table 1-1
Important Horse Terms

Broodmare—mare kept for breeding purposes.

Colt—young stallion under three years of age (four years with Thoroughbreds).

Dam—female parent.

Donkey—beast of burden in the same family as the horse and often known as an ass; scientific name is *Equus asinus*.

Filly—young, immature female horse.

Foal—unweaned young horse of either gender.

Foaling—act of a mare giving birth.

Gelding—male horse castrated prior to sexual maturity.

Hack—horse used for riding on trails and roads; poor quality horse.

Horse breeder—owner of the dam at the time of breeding and the individual responsible for selecting the sire.

Jockey—professional horse rider in races.

Juvenile—horse that is two years old.

Mare—mature female horse four years of age or older (five years with Thoroughbreds).

Mule—the hybrid offspring of a jackass and a mare.

Mustang—horse native to the Western plains of the United States and largely of Spanish breeding.

Pair—term describing two horses ridden side-by-side or hitched together.

Pinto—multi-colored spotted horse.

Plug—horse of poor conformation and common breeding; an old, worn-out horse.

Pony—horse less than 58 inches (14-2 hands) height at the withers.

Sire—male parent.

Stag—male horse castrated after reaching sexual maturity.

Stallion—male horse over four years of age (five years with Thoroughbreds)

Stud (or stud horse)—a stallion used for breeding purposes.

Yearling—a young horse more than one year old but less than two.

History and Development of the Horse Industry

other livestock and are good companions to many different animal species. Horses are multi-purpose animals and have a wide range of uses.

PLEASURE HORSES

Pleasure horses are used for personal enjoyment and include different breeds and types of horses. Personal enjoyment may include trail riding, pleasure riding, group riding, wagon trains, parades, and family affairs. Pleasure horses are a growing industry nationwide. There are a large number of adult and youth activities in 4-H and FFA that involve pleasure horses.

WORK HORSES

Work horses are strong animals used to pull heavy loads, plow, and do many other physical activities. Work horses are a part of history that has affected everyone. Even in modern society, people use horses for work. The Amish continue to use horses in farming, for transportation and business, and for pleasure. Horses have been used to plow fields, mow hay, pull logs, work in coal mines, and pull wagons for transportation. *Draft horses* are a large breed of horses used for work, such as pulling a carriage. Work horse breeds continue to be produced and are used in a variety of ways.

1-4. Draft horses are large horses that stand 14-2 to 17-2 hands, weigh 1400 pounds or more, and are used for work.

BREEDING HORSES

Breeding horses exist for the purpose of producing offspring with certain genetics. The business of breeding has been a vital part of the horse industry for many years. Today, horse breeding is a billion dollar industry that involves all breeds of horses. People breed horses for the purposes of business, for a selection of specific animals with specific traits, and other reasons. Horse breeding is basically the process of selecting a male and female animal with particular characteristics, choosing a method of breeding, and implementing the breeding process. Some well-known horses of specific breeds are highlighted in the following table.

Table 1-2
Examples of Breeding Horses

Breed	Horse's Name
Thoroughbred	Seattle Slew
	Ruffian
	Secretariat
	Petrone
	Boldwood
Standardbred	Hambletonian 10
	Nevele Pride
	Greyhound
	Steady Star
	Bret Hanover
	Dan Patch
Quarter Horse	Wimpy P-1
	Deck Jack
Morgan	Tara's Delight
American Saddle Horse	Plainview's Julia
	Wing Commander
	Will Shriver

Breeds and names courtesy of Thoroughbred, Quarter Horse, and Standardbred breeds associations.

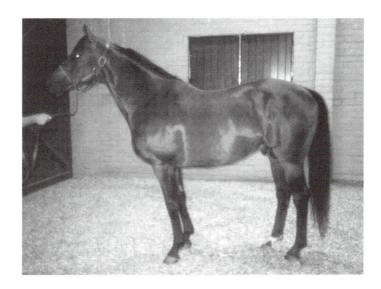

1-5. A breeding stallion. (Courtesy, Harris Farms, California)

SPECIALTY HORSES

Specialty horses are used in nontraditional ways because of their unique traits. One example is the miniature horse. Miniature horses are a growing part of the horse industry. Breeding, feeding, healthcare, facilities, and management businesses that serve the Miniature horse have flourished in the past decade. Associations have been formed specifically for Miniature horses. Many activities, such as shows and sales, are held in this specialized area of equine production.

1-6. Quarter Horses are popular for a variety of uses. (Courtesy, American Quarter Horse Association)

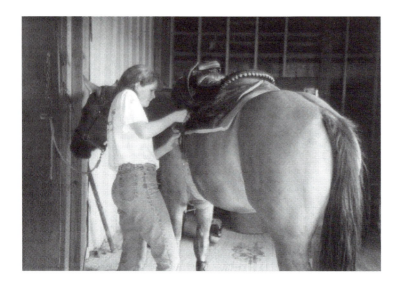

1-7. A saddle, bridle, and blanket, represent needed equipment.

HISTORY OF HORSES

Horses represent a multi-billion dollar, worldwide industry. The development of the horse industry began with the initial ownership of the animal. This was followed by obtaining feed. The proper facilities were required, which usually consisted of a barn or shed, pasture with some type of fence, and a water supply. To use the horse for riding, supplies were needed—saddles, bridles, saddlebags, saddle blanket, horseshoes, etc. To use the horse for

1-8. Barrel racing is a popular activity with some horse owners. (Courtesy, American Paint Horse Association)

work or as transportation, supplies were needed—a carriage, buggy, wagon, sleigh, plow, etc. Breeding and maintaining the health of the horse required either supplies or professional health care.

AGRIBUSINESS AND HORSES

The basic expenses of owning a horse have not changed. These expenses are the foundation in which agribusiness is centered. **Agribusiness is the business that surrounds agriculture**. There are many jobs directly or indirectly related to horses. Can you name some of these jobs? Does a member of your family work in a job related to the horse industry? Although the role of horses has changed, they are very important to the agribusiness industry.

EARLY HISTORY

The modern horse began as a primitive four-toed animal, which was about the size of a small dog (10 inches high). This horse had little resemblance to the horse of today. The Greek term for this horse is **Eohippus**. From the era of Eohippus to the Quarter horse of today, there were many changes in size and shape. The second stage of equine **evolution, the process of change over many years**, was a three-toed horse called **Mesohippus**. This horse was about twice the size (24 inches high) of Eohippus. With further evolution came the three important links to the modern horse. **Parahippus**, the upland horse; **Merychippus**, the desert horse; and **Pliohippus**, the first

1-9. Horses were used many years ago as a source of power to pull farm implements.

1-10. Wild horses in North Carolina.

one-toed horse. With the change in environment came a structural change in the horse. Pliohippus gave rise to Equus or the "True Horse." **Equus** is the typical genus of the contemporary horse family. Today, we use the word Equus in many facets of the horse industry.

HORSES IN NORTH AMERICA

Historians think that Equus originated in North America nearly 60 million years ago and migrated throughout the rest of the world. They also be-

1-11. A market that specializes in horse meat. (Though not widely used for food in North America, France, Italy, and other nations use horses for food. This shows a cheval (French for horse) retail meat counter in an Orleans, France, market. (Courtesy, Jasper S. Lee, Georgia)

lieve that horses became almost extinct about 1 million years ago; however, the reason remains a mystery. Through archeological studies, different types of horse structures have been found to verify the existence of the species. Horses were reintroduced to North America as mounts of the Spanish conquistadors. Wild mustangs roamed the west by the 1800s. Pioneers, explorers, American Indians, and others caught horses to use for many purposes, such as working, riding, selling, and other uses. The East Coast Indians used horses from the Spanish introduction. The colonists brought many horses to the new land and introduced many of the modern breeds we know.

After the new world was founded and began to prosper, the demand for horses increased. Therefore, the Morgan, American Saddlebred, Tennessee Walker, and others were developed to meet the needs—working, pleasure, sports, etc. Our changing environment makes the survival of wild horses more difficult. Herds of wild horses on the coast of North Carolina, Virginia, and Maryland are shrinking. Wild horses in the West are having problems too and horse lovers have developed adoption programs nationwide. Horse owners must take steps to preserve the history and heritage of horses in North America.

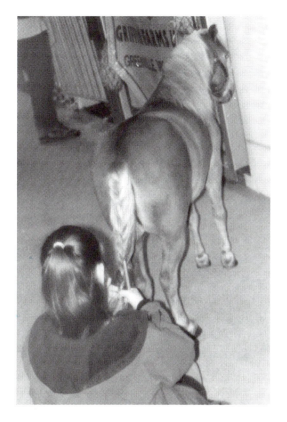

1-12. Grooming horses can be fun. (Courtesy, Jasper S. Lee, Georgia)

EQUINE KNOWLEDGE

Wild horses still run free in a few areas on the coast of Virginia, Maryland, and North Carolina.

REVIEWING

MAIN IDEAS

Horses have been a part of society for many years. The study of evolution places horses on the North American continent over 60 million years ago. Evidence suggests the horse became extinct in North America and was reintroduced by the Spanish and other settlers. After the establishment of new settlements in America, many new breeds of horses were developed to meet the needs of the new world.

The many purposes of horses have ranged from transportation, to working the fields, to pleasure riding, and the related businesses built around the industry. Horses in America are a multi-billion dollar industry, which includes feed, equipment, facilities, health care and products, assorted supplies, breeding, buying, and selling.

Americans today are somewhat uninformed about the importance of the horse industry. The perception regarding horses is that the industry is strictly for pleasure. However, if you evaluate the jobs related to the industry along with the amount of income from the previously mentioned areas, the industry is as viable as any of the more traditional animal science areas. Horses are kept for sport, business, and/or pleasure with various combinations of interests.

There are many opportunities for entrepreneurs in horse production and the industry. These jobs are at all levels of education. Many are available for students in high school and after graduation. Even more jobs are available for students at all levels of higher education.

Horse science and production is an industry of professionals that deal with animal husbandry skills, science skills, business skills, human relation skills, and animal well-being. Equine science offers fascinating career opportunities for students of all backgrounds.

QUESTIONS

Answer the following questions using correct spelling and complete sentences.

1. What is the horse industry? *growing dynamic area*
2. What are the major developments in the history of horse production?
feeding, health, equipment, training, marketing.

History and Development of the Horse Industry

3. What is a draft horse? **large breed of horse used for work.**
4. What are the four uses of horses? Briefly explain each. **Pleasure, work, specialty, breeding**
5. How did horses get to North America? **mounts for spanish conquistadors.**
6. How is the horse industry related to agribusiness? **the expences are centered on agribusiness**

EVALUATING

CHAPTER SELF-CHECK

Match the term with the correct definition. Place the letter by the term in the blank provided.

- a. equine
- b. evolution
- c. Equus
- d. agribusiness
- e. Eohippus
- f. Pliohippus
- g. pleasure horse
- h. work horse

c 1. The genus of the horse family.
g 2. A horse used for personal enjoyment.
f 3. The first one-toed ancestor to the modern-day horse.
e 4. A small, primitive, four-toed ancestor to the modern-day horse.
b 5. The process of change over many years.
a 6. A horse—also the name of a popular magazine.
d 7. The business that surrounds agriculture.
h 8. A strong horse used to plow, pull, and perform other physical activities.

DISCOVERING

1. As a class project, take a field trip to a horse farm. Study the goals of the farm and the characteristics of the farming operation. Prepare a short essay on your visit. Deliver an oral report to the class.

2. Collect information on how the horse industry has changed over the last hundred years. Look at the characteristics of today's horse industry. Compare the two eras of horse production. Prepare a short essay on the results of your work. Deliver an oral report to the class.

3. Examine how horses are linked to agribusiness. Identify specific jobs related to horses. Conduct a shadowing experience with a person who performs one of the identified jobs. Interview the supervisor of the shadowing experience. Prepare a short essay on the results of your shadowing experience. Deliver an oral report to the class.

4. Complete the following survey. Indicate your level of interest in each activity by checking either high, medium, or low. Discuss your results with your teacher and parents. This assessment should be helpful in planning your involvement in current and future activities with the horse industry.

My Interest in Horses

The areas and levels of my interest in horses are:

	HIGH	MEDIUM	LOW
RIDING HORSES	X		
FEEDING HORSES		X	
GROOMING HORSES	X		
SHOWING HORSES	X		
TRAINING HORSES	X		
BREEDING HORSES	X		
EXAMINING HORSES		X	
STUDYING HORSES	X		

After completing the survey, summarize your responses. Which areas were "high"? Which were "low"? Do you think your responses will change after studying about horses? yes

2
EQUINE SCIENCE INDUSTRY AND TECHNOLOGY

Horses are an important part of the United States' animal industry. Although some countries rely on horses as food animals, we do not consider them as a source of food. However, we use horses for many purposes that contribute to the animal industry.

The horse feed industry, for example, generates millions of dollars each year. Horses eat a considerable amount of feed, which includes grain and hay, on a daily basis. Other feed additives, such as minerals, contribute to agriculture economics. The producers of these feedstuffs benefit from this market. Another source of activity is the sale of equipment, such as saddles, bridles, blankets, horse trailers, and trucks.

2-1. Many young people ride horses for pleasure, which in turn supports the animal industry.

OBJECTIVES

This chapter explores the economic contributions and opportunities within the horse industry. The objectives of this chapter are as follows:

1. Explain the role of horses in the animal industry
2. Describe the scope of horses in the United States
3. Explain responsibility and ownership of horses
4. Explain the meaning of horse and animal well-being

TERMS

animal agriculture
animal industry
feed
grain
marketing
responsibility
tack
well-being

EQUINE KNOWLEDGE

A 1,000 pound horse will eat about 30 pounds of feed (hay and grain) per day.

THE ROLE OF HORSES IN THE ANIMAL INDUSTRY

The *animal industry* is all of the activities in producing, buying, selling, and managing animals and the related products and services. Horses have always had important roles in the animal industry. The economic opportunity, with its creation of jobs in the animal industry, due to horses is enormous.

WHY WE HAVE HORSES

Reasons for having horses today are much different from those of the past. Horses were once needed for work and transportation. Today, machinery has replaced most of these uses. We now use horses primarily for pleasure. Showing, racing, and riding are among the purposes of the modern-day horse. Horses have a rich history in America, and they are fun! They have something to offer everyone.

ANIMAL AGRICULTURE

Animal agriculture is the production and marketing of animals. It is one part of the animal industry. For the most part, these animals are produced for human food, though that is not the case with horses. Because horses are not used for food in the United States, many people believe that horses are not

2-2. Pleasure riding is one of the most common purposes of the modern-day horse.

2-3. A horse should be examined to determine its age and health condition before it is bought.

important in animal agriculture. However, upon reviewing the facts, you will find that horses contribute many millions of dollars to animal agriculture. Depending on the level of activity, a horse consumes several pounds of feed and several pounds of hay per day. This alone is a major contribution to animal agriculture. The *tack* (horse equipment, such as saddles and bridles, trailers, and trucks) represents a large amount of money. *Marketing* is the activity of buying or selling. Buying and selling horses is an additional economic aspect of the animal industry.

THE FEED INDUSTRY

Feed is a material that an animal eats for growth, repair, energy, and the maintenance of life. Different animals convert feed at different percentages of efficiency. Because horses are not considered meat animals, they are monitored more for performance purposes. *Grain* is the small, hard seed or fruit produced by cereal plants, such as corn, wheat, oats, and barley. Horses eat feeds made from grains, protein supplements, and other additives, such as molasses. Because horses have the ability to digest roughage, with the enlarged cecum in the small intestine, they eat much hay and grass.

The feed industry is a multi-million dollar industry, which includes production, processing, buying, and selling. New products are continuously developed. Ways to market those products to new and existing customers are explored. The feed industry has a great future and helps the total agriculture industry.

THE EQUIPMENT INDUSTRY

When horses are used for work, harnesses, plows, and different implements are required. When horses are used for transportation, a wide variety of buggies, wagons, carriages, and special hauling rigs are required.

The equipment used today differs from that of the past, but the need for equipment is still viable. Many different saddles, bridles, blankets, shoes, and halters are available to horse owners. The type of equipment needed depends on the type of horse and type of riding. Look at the different types of uses—showing, trail riding, pleasure riding, competitive events, racing, breeding, etc.—and begin to develop a list of equipment needs. You will very quickly see how large and important horse production is to the equipment industry.

2-4. Horse trailers are used to transport horses from one location to another.

THE ANIMAL HEALTH INDUSTRY

Health care is an on-going process and is one of the most important components of horse production. There are two types of health care: preventive and treatment. There are numerous people involved with health care. These include veterinarians, vet technicians, farm managers, pharmaceutical sales people, and horse owners. In addition, there is a large market for health supplies. Although only veterinarians can prescribe drugs, there are many types of health care products that horse owners can purchase and use—dewormers is one example. Equine health care is a vital and important part of the horse industry and the animal industry.

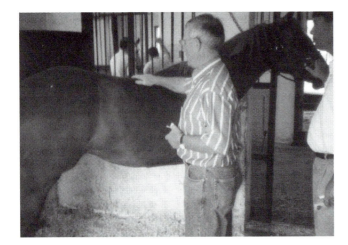

2-5. Veterinarian conducting a health check on a horse.

THE SCOPE OF HORSES IN THE UNITED STATES

The horse industry in the United States is a growing industry. It involves many components mentioned earlier in this chapter. The history of the horse industry shows that the purposes may have changed somewhat over the years, but the interest continues to increase. However, the change in technology over the last several decades caused a decrease in the number of horses in the United States. The number of horses during the early 1900s was approximately 20 million. In the late 1970s, data revealed that the number of horses had dropped to less than 6 million. Today, there are approximately 6.6 million horses in the United States.

The average horse owner spends over $2,500 per year on each horse. Although many horses are used for work and working livestock, the bulk of horses owned in today's society are for pleasure. The industry certainly has numerous horses in the racing arena as well as the show ring, but the U. S. Department of Agriculture census indicates the largest component of horse production is the pleasure horse. Racing, show and sport horses, however, provide for a huge and varied business industry.

THE RESPONSIBILITIES OF HORSE OWNERSHIP

Responsibility is the act of being responsible. Owning a horse is a very big responsibility for several reasons. First, as a horse owner, you are responsible for everything in the horse's life. This includes what and when the horse eats, how much exercise the horse receives, the type of environment in which the horse lives, the type of vaccinations and health care the horse receives, and especially the kind of "TLC" (tender loving care) the horse receives. There are too many cases where people buy a horse with the intention of giving it great daily care, but after the new wears off and the chores of feeding, and exercising continue, the horse begins to get neglected. Eventually, the horse either gets sold or just maintained with very poor care.

The daily attention a horse receives is the most important aspect of the responsibility of a horse owner. Horses are just like any other animal.

2-6. Young people often enjoy feeding and grooming horses.

They need daily care and attention from the owner. If a potential owner cannot give daily care and attention, he or she should not become the owner of an animal. Remember, you are in control of the animal's life. The horse must have food and water on a regular basis just like humans.

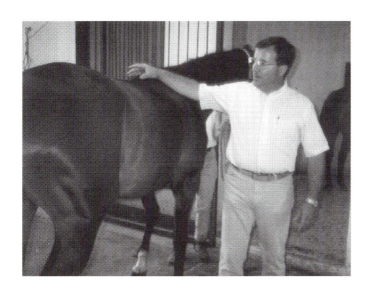

2-7. Examining a horse to determine its condition.

ANIMAL WELL-BEING

Well-being is providing care for a horse so that its basic needs are met without injury to its health. To insure an animal's well-being you are obligated to provide the animal with the best possible care every day. The areas of care include feeding, health, exercise, environment, and daily attention.

Horses are just like other animals in regards to care. The owner should know the things involved in animal well-being before becoming an owner. Horses that are underfed, overfed, not given adequate health care, required to live in an environment less than standard, and not given daily attention are being abused. Adequate shelter, exercise, and hoof care are important. There are numerous places that can provide help and training in all the areas mentioned. The Cooperative Extension Service, local veterinarian, local agriculture teacher, horse and pony clubs, and private stables are available.

It is important to understand animal well-being with horses not only to become a better horse owner but to serve as a steward to the industry as well.

2-8. The University of Minnesota's Equine Facility in Crookston, Minnesota, provides education and research to support the equine industry. (Courtesy, Jasper S. Lee, Georgia)

REVIEWING

MAIN IDEAS

Horses are an important part of the animal industry. Because horses are not used for food in the United States, some individuals believe they do not have a true role in the animal industry. However, the importance of horses to the total animal industry is evident in the important role they play in so many aspects of production.

Equine Science Industry and Technology

The feed industry provides millions of dollars to the agriculture economy in the United States each year. The components of the feed industry include, farmers, feed dealers, equipment production and sales, and all the individual retail outlets for feed.

Other linkages that connect horses to the agribusiness industry include equipment production and sales, such as saddles, bridles, blankets and other riding gear, horse trailers, and trucks.

The health industry is one of the larger connections. Horse care from veterinarians, technicians or owners, and animal health products, such as dewormers, antibiotics, vitamins, and minerals, are just a few.

In general, the horse industry contributes millions of dollars to the national, state, and local economy. It is important that the horse industry be seen as a vital partner to the total agribusiness community. Please talk to your teacher and investigate the contribution horses make to your local community.

QUESTIONS

Answer the following questions using correct spelling and complete sentences.

1. Explain the role of horses in the animal industry. *economic opportunity w/ certin jobs.*
2. Describe the scope of horses in the United States. *millions of dollers*
3. Explain the responsibility of horse ownership. *high matinence*
4. Explain animal well-being. *The state of being well*
5. What is animal agriculture? *marketing animals.*

EVALUATING

CHAPTER SELF-CHECK

Match the term with the correct definition. Place the letter by the term in the blank provided.

- a. animal agriculture
- b. tack
- c. responsibility
- d. grain
- e. well-being
- f. marketing
- g. animal industry
- h. feed

24   EQUINE SCIENCE AND MANAGEMENT

__e__ 1. The state of being well.

__a__ 2. The production and marketing of animals.

__h__ 3. The material an animal eats for growth, repair, energy, and the maintenance of life.

__f__ 4. The activity of buying or selling.

__d__ 5. The seed of any cereal plant, such as corn, wheat, oats, barley, etc.

__c__ 6. The act of being responsible.

__b__ 7. Horse equipment, such as saddles and bridles.

__g__ ~~[illegible]~~ 8. The buying, selling, and management of animals and the products and services related to those activities.

DISCOVERING

1. As a class project, visit a horse farm. Examine the relationship the horse farm has to the entire animal industry. Prepare a short essay on the data you obtain from the owner on your visit or inquiry. Deliver an oral report to the class.

2. Collect information on the horse industry for the entire United States. Collect horse information on your home state and compare the trends of state to national. Prepare a bar graph or pie chart illustrating the scope of the horse industry both state and nationwide.

3. Visit a horse owner and discuss the responsibilities involved with owning a horse. Prepare a short essay on the items you identify that are important to anyone that owns or plans to own a horse. Deliver an oral report to the class.

4. Visit a horse owner and discuss the concept of animal well-being. Prepare a short essay on the things you discover about being a good animal owner. Outline those things you find that are not representative of good animal well-being. Deliver the outline to the class in the form of an oral presentation.

5. Using a variety of resources (World Wide Web, U. S. Department of Agriculture, cooperative extension, etc.), collect data that indicates the economic importance of the horse industry to the total animal science arena. Prepare you report using either bar graphs, or pie charts. Deliver the information to the class in the form of an oral presentation.

6. Write a breeds association and request materials about their breed.

3

BIOLOGY OF THE HORSE

Horse biology is fun! ***Biology*** is the study of life. Studying equine science, the biology of horses, is somewhat different from the study of humans. The biology of horses deals with all aspects of what makes horses live. This includes both the internal and external parts of the horse.

The biology of the horse relates to the physical condition of the animal, which is so critical in performance events. It also connects the major parts of the horse and their functions to specific uses, such as racing, showing, trail riding, and work; and to the animal's physical appearance. In addition, horses are kept for athletic performance.

3-1. Learning biology is fun and horses are great animals to study this science.

OBJECTIVES

To better understand the biology of the horse, the following objectives are included:

1. List the scientific name of the horse
2. Name the major external parts of a horse
3. Name the systems of a horse and describe the functions of each
4. Describe the importance of newborn foal health
5. Explain important factors in body condition
6. Describe how teeth are used in determining the age of a horse
7. Identify four measures used in determining the size of a horse

TERMS

anatomy
biology
bones
circulation
colostrum
conformation
dermatology
digestion
genotype
hormone
January 1 birth date
kinesiology
muscle
nervous system
phenotype
physiology
respiration

EQUINE KNOWLEDGE

Horses can eat hay and grasses because they have an enlarged cecum. They do not have a ruminant stomach. Horses may be classified as nonruminant herbivores.

HORSE BIOLOGY

Horse biology deals with the unique characteristics of the species. This includes the various systems that make the life of a horse possible. These systems in horses differ from those of other farm animals. Biology also deals with the reproduction of the horse. This includes new and innovative ways to conceive and transfer genetic materials from parents to offspring.

In addition, biology deals with the genetics of horses, including phenotype and genotype. **Phenotype** is the physical or outward appearance of an animal. This includes its size, color, and overall body appearance. **Genotype** is the genetic makeup of an animal. This includes its heredity and traits inherited from its parents and likelihood of passing traits to future offspring.

SCIENTIFIC CLASSIFICATION

Horse biology also includes the scientific classification of horses. Scientific classification is based on similarities and differences with other species. The process of classification has resulted in all living things having scientific names. Horses are no different in that they have a scientific name, but their name is different from any other species. The scientific name of the horse is *Equus caballus*. The scientific name is sometimes used in literature about horses.

The ass is in the same family with the horse. Distinction between the ass and horse is evident in the ass's scientific name: *Equus asinus*. Asses are typ-

3-2. A donkey on the research farm of Virginia Tech. (Courtesy, Jasper S. Lee, Georgia)

3-3. A mule pulling a two-wheeled cart. (Mules are said to make wonderful driving animals as individuals or as teams.) (Courtesy, The American Donkey and Mule Society)

ically smaller than horses when mature size has been reached. The male ass (jackass) can be mated with a mare to produce a hybrid offspring known as a mule. Mules have certain qualities of both horses and asses, such as the ability of a horse to pull a heavy load and the ability of the ass to exert effort over a longer time than a horse. Small asses are sometimes known as donkeys.

EXTERNAL PARTS

It is important to know the major external parts of a horse. Many aspects of horse selection, training, care, and health are related to the appearance of external parts. Figure 3-4 shows the major external parts of a horse.

THE SYSTEMS

Anatomy is the science of the structure of a plant or animal. *Physiology* is the study of the function of the body. The horse's body is made of complex systems. It is important to understand the structure and function, which will result in better management and care of the animal. Anatomy and physiology are the sciences of the relationships between the different parts of the horse. The body of the horse consist of the following parts and systems:

1. Skeletal system (bones and cartilage)
2. Muscular system

Biology of the Horse

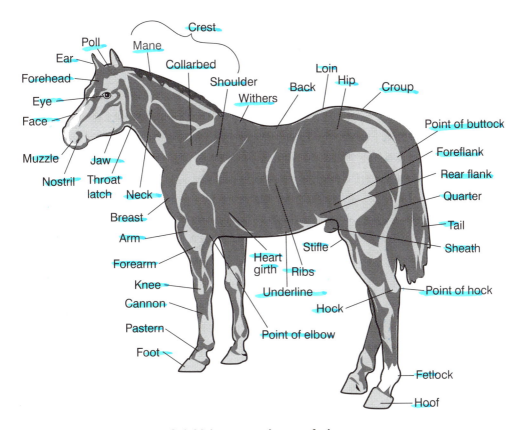

3-4. Major external parts of a horse.

3. Respiratory system (lungs and air movement)
4. Circulatory system (heart and vessels)
5. Digestive system
6. Nervous system (brain, spine, nerves, and senses)
7. Endocrine system (ductless glands and chemical control of the body)
8. Reproductive system (ovaries, testicles, and other organs)
9. Dermatological system (skin)

SKELETAL (BONES)

Bones are the separate parts of the hard tissue that forms the skeleton of most full-grown animals. The bone structure of the horse is very complicated. The bones in the trunk (skull, spinal column, ribs, and breastbone) and legs are connected by ligaments. The skeletal system is most important

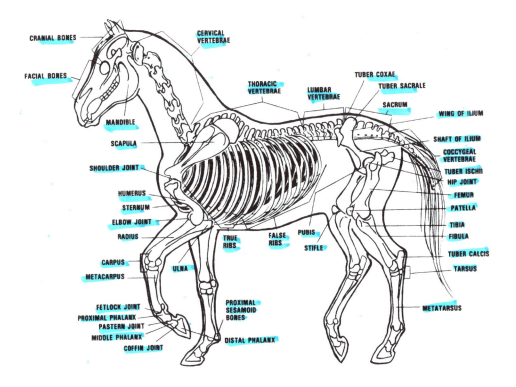

3-5. Skeleton of a horse.

because the horse is used for strenuous activities, such as carrying heavy loads. Bones give the body a shape and protect internal organs. In addition, the bones store minerals and red blood cells are formed in the bones. There are 205 bones in the skeleton of the horse. Bones are classified as long, short, flat, and non-formal.

MUSCULAR

Muscles are body tissues that contract and expand when stimulated to produce bodily movement. The horse has many muscles that conduct a tremendous amount of work. Because of the size of the animal, muscles make up a large portion of the animal's body. *Kinesiology* is the study of muscles and their movement. There are three types of muscles in a horse's system—smooth, cardiac, or skeletal. Muscles are connected to bone by tendons.

The muscles and functions are:

Biology of the Horse

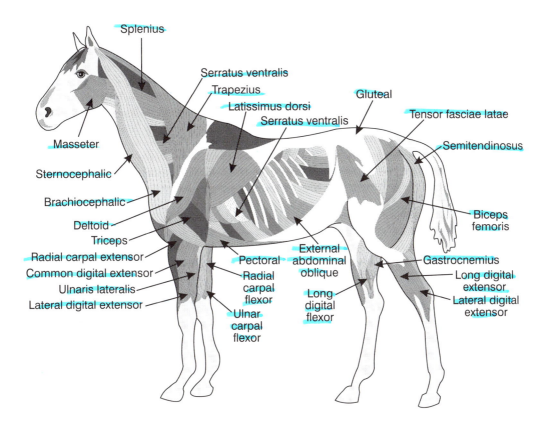

3-6. Muscles of the horse.

- smooth muscles—Smooth muscles are in various organs of the horse's body. Smooth muscles are in the blood vessels, intestines, and walls of the stomach. Smooth muscles function automatically in natural contractions to carry out body processes. These muscles are sometimes known as involuntary muscles because they are not under the conscious control of the brain.

- cardiac muscles—Cardiac muscles are in the heart. They are the major muscles that push blood out of the heart and into the arteries. This causes the blood to circulate throughout the body, bringing nourishing substances to all body cells.

- skeletal muscles—Skeletal muscles give shape to the body of a horse. They hold the bones together and make locomotion (body movement) possible. Such muscles vary greatly in size; muscles around the eyes are quite small while those in the legs are large and strong. Skeletal muscles respond to messages voluntarily sent from the brain, such as when a horse's brain gives the command to move toward the water trough.

RESPIRATORY

Respiration is the act of taking in oxygen and removing carbon dioxide; we think of it as breathing. Oxygen is vital for life. Without the proper amounts of oxygen, the horse will die within minutes. Just as an athlete must have oxygen to survive and to perform, horses must also be able to take in a good supply of oxygen and release carbon dioxide for maximum performance. The major role of the respiratory system is to supply oxygen to body tissue and to remove carbon dioxide. The respiratory system is also important in regulation of body temperature and the elimination of water.

The components of the respiratory system are the:

- nasal cavity—area where air enters; located just past nostrils
- pharynx—portion of the alimentary canal that connects nasal passages and mouth
- larynx—upper part of trachea containing vocal cords
- trachea—passage way between larynx and lungs for passage of air
- bronchi—branches of trachea that extend into the lungs
- lungs—saclike respiratory organs where blood picks up oxygen and releases carbon dioxide

CIRCULATORY

Circulation is movement in a circle or circuit. The movement of blood through the vessels is a result of the heart's pumping action. The body's internal balance is maintained by the circulation of blood. Blood has been called the "seat of the soul" because it bathes the body's tissues with fluids necessary for the support of life. Some of the functions of blood are to:

- transport nutrients
- remove waste products
- transport oxygen
- transport endocrine secretions
- equalize water content
- regulate body temperature
- regulate body acidity
- deliver immune system antibodies
- allergenic reactions

Biology of the Horse

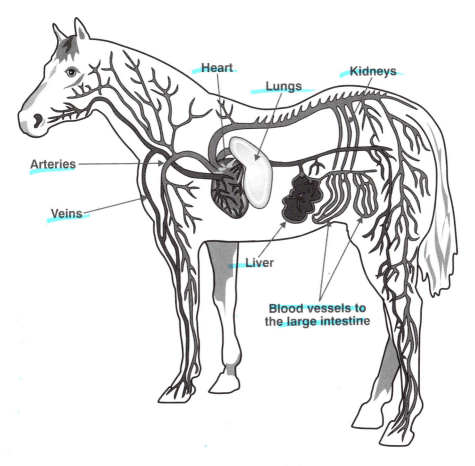

3-7. Circulatory system of a horse.

The circulatory system consists of the:

- heart—a pump
- vessels—movement tubes
- arteries—thick-walled vessels that move blood away from the heart
- arterioles—small arteries
- capillary bed—tissue site of fluid and nutrient exchange
- veins—return blood to the heart

DIGESTIVE

Digestion is the breakdown of foods by the digestive system to allow the nutrients to be utilized by the body. The horse's digestive system is a tube

3-8. Food breakdown in a horse begins in the mouth.

that extends from the mouth to the anus. The tube is approximately 100 feet in length and functions to ingest, grind, mix, digest, and absorb nutrients. It also eliminates the solid waste products. The digestive organs of a horse include the mouth, pharynx, esophagus, stomach, small intestine, cecum, large intestine, and anus.

The first step of the digestive process is to collect the food through the mouth of the horse. Once in the mouth, food is moved through the pharynx through the esophagus to the stomach. When food leaves the stomach, it goes to the small intestine then to the cecum. Since the cecum serves as a stop to breakdown cellulose or roughage, certain kinds of food can spend more time here. The next stop is the large intestine before finally reaching the anus followed by excretion.

Digestion is the process by which a horse takes in food, breaks it down, collects beneficial nutrients, and excretes any waste products. The process is very scientific and begins with the mouth. The horse's teeth begin the breakdown process. While in the mouth, saliva and enzymes begin to breakdown the food. The mixture then goes down the esophagus to the stomach where enzymes and gastric juices further breakdown the food. Most nutrients are collected in the small intestine while the toxic waste products are sent to the liver. The remainder of the solid waste products are sent to the large intestine and finally to the anus for excretion. The digestive process is not totally efficient and does allow some nutrients to be excreted. This is why horse manure can be used for fertilizer on cropland. A unique feature of a horse is that it cannot vomit. Therefore, this affects the management of the horse versus other animals.

Biology of the Horse

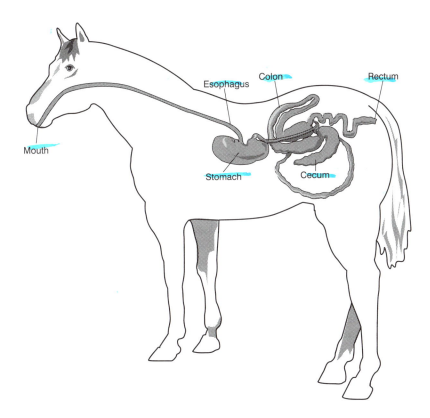

3-9. Equine digestive system.

NERVOUS

The **nervous system** is made up of key components that cause different bodily acts. Horses are controlled by the rider. However, the "control mechanism" inside the horse allows this to happen. The nervous system is a complex set of nerves, organs, and sensory devices that perform in a delicate fashion that allows different behaviors to occur. The central nervous system involves the brain, the brain stem, and the spinal cord. From there, the nervous system has a network of nerves, such as spinal nerves, cranial nerves, and other nerves that either work voluntarily or involuntarily. It is interesting to observe a horse when a fly lands on its head. Watch how it reacts to the stimulus. This is an example of the nervous system working.

The nervous systems divisions are the:

- central nervous system
- peripheral nervous system
- specialized sensory organs

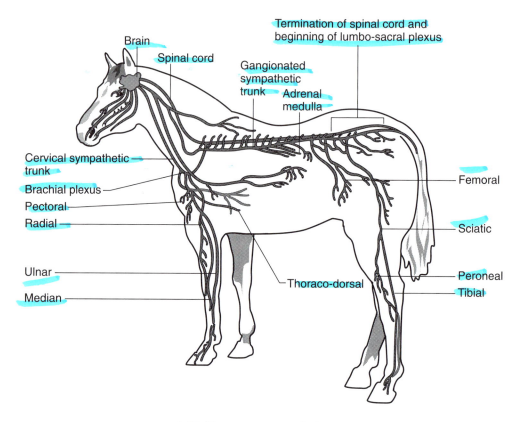

3-10. **Nervous system of a horse.**

The central nervous system consists of the:

- brain
- brain stem
- spinal cord

The peripheral nervous system provides a network of communication between the internal or external environment and the central nervous system. The peripheral system consists of the:

- spinal nerves
- cranial nerves
- sensory ending
- motor ending

The specialized sensory organs consist of the:

- eyes

Biology of the Horse

- ears
- nose

These organs of the nervous system are very important to the internal and external environment of a horse.

The system can also be divided by response. The automatic function controls most body functions.

ENDOCRINE

Hormones are chemicals that are essential for normal growth and development in the body. Hormones are a part of all animals. They are chemicals that the body produces that create a certain response. The best example is testosterone in males and estrogen in females. There are hormones for growth, reproduction, breaking down food, and other bodily functions. This system is called the endocrine system. This system controls such functions as:

- growth
- reproduction
- metabolism
- digestion

REPRODUCTIVE

Reproduction is the process by which offspring are produced. Male and female horses have reproductive organs which make up the reproductive system. The reproductive system is covered in detail in Chapter 7.

DERMATOLOGICAL

Dermatology is the study of the skin and other body covers. It is important to understand the nature and function of the coverings for the following reasons:

- regulates body temperature
- reflects color patterns and other breed characteristics
- protects against disease
- influences health

FOAL HEALTH

Upon the delivery of a foal, it is critical to examine the foal to make sure it is breathing. If necessary, remove debris from the nostrils and administer artificial respiration. The production of a healthy foal is the result of best management practices by the horse owner.

Colostrum is the first milk secreted by the mother's mammary glands for several days after the birth of the foal. It is important to the health of the foal to nurse soon after birth. Colostrum has antibodies that will protect the foal against diseases until the foal builds its own protection system called active immunity. Foals should receive the following management procedures upon delivery: (More details are given in Appendix C.)

- navel care — Management of the navel cord is important. Dip or spray the cord with iodine. This will prevent infection and bacterial problems.
- tetanus shot — After the navel cord is treated, a tetanus shot should be administered to the foal.
- nursing — If the foal is not nursing one hour post-foaling, help should be given.
- defecation — The foal should defecate the meconium, the greenish fecal matter in a fetus, within 2 to 5 hours post-foaling. If this does not happen, an enema should be given.
- eyes — Proper eye care should be given to the foal after birth. The eyelids sometime are turned in. They should be rolled out and a solution should be administered.

3-11. A newborn foal needs colostrum, its mother's first milk.

- diarrhea — Diarrhea can be a problem for newborn foals. If persistent diarrhea occurs, contact your veterinarian immediately.

BODY CONDITION

Horses are athletes and anything that affects their ability to perform to their fullest potential is a problem. The body condition of a horse is the first place to begin in determining soundness. The desired conformation has little value unless the horse can perform. It is important to recognize and to evaluate common defects that occur in horses. Few horses are completely sound. Therefore, horse owners need to be trained to identify and manage these problem areas. The following may be evaluated to determine the body condition of a horse: forelimbs, hind limbs, hooves, head, body, and body systems (e.g., reproductive).

FORELIMBS (front legs)—support the major part of the horse's weight:

- splint—calcification or bony growth along the cannon
- bowed tendon—inflammation and enlargement of the flexor tendon at the back of the front cannon
- sidebone—calcification of the lateral cartilages of the third coffin bone
- ringbone—raised bony ridge usually parallel to the coronary band
- osselets—inflammation of the periosteum on the anterior surface of the fetlock joint
- sesamoiditis—inflammation of the proximal sesamoid bones
- suspensory ligament—common problems with race horses
- navicular disease—injury of the navicular bone of the front foot
- carpitis or popped knee—enlargement of the knee joint
- capped elbow or shoe boil—swelling at the point of the elbow
- sweeney—atrophy of the muscles of the shoulder

HIND-LIMBS (rear legs)—the main propulsive force for the horse:

- knocked-down hip—when one hip is lower than the other due to a fracture of the point of the hip
- stifle lameness—inflammation to the stifle joint
- stringhalt—sudden spasmodic jerking and flexion of one or both hocks
- curb—hard enlargement on the rear of the cannon below the hock
- thoroughpin—soft, fluid-filled enlargement in the hollow on the outside of the hock
- bog spavin—soft distension on the inside portion of the hock

- bone spavin—bony enlargement on the lower interior surface of the hock
- wind galls or wind puffs—soft, fluid-filled enlargements that occur around a joint capsule, tendon sheath, or bursa

HOOVES—support the entire weight of the horse (60 percent of the weight is on the front feet) and serve a critical role in the animal's well-being:

- laminitis or founder—noninfectious inflammation of the sensitive laminae of one or more hooves
- cracked hooves or sand cracks—occur on horses that are unshod or on horses with neglected foot care
- contracted heels—narrow or shrunken frog and the heels tend to close
- quittor—chronic, inflammatory swelling of the lateral cartilage resulting in abscesses

OTHER UNSOUNDNESSES—

- head—blindness, cloudy eyes, cataracts, conjunctivitis
- mouth—improper teeth structure and/or jaws
- nostrils—discharge, reflecting respiratory problems
- poll—poll evil, an inflammation of the bursa
- body—fistula of the withers
  saddle sores
  hernias
  genital abnormalities—tipped vulva, cryptorchid
- feet—thrush

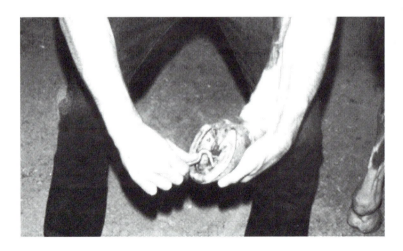

3-12. Regular cleaning of hooves helps prevent lameness.

Biology of the Horse

CONFORMATION

Conformation is the general body form and shape of a horse. It is one of the major considerations in judging and selecting horses. In general, good

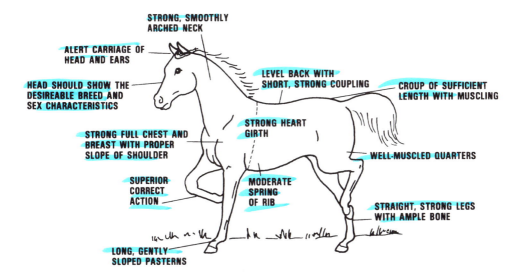

3-13. Desirable conformation of a horse.

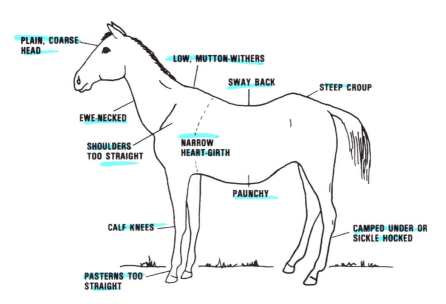

3-14. Undesirable conformation of a horse.

conformation is marked by alert eyes, smooth coat, level back, well-muscled hindquarters, straight legs, and sound feet. Of course, all horses should have easily identified breed and gender characteristics. Skills in identifying these and other characteristics are obtained through practice with horses.

DETERMINING THE AGE OF A HORSE

Age is an important trait of a horse. The value of a horse increases rapidly as it approaches maturity and then declines after eight years. The usefulness of a horse extends beyond eight years and may be much longer if the horse receives good care.

Regardless of the month in which a foal is born, its age is figured as of January 1 of the year in which it was born. This known as the *January 1 birth date*. For example, a foal born June 15, 1999, will be four years old on January 1, 2003.

The number and condition of the teeth of a horse are used in assessing age when its age is unknown. The first four teeth (two upper and two lower in the front) of a foal are temporary teeth and begin appearing 10 days after birth. In some cases, a foal may have teeth at birth. At about 2½ years of age, the temporary teeth begin to be replaced by permanent teeth.

The number of permanent teeth in a mature horse varies by gender, with mares having 36 and males having 40. In some cases, two extra teeth known as wolf teeth may form in the upper and lower gums so that mares have 40 and males have 44 teeth. Of course, older horses may lose teeth due to wear or damage.

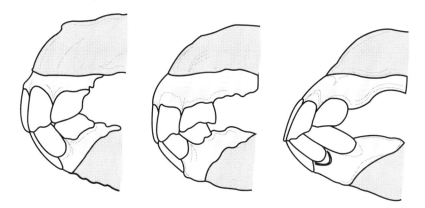

3-15. Side view of teeth of a horse shows how they slant forward as the horse ages. (The teeth shown are, from the left, of horses that are 5, 7, and 20 years old.)

Biology of the Horse

Teeth change with age because of wear from eating and chewing. A trained equestrian can judge the color, shape of the wear, number of teeth, and presence of temporary teeth. Temporary teeth are smaller and whiter than permanent teeth. Permanent teeth are larger and have a darker color.

DETERMINING THE SIZE OF A HORSE

Horse size is important in marketing, fitting saddles and harnesses, and in other ways. Four measures are used to determine the size of a horse:

- weight—Weight is measured on balanced scales and reported in the United States in pounds.
- girth—Girth is the distance around the chest just behind the withers and in front of the back. It is measured in inches in the United States. A large girth is important because it reflects the space available for the heart, lungs, and other organs in that area of the body.
- bone—Bone measurement is made on the rear legs of horses. A tape measure is placed around the cannon bone halfway between the knee and fetlock joint. Bone is reported in inches.
- height—Height is traditionally measured in hands, with a hand equal to 4 inches. A horse, for example, that is 16-1 hands is 65 inches tall. The mea-

3-16. Measuring the height of a horse.

surement is made from the highest point of a horse's withers to the ground. The horse should be standing squarely on level ground.

REVIEWING

MAIN IDEAS

Biology is the study of life. With horses, it is the foundation upon which everything else fits. Equine anatomy studies or identifies the structure and parts of the horse. Whereas, physiology studies or identifies the function of the body parts of the horse. It is important that horse owners know as much as possible in each of these areas.

The horse is a complex animal that works like a finely tuned engine. All the parts of the body have a role and are important to daily existence. From the head to the tail, all the parts are needed. A summary of selected body parts and their functions is:

- Mouth—conducts chewing and provides enzymes to break down food
- Throat—serves as a conduit to move food and oxygen
- Lungs—provides exchange of oxygen and carbon dioxide
- Heart—moves blood throughout the body; a pump
- Esophagus—delivers food and water to the stomach
- Stomach—stores food and assists in the breakdown of food
- Small intestine—assists in the uptake of nutrients from food and delivers it to the body
- Large intestine—stores and breaks down food and water
- Cecum—breaks down roughage, grass, hay, etc.
- Brain—controls the horse; command central
- Nervous system—delivers messages to all parts of the body
- Liver—serves as a filter to remove waste products from the body; removes toxins; serves as an "oil filter" for the body

Newborn foals rely on many factors to survive and live a healthy life. The first ingredient they need is colostrum—the first milk secreted by a mare after foaling. This substance is rich with antibodies, which help protect the foal against disease and other foreign material until the foal can produce its own immunity.

Biology of the Horse

Body condition is how a horse deals with internal and external forces. A horse's body condition is really in the hands of the horse owner or manager. This must be evaluated daily and changes must be made if there are any indicators of negative activity. There are many indicators, such as changes in weight, appearance, and behavior. Behavior is an action or response to stimulation.

Knowing the parts of a horse is the first step in being a proficient horse owner. These parts need to become common knowledge to people that deal with horses.

QUESTIONS

Answer the following questions using correct spelling and complete sentences.

1. What is the scientific name of the horse? *Equus caballus*
2. What are the major external parts of a horse? *Skeletal system, muscular system, Respitory system, Circularty system, Digustive system, Nervous, Reproductive, Derm-*
3. What are the major systems in the body of a horse? What are the functions of each? *a-bigical P. 28-29*
4. What are the three kinds of muscles? What are the functions of each? *Smoothe, cardiac, skeletal P. 31*
5. What are the parts and functions of the digestive system? *mouth, Pharynx, esophagus, Stomach, small intestine, cecum, large intestine, & anus p.34*
6. What is colostrum? Why is it important to a newborn foal? *first milk, protects foals againts diseases until it gets its own protection system P. 38*
7. Why is body condition important to a horse? *ability to pefore to full potential*
8. What is conformation? Identify three desirable and three undesirable conformation characteristics of horses. *Set up of body for a horse form & shape P. 41*
9. How are teeth used in determining the age of a horse? *The number & condition of them.*
10. What four measures are used in determining the size of a horse? *weight, girth, bone, height*

EVALUATING

CHAPTER SELF-CHECK

Match the term with the correct definition. Place the letter by the term in the blank provided.

46 EQUINE SCIENCE AND MANAGEMENT

a. biology	d. digestion	g. bone
b. hormone	e. respiratory system	h. kinesiology
c. anatomy	f. feedstuff	i. physiology

__c__ 1. The study of the function of the body.

__d__ 2. The breakdown of food by the digestive system to allow the nutrients to be utilized by the body.

__a__ 3. The study of life.

__e__ 4. The body system that supplies oxygen to body tissue and removes carbon dioxide.

__g__ 5. The separate parts of the hard tissue that forms the skeleton of most full-grown animals.

__b__ 6. A chemical that is essential for normal growth and development in the body.

__f__ 7. A material, or mixture of materials made into or used as food.

__h__ 8. The study of muscles and their movements.

__i__ 9. The science of the structure of a plant or an animal.

DISCOVERING

1. As a class project, take a field trip to a veterinary clinic or diagnostic lab. Examine the digestive system of a horse and identify parts of the digestive tract and system. Prepare a short essay on the results you find.

2. As a group project, select one physiological system of the horse, research the parts and function using many types of resources. Make a model of the horse and illustrate your selected system in the form of a poster, or stand-up model. Make a group presentation on the findings of your project.

3. Examine the role colostrum has in a newborn foal. Conduct a interview with horse owners, veterinarians, extension agents, or other knowledgeable professionals. Prepare a written essay on your findings and turn into your teacher. Discuss the alternatives if no colostrum is available from the mother.

4. Draw the skeletal (bone) system of the horse.

5. Draw the muscular system of the horse. Participate in a class discussion about form to function—how the horse moves, gaits, way of going, faults.

4

NUTRITION

Nutrition is the process of nourishing or being nourished. A proper diet is one of the basic needs of a horse. Equine nutrition appears simple, but is one of the most complex issues a horse owner must manage.

Horses eat a variety of feedstuff, including grass, hay, grain, minerals, and water. There are many types of hay—orchard grass, timothy, fescue (however, pregnant mares should avoid fescue), mixed-grass hay, and some alfalfa. Providing feeds that contain proper nutrients is an important role of a horse owner.

4-1. Feeding horses is scientific and requires knowledge of feedstuffs and performance.

OBJECTIVES

This chapter is about the nutrition of horses. To better understand this area of horse production, the following objectives are included:

1. Describe acceptable feedstuffs for horses
2. List the major nutrient needs of horses
3. Identify ways to feed horses
4. Balance rations for horses at different stages of production
5. Calculate feed amounts needed to meet nutrient requirements for horses

TERMS

balanced ration
carbohydrate
energy
fat
feedstuff
fiber
founder
glucose
grass
hand-feeding
lactation
legume
maintenance
mineral
nutrient
nutrition
pasture
protein
ration
roughage
self-feeding
supplement
vitamin
water

EQUINE KNOWLEDGE

Horse evolution has always paralleled its soil and vegetation. The ponderous horse of Flanders, progenitor of the modern draft horse, was the product of fertile soils, a mild climate, and abundant vegetation. The Shetland pony evolved on the sparse vegetation native to long, cold winters of the Shetland Isles.

FEEDSTUFFS FOR HORSES

Equine science deals with the nutrition of horses including what they eat and how they digest feedstuffs. **Feedstuff** is the material, or mixture of materials, made into or used as food. Feedstuffs for horses can be categorized into four areas: grain, roughage, water, and supplements. All of these are important. Selecting feedstuffs for the horse requires thought and a basic knowledge of what and how much the animal needs. Many problems can be avoided with careful planning.

GRAIN

Grain is a small hard seed or fruit produced by a cereal plant, such as corn, wheat, oats, and barley. It is best to feed grains to horses in a mixture where the grains are measured in certain proportions. This eliminates any problem that horse owners may create by giving too much of a certain grain. Mixtures may contain corn, oats, sorghum, and pellets of some type. Most complete horse rations are mixed with molasses, which makes the feed more desirable to horses. Most horses are picky eaters and the molasses add a sweet taste that horses like. In addition, there are some small nutrients in the molasses that add to the total diet.

The primary grain sources are corn, barley, oats, and wheat. These supply the necessary energy for a horse's daily requirement. Consideration must be given to the amount of energy yielded by each grain and the cost of the grain.

4-2. Small grains are a feed high in starchy carbohydrates.

Additionally, horse owners must evaluate the digestibility of each grain to determine an accurate value. It is possible for horses to receive enough energy without grain, but make sure by balancing a ration according to size of the animal and level of performance.

ROUGHAGE

Roughage is a coarse feedstuff that is high in fiber. Horses have been surviving on roughage for many years. Because of an enlarged cecum, horses can digest and utilize a certain amount of roughage. However, there are some important factors that one must examine regarding this feeding system.

First, determine the nutrient requirements of the horse based on the animal's age, size, and performance. Then, the kind and quality of roughage should be evaluated by running a feed analysis to determine protein content, etc. Many roughages, such as orchard grass, timothy, fescue, alfalfa, and mixed grasses, are excellent sources of nutrition. The other variable to consider is whether you are feeding dry hay or pasture forage. The moisture content of feed can change the nutritional makeup and can affect the health of the horse. Again, whether it is hay or pasture, samples should be taken and nutrient analysis should be determined.

It is important to feed horses based on their performance status. Horses that are ridden or shown require different diets from a pastured horse. Horse diets should be formulated based on the available feedstuff and the animal's performance data. Good records are essential should you encounter a problem.

Horses can digest roughage because they have an enlarged cecum, which is part of the digestive tract. Horses can maintain their body on good quality hay if they are not on a high workout routine. Horses like many different types of pasture roughage. These include mixed grasses and legumes. A *legume* is a plant, such as a bean, peanut, or clover, with nitrogen-fixing nodules on the roots, which makes the use of atmospheric nitrogen possible. *Grass* is any of various plants having slender leaves. Grass is a common roughage in pasture and hay. A *pasture* is a grassy area designated for grazing. Before letting the horse into a pasture, inspect the plants in it. Poisonous weeds are sometimes harmful to horses. Samples can be identified and assessed for toxic substances.

WATER

Water is a clear, colorless, nearly odorless, and tasteless liquid that is essential for plants and animals. Water is the most important nutrient and feedstuff. A horse can go longer without food than water. A horse needs access to abundant, fresh, clean water. However, water should be rationed when a horse is heavily worked. Excessive consumption of water may damage an overheated horse. Water serves many functions in the body. Those functions include:

- Blood builder
- Temperature regulator
- Nutrient solvent
- Glandular secretions
- Cell builder
- Others

4-3. Horses need access to plenty of clean water at all times.

SUPPLEMENTS

Horses are fed according to their level of activity. Supplements are given to supply adequate amounts of nutrients. A **supplement** is a feed material that is high in a specific nutrient. Some supplements may contain a mixture of nutrients, for example, protein supplements may contain soybean, cottonseed, corn gluten, and sunflower meal. Protein quality is usually less important in ruminants than nonruminants, but since horses are monogastric, horse owners need to be aware of this component. Other very important supplements are salt and minerals, which are needed for normal growth and development.

NUTRIENTS

Nutrients are substances that provide nourishment to the body. They are vital—the body must have nutrients to survive. These consist of carbohy-

4-4. Nutrients listed on horse feed bag.

drates, fats, protein, minerals, vitamins, and water. The condition of a horse reveals the amount and quality of nutrients the horse is receiving. However, by the time you see deficiencies, much damage has been done. This is why it is so important to know the nutrient requirements of horses and make sure the requirements are met. This is done by using a balanced ration that has the correct proportions of nutrients for the needs of that specific animal.

ENERGY

Energy is defined as usable power. Several methods are commonly used to determine the energy content of feeds. Regardless of the method, horse owners need to be aware of the energy being given to the horse. All feedstuffs have some energy value and it is critical to get the appropriate amount of energy into a horse. Again, this varies with the level of work being done by the horse and the age and sex of the horse. For example, a race horse or a breeding horse needs more energy than a pleasure horse on pasture.

Carbohydrates

Carbohydrates are the major components of plant tissues. Besides energy, carbohydrates aid in the use of proteins and fats.

Carbohydrates provide energy for growth, maintenance, work, reproduction, and lactation. There are three types of carbohydrates: sugars, starches,

Nutrition

and fiber. Simple sugars (monosaccharides) and double sugars (disaccharides) are two types of sugars. Glucose and fructose are simple sugars.

Starches are the food supply for plants. Starches and sugars are converted to glucose. *Glucose*, a simple sugar, is the ultimate source of energy for most cells. Starch is an energy reserve found in roots, tubers, and seeds.

Fiber is the material left after the food has been digested. It is made of plant cell walls and cellulose. The purpose of fiber is to help the digestive system run smoothly. Fiber absorbs water and provides bulk.

Fats

Fats provide energy. They contain the highest amount of energy, with 2.25 times more energy than carbohydrates. Fats help supply energy for normal body maintenance. Fats also provide a healthy skin, keep the nervous system healthy, give food a good flavor, and carry fat soluble vitamins A, D, E, and K. Horses do not develop a fat deficiency for energy. However, they can develop a vitamin deficiency.

PROTEIN

Protein is composed of a chain of units called amino acids, which are essential for growth. Amino acids are the building blocks of the body's tissues. Protein needs vary with the age of the horse, especially foals and yearlings. Younger horses require a much higher level of protein for growth and development; whereas, the adult horse needs a maintenance level of protein. Horse diets should be balanced according to these factors and the protein content of available feedstuffs.

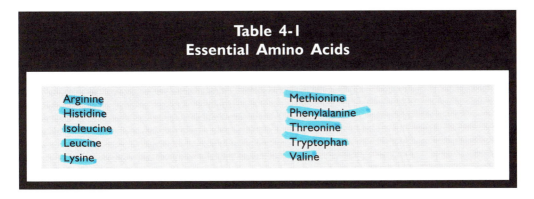

**Table 4-1
Essential Amino Acids**

Arginine	Methionine
Histidine	Phenylalanine
Isoleucine	Threonine
Leucine	Tryptophan
Lysine	Valine

Table
Mineral Functions

Minerals Which May Be Deficient Under Normal Conditions	Conditions Usually Prevailing Where Deficiencies Are Reported	Function of Mineral	Some Deficiency Symptoms	Practical Sources of the Mineral
Major or macrominerals:				
Salt (NaCl)	Negligence, for salt is cheap. The salt requirement is greatly increased under conditions which cause heavy sweating, thereby resulting in large losses of this mineral from the body. Unless it is replaced, fatigue will result. For this reason, when engaged in hard work and perspiring profusely, horses should receive liberal allowances of salt.	Salt serves as both a condiment and a nutrient. Sodium and chlorine help maintain osmotic pressure in body cells, upon which depends the transfer of nutrients to the cells and the removal of waste materials. Sodium is associated with muscle contraction and is important in making bile, which aids in the digestion of fats and carbohydrates. Chlorine is required for the formation of hydrochloric acid in the gastric juice so vital to protein digestion.	In warm or hot weather, workhorses show heat stress. Long-term symptoms of sodium deficiency are depraved appetite, rough hair coat, reduced growth of young animals, and decreased milk production.	Salt provided free-choice, preferably in loose form, or 0.5–1.0% salt added to the ration. It is very difficult for horses to eat very hard block or rock salt. This often results in inadequate consumption. Also, if there is much competition for a salt block, the more timid animals may not get their requirements. Iodized salt should be used in iodine-deficient areas.
Calcium (Ca)	The typical horse ration of grass hay and farm grains—usually deficient in calcium.	Builds strong bones and sound teeth. Very important during lactation. Affects availability of phosphorus. Calcium and phosphorus comprise ¾ of the ash of the skeleton and form $1/3$–$1/2$ of the minerals of milk.	A deficiency of calcium in young animals is generally characterized by poorly formed, soft bone, which may bend or bow; and a severe deficiency may cause rickets. A deficiency of calcium in older animals results in porous, fragile bones. Because deficiency conditions may not be completely reversible, prevention is imperative.	Ground limestone or oystershell flour. When both calcium and phosphorus are needed, use steamed bone meal or dicalcium phosphate. Horses absorb 55 to 75% of the calcium in a typical ration.
Phosphorus (P)	Horses grazed on phosphorus-deficient areas or fed for a long period on mature, weathered forage.	Important in the development of bones and teeth. Essential to metabolism of carbohydrates and fats, and enzyme activation.	Rickets in young horses; osteomalacia in mature horses.	Monosodium phosphate, diodium phosphate, or sodium tripolyphosphate. Where both calcium and phosphorus are needed, use steamed bone meal or dicalcium phosphate. Horses absorb 35–55% of the phosphorus in a typical ration.
Magnesium (Mg)	Horses fed high grain-low forage ration, which characterizes most horses at hard work (as in racing and showing). Lactating mares grazing on lush spring pastures low in magnesium or in which Mg is unavailable.	Reduces stress and irritability. Magnesium is important in enzyme systems, bone formation, and calcium and phosphorus metabolism.	Horses under stress are keyed up, high-strung, and jumpy. Foals fed a purified ration deficient in magnesium develop nervousness, muscular tremors, convulsive paddling of the legs and, in some cases, die. Grass tetany.	Magnesium sulfate Magnesium oxide.
Potassium (K)	When stabled horses are fed high-concentrate rations. Excessive sweating.	Major cation of intracellular fluid where it is involved in osmotic pressure and acid-base balance. Muscle activity. Required in enzyme reaction involving phosphorylation of creatine. Influences carbohydrate metabolism.	Reduced appetite, growth retardation, unsteady gait, general muscle weakness, pica, diarrhea, distended abdomen, emaciation, followed by death. Fatigue. Abnormal electrocardiograms.	Potassium chloride. Roughages usually contain ample potassium.
Sulfur (S)		Sulfur is an integral part of the amino acids methionine and cystine.		

4-2. and Deficiencies

Classes/Function	Nutrient Requirements[1,2]				Nutrient Allowances[1,2]				Comments
	Per Horse Daily (g)	In Ration A-F (%)	Per Ton Ration A-F (lb)	(kg)	Per Horse Daily (g)	In Ration A-F (%)	Per Ton Ration A-F (lb)	(kg)	
Maintenance: 1,000-lb (454-kg) horse	85	0.5–1.0	10–20	4.5–9.1	85	0.75	15	6.8	Horses require both sodium and chlorine, but the requirement for chlorine is approximately half that of sodium. Generally, the chlorine requirements will be met if the sodium needs are adequate.
Gestation/Lactation: 1,000-lb (454-kg) mare	85	0.5–1.0	10–20	4.5–9.1	85	0.75	15	6.8	Sodium and chlorine are low in feeds of plant origin.
Growth: 450-lb (204.5-kg) weanling	41	0.5–1.0	10–20	4.5–9.1	41	0.75	15	6.8	There is little danger of overfeeding salt unless a salt-starved animal is suddenly exposed to too much salt, or if liberal amounts of water are not available.
Working: 1,000-lb (454-kg) horse	85	0.5–1.0	10–20	4.5–9.1	85	0.75	15	6.8	Excessive salt intake may result in high water intake, excessive urine excretion, digestive disturbances, or death from salt cramps.
Maintenance: 1,000-lb (454-kg) horse	20	0.175	3.5	1.6	23	0.21	4.1	1.8	The calcium-phosphorus ratio should be maintained close to 1.1:1 although 2:1 is acceptable. Narrower ratios may cause osteomalacia in mature horses. When there is a shortage of calcium in the ration, it is withdrawn from the bones.
Gestation/Lactation: 1,000-lb (454-kg) mare	56	0.495	9.9	4.5	64	0.57	11.3	5.1	
Growth: 450-lb (204.5-kg) weanling	36	0.66	13.2	6.0	41	0.76	15.1	5.8	Feeding excess calcium interferes with the utilization of magnesium, manganese, and iron—and perhaps in the utilization of zinc.
Working: 1,000-lb (454-kg) horse	40	0.35	7.0	3.2	46	0.41	8.1	3.7	
Maintenance: 1,000-lb (454-kg) horse	14	0.125	2.5	1.1	16.1	0.14	2.8	1.3	For the growing horse, the calcium-phosphorus ratio should be maintained close to 1.1:1, although 2:1 is acceptable.
Gestation/Lactation: 1,000-lb (454-kg) mare	36	0.315	6.3	2.9	41.4	0.37	7.3	3.3	The mature horse can tolerate a Ca:P ratio as wide as 4:1 or 5:1 provided adequate levels of phosphorus are available.
Growth: 450-lb (204.5-kg) weanling	19	0.35	7.0	3.2	21.9	0.4	8.0	3.7	Excess phosphorus can cause bighead.
Working: 1,000-lb (454-kg) horse	29	0.255	5.1	2.3	33.4	0.3	5.9	2.7	If plenty of vitamin D is present, the ratio of calcium to phosphorus becomes less important.
Maintenance: 1,000-lb (454-kg) horse	7.5	0.065	1.3	0.6	8.6	0.08	1.5	0.7	Excess of magnesium upsets calcium and phosphorus metabolism. Rations containing 50% forage will likely contain sufficient magnesium for unstressed horses.
Gestation/Lactation: 1,000-lb (454-kg) mare	10.9	0.096	1.92	0.9	12.5	0.11	2.2	1.0	
Growth: 450-lb (204.5-kg) weanling	5.7	0.105	2.1	1.0	5.5	0.12	2.4	1.1	
Working: 1,000-lb (454-kg) horse	15.1	0.135	2.7	1.2	17.4	0.16	3.1	1.4	
Maintenance: 1,000-lb (454-kg) horse	25.0	0.22	4.4	2.0	28.8	0.26	5.1	2.3	A ration that contains at least 50% forage can be expected to meet potassium requirements.
Gestation/Lactation: 1,000-lb (454-kg) mare	46.0	0.405	8.1	3.7	52.9	0.47	9.3	4.2	
Growth: 450-lb (204.5-kg) weanling	18.2	0.335	6.7	3.0	20.9	0.39	7.7	3.5	
Working: 1,000-lb (454-kg) horse	49.9	0.44	8.8	4.0	57.4	0.51	10.1	4.6	
Maintenance: 1,000-lb (454-kg) horse					17.0	0.15	3.0	1.36	The precise sulfur requirement is not known, but an allowance of 0.15% of the total ration appears to be adequate.
Gestation/Lactation: 1,000-lb (454-kg) mare					17.0	0.15	3.0	1.36	If the protein requirement of the ration is met, the sulfur intake will usually be at least 0.15%, which appears to be adequate.
Growth: 450-lb (204.5-kg) weanling					8.2	0.15	3.0	1.36	
Working: 1,000-lb (454-kg) horse					17.0	0.15	3.0	1.36	

(Continued)

Table 4-2

Minerals Which May Be Deficient Under Normal Conditions	Conditions Usually Prevailing Where Deficiencies Are Reported	Function of Mineral	Some Deficiency Symptoms	Practical Sources of the Mineral
Trace or microminerals:				
Cobalt (Co)	Animals grazed in cobalt-deficient areas, such as Australia, Western Canada, and the following states of U.S.: Florida, Michigan, Wisconsin, New Hampshire, Pennsylvania, and New York.	Cobalt is required for the synthesis of vitamin B-12 in the intestinal tract of the horse.	Anemia. Severe weight loss.	Cobaltized mineral mix made by adding cobalt at the rate of 0.2 oz/100 lb (5.7 g/45.4 kg) of salt as cobalt chloride, cobalt sulfate, cobalt oxide, or cobalt carbonate. Also, several good commercial cobalt-containing minerals are on the market.
Copper (Cu)	Suckling foals. Mare's milk, along with milk from other species, is low in copper. Deficiency occurs in regions where soils contain too little copper or where horses are getting an excess of molybdenum, sulfur, or zinc.	Copper, along with iron and vitamin B-12 is necessary for hemoglobin formation, although it forms no part of the hemoglobin molecule (or red blood cells). Closely associated with normal bone development in young growing animals.	Anemia, characterized by fewer than normal red cells and less than normal amount of hemoglobin. Abnormal bone development in young equines, including an increased incidence of epiphysitis, contracted tendons, and osteochondritis dissecans (OCD).	Trace mineralized salt containing copper sulfate or copper carbonate.
Iodine (I)	Iodine-deficient areas or soils (in Northwestern U.S. and in the Great Lakes region) when iodized salt is not fed. Use of feeds that come from iodine-deficient areas.	Iodine is needed by the thyroid gland in making thyroxin, an iodine-containing compound which controls the rate of body metabolism or heat production.	Foals born dead, or very weak with enlarged thyroid glands (goiter) and unable to stand or nurse. Higher than normal incidence of navel ill.	Stabilized iodized salt containing 0.01% potassium iodide (0.0076% iodine). Calcium iodate.
Iron (Fe)	Suckling foals kept away from soil and feed other than milk. Horses subjected to pressure from racing, showing, or other heavy use. Such animals require added iron in their daily ration. Excessive blood loss from a wound or heavy parasite infestation.	Necessary for formation of hemoglobin, an iron-containing compound which enables the blood to carry oxygen. Also, important to certain enzyme systems.	Iron-deficiency anemia, characterized by fewer than normal red cells and less than normal amount of hemoglobin. Anemic horses tire easily. **NOTE:** Iron deficiency anemia may also result from heavy parasitization.	Ferrous sulfate administered orally. Trace mineralized salt. Cane molasses. Iron oxide should not be used as a source of iron for horses because it is poorly absorbed.
Manganese (Mn)	Excess calcium and phosphorus which decreases absorption of manganese.	Essential for normal bone formation (as a component of the organic matrix). Thought to be an activator of enzyme systems. Growth and reproduction.	Poor growth. Lameness, shortening and bowing of legs, and enlarged joints. Impaired reproduction (testicular degeneration of males; defective ovulation of females).	Trace mineralized salt containing 0.25% manganese (or more).
Selenium (Se)	Muscle disorders and lowered serum selenium.		Infertility. Myositis (muscular discomfort or pain).	Forages or grains grown on soils known to have adequate selenium. Sodium selenate Sodium selenite.
Zinc (Zn)	Feeds low in zinc. Excess calcium may reduce the absorption and utilization of zinc.	Important in many enzyme systems. Required for normal protein synthesis and metabolism. Imparts gloss or bloom to the hair coat.	Rough, dull hair coat. Loss of appetite.	Zinc carbonate. Zinc sulfate.

[1] All "nutrient requirements" given in this table were adapted from Nutrient Requirements of Horses, 5th rev. ed., NRC—National Academy of Sciences. The "nutrient allowances" given in this table represent the best judgment based on current research; it is intended that they meet the nutrient requirements, and provide adequate margins of safety in addition.
[2] Feed consumption of a mature 1,000-lb (454-kg) horse estimated at 25 lb (11.36 kg) per day. Feed consumption of a 450-lb (204.5-kg) weanling estimated at 12 lb (5.45 kg) per day.

Nutrition

(Continued)

Classes/Function	Nutrient Requirements[1,2]			Nutrient Allowances[1,2]			Comments
	Per Horse Daily	In Ration A-F	Per Ton Ration A-F	Per Horse Daily	In Ration A-F	Per Ton Ration A-F	
	(mg)	(ppm, or mg/kg)	(g/ton)	(mg)	(ppm, or mg/kg)	(g/ton)	
Maintenance:							The disease called salt sick in Florida is due to a cobalt deficiency associated with a copper deficiency.
1,000-lb (454-kg) horse	1.13	0.1	0.091	1.3	0.11	0.104	
Gestation/Lactation:							The cobalt requirement for horses is very low, for horses have remained in good health while grazing pastures so low in cobalt that ruminants confined to them have died.
1,000-lb (454-kg) mare	1.13	0.1	0.091	1.3	0.11	0.104	
Growth:							
450-lb (204.5-kg) weanling	0.54	0.1	0.091	0.6	0.11	0.100	
Working:							
1,000-lb (454-kg) horse	1.13	0.1	0.091	1.3	0.11	0.104	
Maintenance:							A copper deficiency in horses has been reported in Australia. In high-molybdenum areas, more copper may be added to horse rations; but excesses and toxicity should be avoided.
1,000-lb (454-kg) horse	113.4	10.0	9.070	283.4	25	22.675	
Gestation/Lactation:							
1,000-lb (454-kg) mare	113.4	10.0	9.070	340.1	30	27.210	
Growth:							
450-lb (204.5-kg) weanling	54.4	10.0	9.070	217.7	40	36.280	
Working:							
1,000-lb (454-kg) horse	113.4	10.0	9.070	283.4	25	22.675	
Maintenance:							Enlargement of the thyroid gland (goiter) is nature's way of trying to make enough thyroxin (an iodine-containing hormone) when there is insufficient iodine in the feed. Feeding excess iodine continuously will also produce goiter in foals.
1,000-lb (454-kg) horse	1.13	0.1	0.091	1.3	0.11	0.104	
Gestation/Lactation:							
1,000-lb (454-kg) mare	1.13	0.1	0.091	1.3	0.11	0.104	
Growth:							Iodine deficiency seldom occurs in coastal areas because of the abundance of iodine from spray drift from ocean or sea water.
450-lb (204.5-kg) weanling	0.54	0.1	0.091	0.6	0.11	0.100	
Working:							
1,000-lb (454-kg) horse	1.13	0.1	0.091	1.3	0.11	0.104	
Maintenance:							The horse's body contains about 0.004% iron. Milk is deficient in iron, and the iron content of the mother cannot be increased through feeding iron. Thus, foals should be individually or creep fed as soon as they are old enough. A variable store of both iron and copper is located in the liver and spleen, and some iron is found in the kidneys. Too much iron may be harmful.
1,000-lb (454-kg) horse	453.5	40	36.280	453.5	40	36.280	
Gestation/Lactation:							
1,000-lb (454-kg) mare	453.5	50	45.350	1,020.4	90	81.630	
Growth:							
450-lb (204.5-kg) weanling	217.7	50	45.350	489.8	90	81.630	
Working:							
1,000-lb (454-kg) horse	453.5	40	36.280	680.3	60	54.420	
Maintenance:							Most natural feedstuffs are rich in manganese.
1,000-lb (454-kg) horse	453.5	40	36.280	521.5	46	41.720	
Gestation/Lactation:							
1,000-lb (454-kg) mare	453.5	40	36.280	521.5	46	41.720	
Growth:							
450-lb (204.5-kg) weanling	217.7	40	36.280	250.4	46	41.720	
Working:							
1,000-lb (454-kg) horse	453.5	40	36.280	521.5	46	41.720	
Maintenance:							Excess selenium results in selenium poisoning, or alkali disease.
1,000-lb (454-kg) horse	1.13	0.1	0.091	1.3	0.11	0.104	
Gestation/Lactation:							
1,000-lb (454-kg) mare	1.13	0.1	0.091	1.3	0.11	0.104	
Growth:							
450-lb (204.5-kg) weanling	0.54	0.1	0.091	0.6	0.11	0.100	
Working:							
1,000-lb (454-kg) horse	1.13	0.1	0.091	1.3	0.11	0.104	
Maintenance:							If zinc in the feed is on the low side, the addition of zinc should improve the hair coat.
1,000-lb (454-kg) horse	453.5	40	36.280	907.0	80	72.560	
Gestation/Lactation:							Excess zinc prevents calcium utilization and produces signs of calcium deficiency.
1,000-lb (454-kg) mare	453.5	40	36.280	1,133.8	100	90.700	
Growth:							The toxicity level exceeds 1,000 ppm.
450-lb (204.5-kg) weanling	217.7	40	36.280	544.2	100	90.700	
Working:							
1,000-lb (454-kg) horse	453.5	40	36.280	1,020.4	90	81.630	

MINERALS

Minerals are inorganic substances occurring naturally in the earth. Minerals are essential to a horse's well-being. Minerals can be available to horses either in a block or blended in their grain. Most horse owners use mineral blocks where horses have free-choice access. Sodium chloride (salt) should be provided by free choice.

Calcium and phosphorus are two critical minerals in a horse's diet. This is not to say the other minerals are not important, but these two play a major role in bone development—indispensable for a foal. Deficiencies or the wrong calcium phosphorus ratio can result in many developmental problems. The diet of a horse should be based on the needs of the individual animal and then appropriate amounts of minerals added to the diet. Other important minerals are magnesium, potassium, iodine, iron, zinc, selenium, salt, copper, fluorine, and lead.

VITAMINS

A *vitamin* is a substance essential for animal growth and development. Vitamins are very important in the diet of a horse. Again, each horse diet should be based upon the needs of the individual. Critical vitamins are: vitamin A, vitamin D, vitamin E, B vitamins, thiamin, riboflavin, vitamin B12, and ascorbic acid.

FEEDING HORSES

When is the best time to feed horses? What are the variables we look at when determining the amount of feed to provide to a given horse? Are some feedstuffs better than others and how does the cost of feed affect the nutrition of a horse? These are questions that all horse owners face and these questions should not be taken lightly.

4-5. Feed mills make feed that provides a balanced ration for horses.

Two general approaches are used in feeding horses: self-feeding and hand-feeding.

Self-feeding involves placing a large quantity of feed in a feeder and allowing the horse to eat as much and as frequently as the horse wishes. Horses have access to the feed all of the time. Unfortunately, horses sometimes do not know when they have had all that they need. With high-energy rations (those high in grain), horses may overeat and suffer founder or other disease problems. Some people do not recommend self-feeding because of potential health problems. Of course, horses on pasture and other low-energy rations usually are given free access to the feed. Minerals and salt may be self-fed.

Hand-feeding is providing the horse with a given amount of feed each day. The portions are usually divided for three feedings—one in the morning, one at noon, and one at night. Approximately one-third of the ration is fed at each feeding. Horses that are working may have higher energy foods in the morning and at noon and lower energy foods such as hay at night.

The amount to feed a horse is based on its weight and activity. For a mature 1,000-pound horse doing no work or light work, provide 12 to 15 pounds of hay and 4 to 5 pounds of grain. The amount would be increased proportionately with larger horses and reduced for smaller horses. Active, working horses receive about the same amount of hay, but the grain is increased. A mature 1,000-pound horse doing heavy work will need 12 to 14 pounds of grain each day.

It is important to know your horse's feed requirements. These vary from activity to activity. Secondly, horses are creatures of habit and should be fed at the same time every day—preferably, twice per day so they know when to

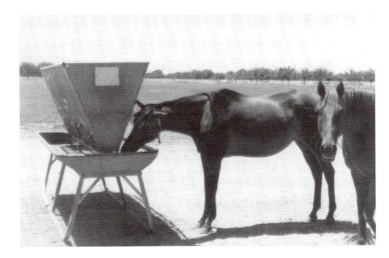

4-6. Hay is fed on a regular schedule at this California ranch. (Courtesy, Jasper S. Lee, Georgia)

expect their meal. Although feeding horses can be expensive, it is very important that you provide the best quality feed. Bargains are okay if of good quality. All feeds can be tested for quality through your local extension agent. They can also assist you in locating feed sources, such as hay and pasture. Some feedstuffs are better than others and some you need to stay away from because of problems with diseases. Whether it is pasture and weeds or buying prepared feed, horse owners need to first know their horse's nutrition requirements. Then, determine which feed to provide followed by the correct method of feeding on a daily basis.

Too much nutrition, including unlimited grazing can result in obesity and founder. *Founder* is an inflammation of the sensitive tissue under the horny wall of the hoof. Horses can develop founder on grass, especially lush clover pastures. Brood mares should not as a rule be given fescue grass hay nor put into pastures with fescue grass.

RATION BALANCING

A *ration* is the amount of feed that an animal is given. The amount of each essential nutrient is figured into the ration. Comparing this with the nutrient requirements of the animal yields how much roughage, grain, and supplement is needed. This can be done with a calculator and the nutrient requirements or with a computer ration balancing program. Feed specialists and extension specialists can assist any horse owner with specific needs.

A *balanced ration* is a feed that has all of the required nutrients for a specific horse or animal. Horse owners may purchase complete feed already mixed. It is important to become familiar with the nutrient requirements of various horses according to their level of work. A mature show horse compared to a horse on pasture demonstrates a marked difference of feed amounts and nutrient requirements. NRC, National Research Council, provides an updated list of animal nutrient requirements. All horse owners should be aware of this reference. Some people produce their own feeds and balance their own rations. It is essential to use quality feed stuffs and mix the appropriate amounts for the specific horse. The nutrient needs of a horse should be determined before trying to prepare a balanced ration.

NUTRIENT NEEDS OF HORSES

Through research, scientists have been able to determine the amounts of various nutrients horses need in a daily ration. Nutrient needs vary with age and activity of an animal as well as its reproductive condition.

Nutrition

Table 4-3
Summary of Nutrient Allowances for Horses

	Young Horses			
body weight =	Creep Feed* (250 lbs.)	Weanlings (450 lbs.)	Yearlings (650 lbs.)	2–3 Year Olds (800 lbs.)
Total Digestible Nutrients (TDN) (%)	75.0	75.0	70.0	60–65
Crude Protein (%)	18.0	16.0	14.0	13.0

	Mature Horses				
	Idle/Light Work	Heavy Work	Stallions (breeding season)	Mares (90 days before foaling)	Mares (lactating)
Total Digestible Nutrients (TDN) (%)	55.0	62.5	75.0	62.5	75.0
Crude Protein (%)	9.0	11.0	14.0	13.0	14.0

*Not weaned and allowed access to feed restricted from mature horses.

Source: Adapted from: Ensminger, M. E. *Horses and Horsemanship*. Danville, IL: Interstate Publishers, Inc., 1999.

Young horses typically need feed with a higher percentage of protein than older horses. This is because protein is needed to form new tissue and keep the young horse healthy. Breeding stallions, pregnant mares, and lactating mares need more protein than horses that are idle or doing light work. Table 4-3 presents sample information on the nutrient needs of horses based on maturity and activity.

NUTRIENTS IN FEEDSTUFFS

Scientists have analyzed various feedstuffs commonly used with horses and other animals to determine the nutrients. A wide range of approaches have been used in analyzing feedstuffs. In most cases, the analyses are de-

Table 4-4
Protein Content of Selected Feedstuffs

Feedstuff	Crude Protein (%)
alfalfa hay (sun dried)	14.5
bahiagrass pasture	2.6
barley (grain)	11.7
Bermudagrass (Coastal) (pasture)	4.4
bluegrass (Kentucky) (pasture)	5.4
clover (white) (pasture)	5.0
corn (yellow dent) (grain)	9.9
cotton seed meal	37.2
oats (grain)	11.9
rye (grain)	12.0
sorghum (grain)	11.5
soybean meal	49.7
timothy (pasture)	3.4

Source: Adapted from: Ensminger, M. E. *Horses and Horsemanship*. Danville, IL: Interstate Publishers, Inc., 1999.

signed to determine the percentage of crude protein, dry matter, vitamins, and minerals.

A ration prepared for horses must provide the nutrients needed for the animal to prosper. Protein is one of the most essential nutrients for growing animals and those that are used for breeding or are lactating. Reports often show information on protein as "crude protein" and "digestible protein." Digestible protein is that which is actually available to an animal.

Table 4-4 shows crude protein content in selected feedstuffs that horses might eat. This table presents only a few ingredients that comprise the ration of a horse. Information in tables such as this can be used in preparing a balanced ration for a horse. (For more information, refer to *Animal Science Digest* or *Horses and Horsemanship* available from Interstate Publishers, Inc.)

Nutrition

PEARSON SQUARE METHOD OF RATION BALANCING

The Pearson Square Method is an easy-to-use approach in ration balancing. Here is an example.

Given two feeds of varying protein levels, calculate the proper percentage of each for a mixed feed of desired protein percentage and convert those percentages to the pounds of feed required to make a given weight of feed. The example here is for a 450-pound weanling colt. Table 4-3 shows that 16 percent protein is needed.

The procedure consists of six steps:

Step 1. Draw a rectangular box.

Step 2. In the center of the box, place the desired protein percentage.

Step 3. At the two lefthand corners of the box place the protein percentage of the feeds A and B from the feedstuffs.

Step 4. Draw diagonal lines from the upper lefthand corner to the lower right and from the lower left to the upper right corner.

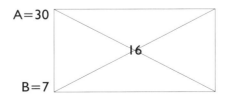

Step 5. Subtract the figures connected along each diagonal line and place the result at the end of that diagonal line.

Step 6. Draw a horizontal line from the figures on the outside right-hand side of the box back to the original feed started with on the left side of the box. This will give the ratios of the respective feeds to use.

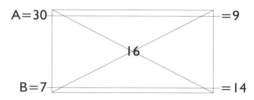

9 parts of Feed A
14 parts of Feed B

4-7. Hoof of a horse with founder or laminitis.

Ration balancing is important to those who either purchase feed ingredients and/or produce feed ingredients then mix rations for horses. Nutritional information about feeds is used to formulate rations.

In ration formulation, the feedstuffs are selected on availability and cost. Computer programs calculate the feed ration that contains the amount of nutrients necessary for the individual horse's needs. It is important to note when a balanced ration is not fed, nutritional diseases can occur, such as founder. There are many unpleasant stories of horses that did not receive adequate nutrition.

DETERMINING NUTRIENT REQUIREMENTS

Animals use different kinds and amounts of feeds to meet their needs. Through the blood, nutrients are carried throughout the body to nourish the entire animal. The goal is to provide the horse with adequate nutrition regardless of the phase of production. The major phases of production are:

- Growth and Development
- Work
- Maintenance
- Reproduction
- Lactation

In the growth and development phase, there are specific nutrients necessary for bone development, muscle development, nervous system development, and other critical things for the young horse to mature with a healthy body.

The work phase requires high-energy feed. In most cases, carbohydrates and fats supply this needed requirement. The other important feed necessity is a good supply of water. An overheated horse should not have access to water until the animal is cooled.

4-8. Good quality hay can provide many nutrients for horses. (Courtesy, American Quarter Horse Association)

Maintenance is no loss or gain, to keep in a certain condition. Nutrients are required to continue the daily operation of the horse's body. Animals re-

4-9. Horses need plenty of good drinking water. (Courtesy, Jasper S. Lee, Georgia)

quire energy for internal workings of the body, heat to maintain body temperature, and small quantities of vitamins, minerals, and protein.

Adequate nutrition is critical in the phase of reproduction. Not only is the existence of the horse important, but the development of the foal is a major focus. During the first trimester of pregnancy, the fetus requires large amounts of protein, vitamins, and minerals. The second and third trimester also have special requirements. The mother or mare must have adequate nutrition to maintain her health and to supply nutrients to the foal.

Once the foal is born, the mare must provide adequate milk for the continued development of the foal. **Lactation** is the production of milk after parturition. Mares must have additional nutrients to produce large quantities of milk. Since milk is high in protein, calcium, and phosphorus, lactation diets need these nutrients.

REVIEWING

MAIN IDEAS

Adequate nutrition is essential for survival. Nutrition is the process by which a horse eats and uses various feedstuffs. The feed allows the animal to function in all the phases of production—growth and development, work, maintenance, reproduction, and lactation. The nutrients required are water, carbohydrates, fats, proteins, minerals, and vitamins. The first step in providing proper nutrition is to determine the horse's daily requirements, which are based upon the age and sex of the animal and especially the level of work. In the second step, identify proper feedstuffs and know what kind of nutrients the feedstuffs will provide. The final step in providing proper nutrition is the routine of daily feeding, cleaning the facilities, and monitoring the animal for any problems.

Balanced rations can be purchased from a feed dealer or horse owners can purchase or produce ingredients and balance their own rations. Regardless of how you prepare your horse's feed, you should contact your local extension agents and periodically test your feed by running a feed quality analysis.

Pasture and hay form the basics for most feed programs. Grain (mixed feed) can be used to balance the ration. The horse owner should know the kind of forage in the pasture. Horses can be overfed, underfed, and/or improperly fed. All horses require water, some roughage and usually iodized salt (NaCl). All feed should be clean, fresh, free of mold, and as free of dust as possible.

Nutrition

Regardless of the method and source, always know the nutritional requirements and whether your horse is getting the recommended daily allowance as outline by the National Research Council.

QUESTIONS

Answer the following questions using correct spelling and complete sentences.

1. What is a feedstuff? *mixtures used for food*
2. What are the acceptable feedstuffs for horses? Briefly describe each. *Grain, Roughage, Water p. 49-51*
3. What is a nutrient? *Substance that provides nutrience*
4. What are the essential nutrients of horses? *carbohydrates, fats, protein, minerals, vitamins & water*
5. What two general approaches are used in feeding horses? *Self-feeding & hand-feeding*
6. What is a ration? *amount of feed an animal is given.*
7. What is ration balancing for horses? *feed w/ all required nutrients*
8. How do the nutrient requirements differ for young and mature horses? *Young- more protien than mature horses*

EVALUATING

CHAPTER SELF-CHECK

Match the term with the correct definition. Place the letter by the term in the blank provided.

- a. nutrition
- b. nutrient
- c. roughage
- d. supplement
- e. lactation
- f. ration
- g. legume
- h. water
- i. maintenance
- j. minerals

__C__ 1. A coarse feed that is high in fiber.

__g__ 2. Plants, such as beans, peanuts, clover, with nitrogen-fixing nodules on the roots, which makes the use of atmospheric nitrogen possible.

__e__ 3. The production of milk after parturition.

__h__ 4. A clear, colorless, nearly odorless, and tasteless liquid that is essential for plants and animals.

__d__ 5. A feed material that is high in a specific nutrient.

__f__ 6. The amount of feed an animal is given.

__i__ 7. No loss or gain, to keep in a certain condition.

__a__ 8. The process of nourishing or being nourished.

__j__ 9. An inorganic substance occurring naturally in the earth.

__b__ 10. A substance that provides nourishment to the body.

DISCOVERING

1. Have your local extension office send a feed sample to the university lab for analysis. Discuss your finding in class.

2. Visit your local feed store and examine the feed tag on a bag of horse feed. Specifically evaluate:
    1. Growing diets
    2. Maintenance diets
    3. Gestating diets
    4. Lactating diets
    5. Other

3. Using the Internet, visit a feed company's site and locate the nutrient requirements for a pregnant mare in her second trimester.

4. As a group project, determine the nutrient requirements for a show horse, then prepare a ration for the horse. Share your findings in class.

5

PASTURE MANAGEMENT

Managing a pasture is more than just fencing in horses! Good pasture plants are needed. Horses like to graze in a lush, green pasture. It is a perfect picture to see horses running free and grazing in a nice pasture. But is everything nutritionally sound for those animals? Many questions should be answered to assure the horses in the pasture are getting the correct nutrition. Some of these questions are:

1. What kinds of grasses are growing in the pasture?
2. Are poisonous weeds or vines present?
3. How many acres of pasture are needed for each horse?
4. Should a rotation system be used to allow the grass to catch up with the grazing demands?
5. Has the forage been tested for nutritional value?
6. Is grain needed to supplement the pasture?
7. Is shade or protection from the weather available?
8. Is suitable water available?

5-1. A good pasture promotes health and well-being.

OBJECTIVES

This chapter explores nutritional requirements for horses on pasture. The objectives of the chapter are as follows:

1. Identify the common forages used for horses
2. Discuss management techniques with horse pastures
3. Describe fences used with horse pastures

TERMS

fence
forage
grazing pressure
paddock
pasture renovation
rotational grazing
toxic
weed

EQUINE KNOWLEDGE

A wooden fence around a horse pasture should be 72 inches high with five 2×6 boards. (Note: Check county and state laws about fencing requirements.)

COMMON FORAGES

Forage is food, primarily from the leaves of plants, for domestic animals. It is a very important part of any horse feeding program. Good pasture, water, and trace minerals can provide complete nutrition for many classes of horses—mature, nonworking, yearlings, and pregnant mares. Performance horses, lactating mares, and weanlings may require feeds in addition to pasture, but they still benefit from good pasture.

There are many sources of forage for horses, but the primary ones are bluegrass, orchard grass, bluestem, brome grass, and cereal grasses. In very warm climates, pangola grass, Bahiagrass, carpet grass, or Para grass is often used. Legumes, such as alfalfa, red clover, white clover, and birds-foot trefoil are often inner seeded with grasses. The mixture is more desirable and more palatable. The key is to know the nutrient values for all sources used in a pasture so you can maximize the pasture productivity.

Some pastures have weed problems. A *weed* is any undesired, uncultivated plant. Whether the weed is *toxic* (poisonous) or not, it takes the place of the desired plants. The specific weeds that are poisonous to horses are nightshades, yellow star thistle, horse nettle, and ragwort. Horse owners should be cognizant of the plants growing in a pasture and practice good management to prevent weed growth, which includes a schedule that involves regular weed identification. Weeds can be identified by taking specimens to the local extension office. Timing is very important. If you are in question as to how and when to take a sample, call your extension agent and have a professional come out and show you how to take the sample. They

5-2. Horses enjoy running free and grazing in a good pasture.

5-3. A good pasture is clean of weeds.

will send the sample to the appropriate lab and contact you when the results are available. With modern technology, the results should be available in a few days. Usually there is minimal charge for this procedure. Poisonous weeds can cause sickness or death in horses. So, do not minimize this management item.

PASTURE MANAGEMENT

Pasture is very important in any horse feeding program. A pasture is a grassy area designated for grazing. A *paddock* is a small field or enclosure near a stable. Several factors, such as pasture management, species of plant, amount of land, and the determination of nutrition per acre of pasture is necessary.

MANAGEMENT TECHNIQUES

Good pasture management consists of several important practices:

1. Do not overgraze (also called overstocking). Limit the number of horses per paddock! Recommendation: 2 to 3 acres per horse.

5-4. Horses like to graze in a lush, green pasture.

Pasture Management 73

2. Clip pastures on a regular basis to prevent plant material from becoming too mature. Help maintain a balance between legumes and grasses. This will assist in weed control.
3. Spread manure droppings with a chain harrow. A ton of well-preserved horse manure, free of bedding, contains plant food nutrients equal to about 100 pounds of 13-2-12 fertilizer.
4. Keep pasture free of mechanical hazards, such as wire and nails.
5. Keep pasture free of weeds, particularly poisonous weeds.
6. During extreme weather, keep horses out of the pasture to avoid soil compaction and damage to the forage.
7. Practice **rotational grazing**, which is a system of heavy grazing followed by periods of no grazing. The horses are moved to a new pasture after heavy grazing. This permits the pasture forage to recover and grow again.
8. Conduct a planned internal parasite control and prevention program.

GRAZING MANAGEMENT

Grazing management has been a difficult concept for horse owners to identify and use. Many people put several horses in a small lot and wonder why they cannot get a good stand of grass. The problem is they do not have an effective grazing plan.

Good pasture can be an important part of the horse management program. However, good pasture means different things to different people. Some horse owners refer to pasture as an exercise and exhibition lot, which

5-5. Establishing a good horse pasture is an important part of a horse management program.

plays no role in the nutrition of the horse. Others refer to the image of a horse farm with the lush, green pasture, which may or may not have nutritional value. The first thing a horse owner must do is to establish the goal of the pasture. If it is for nutritional purposes, then a plan must be put together that involves the type of forage to be used, the kind of fencing around the pasture, the number of horses to be placed in the pasture, and finally, a rotational schedule to manage the pasture. All of this can be done with much success! A good forage program can reduce feed costs.

Good forage is high in digestible nutrients, is perennial, is harvested by the horses, requires no storage, provides exercise, and requires limited labor. The forage produced by the pasture is usually less expensive and provides more nutrients than hay.

The pasture should have good shade for the horses. A source of fresh, clean water and available salt should be included. The pasture should be clean of any debris or sharp objects and holes. It should be fenced with a good type of fence that is not harmful to the horse.

Stocking rate is very important and is usually 2 to 3 acres per horse. More acres will be needed if the forage is not good. The choice of grasses and legumes will be influenced by the geographical location in which you live. Your extension agent can be a great source of help in determining the forage that is good for your location.

After you have established a good pasture, management is the key to keeping a good pasture. Management should include proper fertilization, clipping to control growth, scheduling rotational grazing, and monitoring the grazing pressure of the herd. **Grazing pressure** is the animal-to-forage ratio at a specific time. To maximize the benefits of a pasture, horse owners should plan a pasture calendar for a full year. Your county extension agent has many pasture management calendars and will be glad to assist you.

FENCES FOR HORSES

A *fence* is a barrier that limits the distance an animal can travel or move. Good fences confine horses to the desired area. Pastures are very important for horses and require an effective fence. First, there is no perfect fence for horses. The mere nature of a horse is to move around naturally and not be restricted. But, a horse must be safely contained to a given location without hurting the horse. Several types of fences can be used. All horse areas must have safe fences and gates. Cattle guards are not recommended. Before constructing a horse fence, consider the objectives of your operation, the types of

Pasture Management

horses you have, and the amount of money you can spend on fencing materials.

UTILIZING DIFFERENT FENCES

The secret to a good horse fence is strength, height, and tightness. This is accomplished by correctly setting the posts. Traditionally, board fences have been the horse fence of choice. However, horse fences are also constructed of split rail, wire, pipe, rubber nylon, chain link, concrete, and cable.

1. **Board fences** are rugged and have the advantage of being easily seen by the horse. Originally, these fences were constructed from trees on the farm. Today, these fences are expensive. They require much maintenance whether by painting or treating. Also, horses chew on the fence and it splinters and breaks. Board fences should be made of four or five 2-inch × 6-inch boards with posts no more than 8 feet apart. A board fence with a top board that is 48 to 53 inches high is adequate for horses. The bottom board should be 5 to 6 inches above the ground. Wooden posts should be of long-lasting, strong timber. Posts should extend 5 feet above the ground and be placed in holes 4 to 6 feet deep. Sawed, 4-inch × 4-inch wood is recommended. (Some farms use vinyl fencing instead of boards. Vinyl material is attractive and durable. Unfortunately, vinyl material becomes brittle in very cold weather and may snap if a horse pushes on it.)

2. **Post and rail fences** add beauty to a farm, but they are expensive to install. The split rails are excellent because they are rugged and durable. Treated lumber is used, which discourages chewing by the horse and reduces wear.

3. **Wire fences** are less expensive and faster to build than board; however, they are not as safe. Wire fences should be strung tightly and the strands need to be close together. Do not use barbwire with horses. The barbs will cut horses' legs and other parts of their body.

4. **Pipe fences** are strong and safe for horses, but they are very expensive. Pipe fences are excellent for corrals and paddocks, but for large areas, the cost is extreme.

5. **Rubber nylon fences** are safe and attractive. The rubber nylon belting is 2 to 4 inches wide and, from a distance, gives the appearance of black board fence. This fence requires minimum maintenance, is easy to install, and is relatively inexpensive.

6. **Electric fences** can be used with other fencing materials or alone. Electric fences have been used successfully, but have not been accepted by the entire horse industry. These fences work very well if correctly constructed and regu-

5-6. Pipe fencing around a pasture.

larly maintained. They are inexpensive and easy to install, but you should seek advice from electrical professionals.

7. **Chain link fences** are good for stallion pens and other small paddocks. The top of this fence should be smooth. The fence will stretch if kicked and is expensive to install and maintain.

8. **Precast concrete fences** are made to like post and rail and are very attractive. They are white, weather resistant, durable, and never need painting. However, concrete is difficult to obtain and very expensive to install.

9. **Post and cable fences** are expensive, but they are strong, safe, and durable. The cable is threaded through the middle post and attached by a turnbuckle or spring to the corner post.

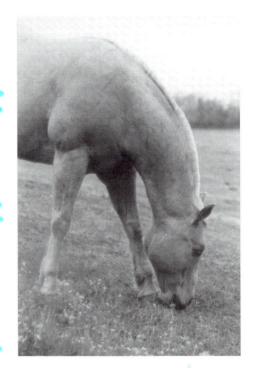

5-7. This horse is grazing a short pasture with weeds and needs supplemental feed. (Courtesy, Jasper S. Lee, Georgia)

Pasture Management 77

REVIEWING

MAIN IDEAS

Pastures are very important to the horse farm. Pastures supply a nutritious, low-cost, labor-saving feed source that improves the health and disposition of the horse. Pasture forage is good for all horses regardless of age.

Pasture management is necessary to maximize the potential of the forage. Weeds can be a problem and can cause sickness and even death to horses. A pasture management calendar of events should include weed identification and fertilization.

Correct pasture management consists of goal setting for the given pasture. Horse owners should determine if the pasture is to be used as a source of nutrition, an exercise lot, or just a place to keep horses. Once this has been determined, a management plan can be put in place.

Horses should have a grazing system, which includes rotational grazing, on any pasture. In addition, stocking rates should be 2 to 3 acres per horse. This will eliminate destruction of the pasture as a result of too many hooves and horses.

The kind of fence you choose to use around the pasture is a big decision. After you have reviewed all types and expenses, develop a plan to maximize the kind you choose. The Cooperative Extension Service has an abundance of materials on fencing and an agent will assist you in choosing and finding the correct fence.

QUESTIONS

Answer the following questions using correct spelling and complete sentences.

1. What are the common forages used in a pasture for horses? *blue grass, orchardgrass, blue stem, carpet grass, white clover. (p71)*
2. What is grazing pressure? *animal-to-forage ratio @ a specific time*
3. List the proper pasture management techniques for a horse pasture. *Pasture management, plants, lands, & nutrition*
4. Describe the different grazing systems for horses. *rotational grazing (p73)*
5. List the different types of fences used around a horse pasture. *Board, post & rail, wire, pipe, rubber, nylon electric, chain link, pre cast concrete, post & cable*

EVALUATING

CHAPTER SELF-CHECK

Match the following term with the correct definition. Place a letter by the term in the blank provided.

a. fence
b. paddock
c. grazing pressure
d. forage
e. toxic
f. rotational grazing
g. roughage
h. weed

_g_ 1. A coarse feed that is high in fiber.
_b_ 2. A small field or enclosure near a stable.
_e_ 3. Poisonous.
_c_ 4. The animal-to-forage ratio at a specific time.
_d_ 5. Food primarily from the leaves of plants for domestic animals.
_h_ 6. Any undesired, uncultivated plant.
_a_ 7. A barrier that confines and limits animal movement.
_f_ 8. A system of heavy grazing followed by periods of no grazing.

DISCOVERING

1. Visit a local horse farm and discuss pasture management. Ask about the management techniques needed to renovate a horse pasture and the techniques to establish of a new pasture. Determine the plant species used and how weeds are controlled.

2. Conduct a job-shadowing project and follow a soil conservationist around for a day.

3. Using the Internet, find five types of grasses and or legumes used in a horse pasture.

4. In a group, take a plot of ground, and using management techniques, identify the type of vegetation and determine the nutrient needs to maximize growth. Send a sample to the extension office. When you receive the report, make a class presentation about your findings.

6

HEALTH MANAGEMENT

A healthy horse is a happy horse! **Health** is the overall condition of a horse at a given time. Managing the health of a horse is an on-going process. Horse owners must be aware of health issues at all times. Prevention is the key to success with horses. Although treatment is a large part of the health industry, you do not want to be in a treatment mode.

Get to know the characteristics of a healthy horse. Observe the appearance and behavior of healthy horses. Good health is evident by bright eyes, clear nostrils, a shiny coat, and normal horse movement and behavior.

6-1. Studying horse health is fun, but should be taken seriously!

OBJECTIVES

Keeping a horse healthy is an important part of horse management. To better understand horse health management, the following objectives are covered:

1. Explain the meaning of horse behavior
2. Describe some common diseases and parasites of horses
3. Identify routine examination procedures for horses
4. Describe the proper techniques used in examining horses
5. Describe foot structure and care
6. Explain disease prevention

TERMS

aggressive behavior
bacteria
colic
contactual behavior
contagious disease
disease
dominance behavior
elimination behavior
environmental behavior
external parasite
frog
fungi
health
hoof
infection
ingestive behavior
internal parasite
noncontagious disease
parasite
pathogen
sexual behavior
thrush
vaccination
veterinarian
virus
vital signs

EQUINE KNOWLEDGE

Horse vital signs are:
  Pulse rate is 32 to 44 beats per minute
  Normal temperature is 100.5
  Normal respiration rate is 8 to 16 respirations per minute

HORSE HEALTH

Horse health management deals with vaccinations, hygiene, feed handling, facilities, deworming, handling techniques, and equipment. ***Vaccinations*** are inoculations with a vaccine to protect against disease. Management of health care is the responsibility of the horse owner. It deals with knowing the common disease problems, correct daily examinations, and using common sense.

Horse owners should know toxic plants, parasites, and other foreign things that will cause problems. Record keeping is a must and should consist of prevention and treatment plans. A plan for dealing with an emergency should also be in place. Studying horse health is fun, yet it should be taken very seriously. Get involved not only in the classroom but with your local veterinarian, extension agent, farrier, and feed dealer. In addition, if you have access to a local Department of Agriculture diagnostic laboratory, make an appointment and visit to find out about the problems that it encounters.

Veterinarians and owners work hard to establish a health care plan that will keep your horse healthy and prevent any unpleasant circumstances you may have to deal with regarding health. A ***veterinarian*** is an animal health care professional.

CATEGORIES OF BEHAVIOR

Behavior is an action or response to stimulation, such as pulling the bridle a certain way. Behavior in horses is complex. There are many stories that horse owners tell about certain horses they have owned. The behavior of horses is very obvious, but the reasons for such behavior may be speculation. We can categorize horse behaviors as follows:

- ***Contactual behavior*** is the result of seeking affection or protection—often from a groomer or rider.
- ***Ingestive behavior*** is the taking of food or water into the digestive tract.
- ***Elimination behavior*** is the establishment of an elimination area in the pasture or paddock. (Horses will not graze that area until there is no source of feed. Horses will usually walk some distance to urinate or defecate in this area.)
- ***Sexual behavior*** is associated with the mating process, including courtship and territory. (Sexual behavior is not confined to mares and stallions. Geldings will definitely show signs of sexual behavior, especially if castrated after puberty. Hormones and learned behaviors are a large part of sexual behavior.)

6-2. This horse is kneeling in response to stimulation from the rider.

- *Environmental behavior* deals with the surroundings of horses, such as pastures and other horses they are around.
- *Aggressive behavior* is associated with conflict, submission, and fighting. (A pecking order is established through many aggressive acts.)
- *Dominance behavior* is the establishment of hierarchy within a group of horses. (The establishment of dominance may be very traumatic for horses. This is an innate, or naturally existing, behavior that will not change.)

IDENTIFICATION OF HEALTH PROBLEMS

A good health program is important in horse management. The identification of health conditions, both good and bad, is essential for the horse owner to conduct management on a daily basis. A physical examination and an accurate history of the horse is needed to determine if the horse is sick and how to treat the problem. Whether your veterinarian or anyone else is administering health treatment, the history is essential. A horse owner must do the following:

1. Identify any problems that may arise.
2. Keep accurate records.
3. Know about horse diseases and how to locate information on health.
4. Know who to refer to as a reference or resource person.
5. Plan an organized vaccination program.

Health Management

6-3. Health examinations should be done on a daily basis.

6. Plan a preventative health program to avoid conditions or situations that place the horse at risk for sickness.

The general appearance of a horse should be monitored daily for health indicators. Does the animal appear energetic and active? How does the animal respond to you? Is the horse alert or does the horse appear in need? Look at the body condition. Does the horse have a shiny hair coat or does it look rough? How does the coat look according to the season of the year? Behavior is another indicator—horses should mix well. Routinely examine legs and back for swelling, which can be a sign of health problems. Examine the teeth. Also, frequent urination or defecation (diarrhea) are problem signs. Respiration of the horse should be viewed. How is the horse breathing? Horse owners can watch the heart girth for the movement of the body cavity and rib cage for normal movement. Finally, all these factors must be based on the environment in which they are watched. Questions to raise are what season of the year is it? What time of the day are you monitoring? What condition is the horse undergoing?

If you suspect any problem, take action! If you feel comfortable relying on your ability, fine. If not, contact a resource person who can help you.

VITAL SIGNS

The vital signs of a horse are measurements of health. These signs reflect normal or abnormal body conditions. **Vital signs** consist of body temperature, pulse rate, and respiration. These are the first things measured when examining a horse. A horse's normal rectal temperature can range from 99.0 to 100.8°F, with an average of 100.5°F. The normal pulse rate for a horse is 32 to 44 beats per minute. A horse's normal respiration rate ranges from 8 to 16 respirations per minute when at rest.

HEALTH PROBLEMS

Many times we take horse health for granted. Every animal is susceptible to health problems. They need vaccinations, a clean and safe environment, and a daily management plan to keep them healthy. Horse owners need a good health management program for their animals and a health plan to treat problems as needed. The health plan should be recommended and approved by your equine veterinarian.

Disease is as an abnormal condition of an animal or an organism. It is a condition that affects the well-being of a horse. It is the absence of good health and may affect any or all of the anatomical parts and functions of a horse. Health is an abstract term that is relative according to the individual that is defining the animal.

DISEASES

There are many diseases that affect animals. Horses are susceptible to some general diseases. They also have some diseases that are unique to their species.

Three microorganisms that affect the health of animals are bacteria, fungi, and viruses. *Bacteria,* also called germs, are one-celled organisms that enter the body and cause many problems. Many bacteria produce spores that are hard to control. They grow on food and other energy sources. Bacteria must be treated with antibiotics and this is not always effective. *Fungi* are unicellular organisms that cause disease on the exterior of the body. Treatment or control of fungi is coverage with a fungicide. *Viruses* are so tiny that they cannot be seen with an ordinary microscope. These contagious organisms enter the body through the air, the blood, water, or other conduits. A vaccination can be used for protection against a virus. These organisms must be respected and proper health management practices observed.

Diseases may further be classified in two categories: contagious and noncontagious. Knowing the distinction is important in the prevention and treatment of a given disease. It is especially useful in keeping horses healthy.

Health Management

Noncontagious diseases are not spread by casual contact. They are caused by nutritional, physiological, environmental, or morphological problems. Most nutritional diseases result from an unbalanced diet. Physiological disease results from a defect of a tissue, organ, or organ system. Morphological problems are a result of poor management, such as cuts, scrapes, bruises, and broken bones.

Contagious diseases are spread by direct or indirect contact with people and/or animals. Disease pathogens, such as viruses, bacteria, fungi, and parasites, cause contagious diseases. *Pathogens* are microorganisms or viruses that can cause disease.

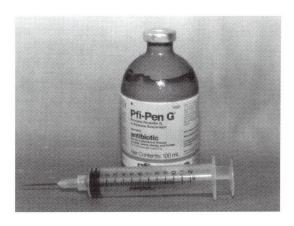

6-4. Antibiotics may be injected into an animal using a syringe and hypodermic needle to treat some diseases.

Horses owners need to be knowledgeable of the following diseases:

1. **Foalhood speticemias** — A disease that affects foals. Bacteria enters the blood system via the umbilical cord. This is why the naval should be disinfected at birth.
   Symptoms: inflammation of the intestine
   Treatment: cut naval and treat soon after birth
2. **Strangles (distemper)** — An acute, contagious disease caused by infection with streptococcus. The respiratory system is affected. An *infection* is an invasion of the body by microorganisms.
   Symptoms: swelling of nodes, creamy discharge, increased body temperature
   Treatment: isolation of animal, good feed, antibiotics, and good hygiene are essential
3. **Pneumonia** — A disease that refers to any inflammatory disease of the lungs. There are many types of pneumonia.
   Symptoms: nasal discharge, difficulty in breathing, increased temperature, and lung congestion
   Treatment: antibiotics, good hygiene, and clean environment
4. **Influenza** — A disease that is caused by myxoviruses.
   Symptoms: respiratory inflammation, fever, muscle soreness, and often a loss of appetite
   Treatment: no exercise, antibiotics, sulfa drugs
5. **Equine viral rhinopneumonitis (EVR)** — This disease is caused by a herpes virus. Although, secondary bacterial infection is often a factor.

Symptoms: high temperature, nasal discharge, and abortions
Treatment: no good treatment—antibiotics help and vaccination may be recommended

6. **Viral arteritis** — An acute, upper-respiratory tract infection caused by a specific herpes virus.
Symptoms: high fever, nasal discharge
Treatment: natural immunity and hygiene

7. **Equine encephalomyelitis** (sleeping sickness) — This inflammatory disease of the brain and spinal cord is transmitted by mosquitoes from an infected horse to a susceptible horse or to humans. Of all horse diseases, this one has received more publicity than any equine disease in recent years. This disease can be transmitted by humans. There are three common types of equine encephalomyelitis: Venezuelan (VEE), Eastern (EEE), and Western (WEE).
Symptoms: high temperature, nervousness, restlessness, dropping ears, paralysis
Treatment: no effective treatment, provide water

8. **Equine infectious anemia (EIA) (swamp fever)** — A viral disease transmitted in the blood. This disease has also received much attention. There is no vaccine available, but a reliable diagnostic test is available. The Coggins test will detect if your horse has this organism.
Symptoms: high fever (104 to 108°F), severe depression, loss of appetite, loss of weight, jaundice, enlarged spleen
Treatment: no effective treatment

9. **Tetanus (lockjaw)** — A wound-infection disease caused by *Clostridium tetani*. This bacteria can be found in the feces of horses and in soil contami-

6-5. A veterinarian may have to come to the horse farm. This photograph shows a well-equipped truck for veterinary medicine work.

Health Management

nated by horse feces. The bacteria enters the body through a wound or the navel cord. This disease can be prevented through a vaccination program. People as well as horses need to have regular vaccinations.
Symptoms: difficulty walking, poor posture, and prolapse of the third eyelid
Treatment: place in a sling, large doses of antitoxin

10. **Anthrax** — An acute disease caused by *Bacillus anthracis*.
    Symptoms: colic-like signs, swelling of throat, lower chest pain, other swelling
    Treatment: large doses of antibiotics in early stages

11. **Scratches (grease-heel)** — An eczema that affects the fetlock and heel areas.
    Symptoms: scratching, loss of hair, and infection
    Treatment: throughly clean and clip hair, remove skin debris, apply ointment and antibiotics

12. **Thrush** — *Thrush* is an inflammation of the frog. The *frog* is the triangular-shaped formation in the sole of the horse's hoof.
    Symptoms: a black discharge and a foul odor
    Treatment: clean and trim frog, prevent environment conditions that cause this disease by cleaning stables and treat the hoof area with antibiotics

13. **Colic** — *Colic* is a disease that causes abdominal pain. Colic is the number one killer of horses, and it is caused by the presence of internal parasites or excessive intake of feed, especially grain.
    Symptoms: restlessness, pawing, kicking at the belly, getting up and down, and rolling
    Treatment: walk to relieve anxiety, prevent from rolling, analgesics (pain-relieving drugs) may be adequate in some cases, surgery may be required

14. **Pulmonary emphysema (heaves)** — A disease in which air is trapped in the lungs and the lungs become distended.
    Symptoms: coughing, wheezing, nasal discharge, and high flank movement
    Treatment: no treatment is known for complete recovery—pasturing a horse in fresh air is the best treatment

15. **Roaring (laryngeal hemiplegia)** — Roaring is caused by damage to the laryngeal nerve and results in lack of muscular control of the vocal cords.
    Symptoms: enlarged lymph nodes, tumors, and abscesses
    Treatment: no known treatment

16. **Laminitis (founder)** — A disease that affects the coffin bones due to excessive intake of feed. This is a very common problem and is of serious concern.
    Symptoms: feet problems, extreme heat of the hooves, restlessness
    Treatment: cool feet immediately, call veterinarian for treatment

17. **Other** — Rabies: common to all animals, including humans.

Note: Most vaccinations are for prevention and are not always 100 percent effective.

Table
Equine

Disease	Species Affected	Cause	Symptoms (and age or group most affected)	Distribution and Losses Caused by
Alkali disease (see selenium poisoning)				
Anemia, nutritional	All warm-blooded animals, including humans.	Commonly an iron deficiency, but it may be a deficiency of copper, cobalt, or certain vitamins—especially B-12.	Loss of appetite, poor performance, progressive emaciation and death. Most prevalent in suckling young.	Worldwide. Losses consist of retarded growth and deaths.
Azoturia (hemoglobinuria, Monday morning disease, blackwater, tying up)	Horses.	Sudden exercise, following a day or two of rest during which time the horse has been on full feed, resulting in partial spasm or "tie-up." Thought to be caused by an abnormal amount of glycogen stored in the muscle. As the glycogen breaks down, lactic acid is formed. The lactic acid builds up in the muscle, causing a myositis which manifests itself as partial spasm, or "tie-up."	Profuse sweating, abdominal distress, wine-colored urine, stiff gait, reluctance to move, and lameness. Finally, animal assumes a sitting position, and eventually falls prostrate on side.	Worldwide, but the disease is seldom seen in horses at pasture and rarely in horses at constant work.
Colic	Horses	Internal parasites are the number one cause of colic. Additional causes are improper feeding, working, or watering.	Excruciating pain; and depending on the type of colic, other symptoms are: the horse looking at its belly, distended abdomen, increased intestinal rumbling, violent rolling and kicking, profuse sweating, constipation, and refusal of feed and water.	Worldwide. Colic is the most common ailment among horses and is the leading cause of death.
Fescue foot	Horses. Cattle. Sheep.	The fungus, *acremonium coenophialum*, which lives in the leaves, stems, and seed of tall fescue.	Decrease or absence of milk production, prolonged gestation, abortion, and thickened placenta.	Wherever tall fescue is grown.
Fluorine poisoning (fluorosis)	All farm animals, fish, poultry, and humans.	Ingesting excessive quantities of fluorine through either the feed, air, water, or a combination of these.	Abnormal teeth (especially mottled enamel and excessive wear); abnormal bones (bones become thickened, rough, and soft); stiffness of joints; loss of appetite; emaciation; reduction in milk flow; diarrhea; and salt hunger.	The water in parts of Arkansas, California, South Carolina, and Texas has been reported to contain excess fluoride. Occasionally, throughout the U.S., high-fluorine phosphates are used in mineral mixtures. Areas near certain industries which heat earthy materials or burn high-fluoride coal may be a problem.
Founder (laminitis)	Horses. Cattle. Sheep. Goats.	Overeating, (grain; or lush legume grass—known as "grass founder"), overdrinking, or from inflammation of the uterus following parturition. Also intestinal inflammation. Too rapid change in the ration.	Extreme pain, fever (103° to 106°F), and reluctance to move. If neglected, chronic laminitis will develop, resulting in a dropping of the hoof soles and a turning up of the toe walls.	Worldwide. Actual death losses from founder are not very great, but usefulness may be affected.
Goiter (see iodine deficiency)				
Heaves	Horses. Mules.	Exact cause unknown, but it is known that the condition is often associated with the feeding of damaged, dusty, or moldy hay. It often follows severe respiratory infection such as strangles. Probably an allergy.	Difficulty in forcing air out of the lungs, resulting in a jerking of flanks (double flank action) and coughing. The nostrils are often slightly dilated and there is a nasal discharge.	Worldwide. Losses are negligible.
Iodine deficiency (goiter)	All farm animals and humans.	A failure of the body to obtain sufficient iodine from which the thyroid gland can form thyroxine (an iodine-containing hormone).	Foals may be weak.	Northwestern U.S. and the Great Lakes region; also reported in California and Texas. Also goiter areas are scattered all over the world.
Night blindness (nyctalopia)	All farm animals and humans.	Deficiency of vitamin A.	Slow dark adaptation progressing to night blindness.	Worldwide. Especially prevalent during an extended drought, or when winter feeding bleached grass or hay.

Health Management

6-1. Diseases

Treatment	Prevention	Remarks
Provide dietary sources of the nutrient or nutrients the deficiency of which is known to cause the condition.	Supply dietary sources of iron, copper, cobalt, and certain vitamins—especially B-12. Keep suckling animals confined to a minimum and provide supplemental feeds at an early age.	Anemia is a condition in which the blood is either deficient in quality or quantity (a deficient quality refers to a deficiency in hemoglobin and/or red cells). Levels of iron in most feeds believed to be ample, since most feeds contain 40 to 400 mg/lb.
Absolute rest and quiet. While awaiting the veterinarian, apply heated cloths or blankets, or hot-water bottles to the swollen and hardened muscles. The veterinarian should determine treatment. In mild cases, he/she may use a tranquilizer or sedative. In severe cases he/she may use muscle relaxers or sodium bicarbonate in solution to readjust the acid balance in the muscles.	Restrict the ration and provide daily exercise when the animal is idle. Give a wet bran mash the evening before an idle day or turn the idle horses to pasture. Some believe that a diuretic (a drub which will increase the flow or urine) will prevent the tie-up syndrome. This is a common treatment of racehorses. Others feel that increased B vitamins will prevent the lactic acid buildup.	The chances of recovery are good for horses that remain standing, are not forced to move after the signs are noticed, and whose pulse returns to normal within 24 hours.
Call a veterinarian. To avoid danger of inflicting self-injury, (1) place the animal in a large, well-bedded stable, or (2) take it for a slow walk. Depending on diagnosis, the veterinarian may use one or more of following: sedatives; laxatives, such as mineral oil; drugs, or surgery.	Parasite control. Proper feeding, working, watering.	Colic is also a symptom of abdominal pain that can be caused by a number of different conditions. For example, bloodworms cause colic due to damage in the wall of blood vessels. This results in poor circulation to the intestine.
There is no effective treatment.	Seeding of fungus-free fescue seed. Where fescue foot is a problem, gestating mares should be removed from fescue pasture the last 2 to 3 months of pregnancy.	
Discontinue the use of feeds, water, or minerals containing excessive fluoride. Any damage may be permanent, but animals which have not developed severe symptoms may be helped to some extent if sources of excess fluorine are eliminated.	Avoid the use of feeds, water or mineral supplements containing excessive fluorine. The National Academy of Sciences uses the figure of 60 ppm fluoride as the dietary fluoride tolerance of horses, or dietary level that can be fed without clinical interference with normal performance.	Fluorine is a cumulative poison.
Pending arrival of the veterinarian, the attendant should stand the animal's feet in a cold-water bath. Antihistamines, restricting the diet, use of diuretics, and antiinflammatory agents such as corticosteroids or phenylbutazone, may speed recovery and alleviate serious after effects.	Alleviate the causes; namely, (1) overeating, (2) overdrinking (especially when hot), and/or (3) inflammation of the uterus following parturition. Veterinary attention should be given if mares retain the afterbirth longer than 12 hours.	Unless foundered animals are quite valuable, it is usually desirable to dispose of them following a case of severe founder.
Antihistamine granules can be administered in feed to control coughing due to lung congestion. Affected animals are less bothered if turned to pasture. If used only at light work, if fed an all-pelleted ration, or if the hay is sprinkled lightly with water at feeding.	Avoid the use of damaged feeds. Feed an all-pelleted ration, thereby alleviating dust.	Unlike humans, a horse cannot breathe through its mouth. Basically, heaves is a rupture of some of the alveoli in the lungs, of which the specific cause is unknown. Heaves in horses is similar to emphysema in people.
At the first signs of iodine deficiency, and iodized salt should be fed to all horses. Once the iodine-deficiency symptoms appear in farm animals, no treatment is very effective.	In iodine-deficient areas, feed iodized salt to all horses throughout the year. Salt containing 0.01% potassium iodide is recommended.	The enlarged thyroid gland (goiter) is nature's way of attempting to make sufficient thyroxine under conditions where a deficiency exists. Large excesses of iodine may cause abortions.
Correcting the vitamin A deficiency.	Provide good sources of carotene in the ration, or add stabilized vitamin A to the ration.	High levels of nitrates interfere with the conversion of carotene to vitamin A.

(Continued)

Table 6-1

Disease	Species Affected	Cause	Symptoms (and age or group most affected)	Distribution and Losses Caused by
Nitrate poisoning (oat hay poisoning; corn stalk poisoning)	Primarily cattle, but it may affect horses and sheep.	Forages (vegetative part) of most grain crops, Sudangrass, and numerous weeds. Inorganic nitrate or nitrite salts, or fertilizer left where animals have access to them, or where they may be mistaken for salt. Pond or shallow well into which surface runoff from barnyard or well-fertilized soil drain.	Accelerated respiration and pulse rate; diarrhea; frequent urination; loss of appetite; general weakness; trembling and staggering gait; frothing from mouth; abortion; blue color of the mucous membrane and muzzle due to lack of oxygen in blood; death within 4½ to 9 hours after consuming nitrates. A rapid and accurate diagnosis of nitrate poisoning may be made by examining blood. Normal blood is red and becomes brighter when exposed to air, whereas blood from animals toxic with nitrates is a brown color due to formation of methemoglobin.	Excessive nitrate content of feeds is an increasingly important cause of poisoning in farm animals, due primarily to more and more high-nitrogen fertilization. But nitrate toxicity is not new, having been reported as early as 1850, and having occurred in semiarid regions of this and other countries for years.
Osteomalacia	All farm animals and humans.	Inadequate phosphorus (sometimes inadequate calcium). Lack of vitamin D. Inadequate intake of calcium and phosphorus. Incorrect ratio of calcium to phosphorus.	Phosphorus deficiency symptoms are: depraved appetite (gnawing on bones, wood, or other objects; or eating dirt); lack of appetite, stiffness of joints; failure to breed regularly; and an emaciated appearance. Calcium deficiency symptoms are: fragile bones; reproductive failures; and lowered lactations. Mature animals most affected. Most of the acute cases occur during pregnancy and lactation.	Southwestern U.S. is classed as a phosphorus-deficient area whereas calcium deficient areas have been reported in parts of Florida, Louisiana, Nebraska, Virginia, and West Virginia.
Periodic ophthalmia (moon blindness)	Horses. Mules. Asses.	It may be caused by (1) lack of riboflavin; (2) an autoimmune reaction; (3) an allergic reaction; (4) genetics; (5) leptospirosis, brucellosis, or strangles; (6) parasitic infections; or (7) fungal infections.	Periods of cloudy vision, in one or both eyes, which may last for a few days to a week or two and then clear up; but it recurs at intervals, eventually culminating in blindness in one or both eyes.	In many parts of the world. In the U.S. it occurs most frequently in Northeastern U.S.
Rickets	All farm animals and humans.	Lack of calcium, phosphorus, or vitamin D; or an incorrect ratio of the two minerals.	Enlargement of the knee and hock joints, and the animal may exhibit great pain when moving about. Irregular bulges (beaded ribs) at juncture of ribs with breastbone, and bowled legs. Rickets is a disease of young animals, including foals.	Worldwide. It is seldom fatal.
Salt deficiency (sodium chloride deficiency)	All farm animals and humans.	Lack of salt (sodium chloride).	Loss of appetite, retarded growth, loss of weight, a rough coat, lowered production of milk, and a ravenous appetite for salt.	Worldwide, especially among grass-eating animals.
Salt poisoning (sodium chloride)	All farm animals, including horses, but swine and sheep most frequently affected.	When excess salt is fed after a period of salt starvation. When salt is improperly used to govern self-feeding of concentrates.	Sudden onset—1 to 2 hours after ingesting salt; extreme nervousness; muscle twitching and fine tremors; much weaving and wobbling, staggering, and circling; blindness; weakness; normal temperature; rapid but weak pulse; and very rapid and shallow breathing; diarrhea; death from a few hours to 48 hours.	Salt poisoning is relatively rare.
Selenium poisoning (alkali disease)	All farm animals and humans.	Consumption of plants grown on soils containing high levels of selenium.	Loss of hair from the mane and tail in horses. In severe cases, the hoofs slough off, lameness occurs, feed consumption decreases, and death may occur by starvation.	In certain regions of western U.S.—especially certain areas in South Dakota, Montana, Wyoming, Nebraska, Kansas, and perhaps areas in other state in the Great Plains and Rocky Mountains. Also, in Canada.
Urinary calculi (gravel, stones, water belly)	Horses. Cattle. Sheep. Goats. Mink. Humans.	Unknown, but it seems to be nutritional. Experiments have shown a higher incidence of urinary calculi when there is (1) a high intake of potassium, (2) more phosphorus than calcium in the ration, or (3) a high proportion of beet pulp or grain sorghum in the nation.	Frequent attempts to urinate, dribbling or stoppage of the urine, pain and renal colic. Usually only males affected, the females being able to pass the concretions. Bladder may rupture, with death following. Otherwise, uremic poisoning may set in.	Worldwide. Affected animals seldom recover completely.

Health Management

(Continued)

Treatment	Prevention	Remarks
A 4% solution of methylene blue (in a 5% glucose or a 1.8% sodium sulfate solution) administered by a veterinarian intravenously at the rate of 100 cc/1000 lb liveweight.	More than 0.9% nitrate nitrogen (dry basis) may be considered as potentially toxic. Feed should be analyzed when in question. Nitrate poisoning may be reduced by (1) feeding high levels of grains and other high-energy feeds (molasses) and vitamin A, (2) limiting the amount of high-nitrate feeds, (3) ensiling forages which are high in nitrates.	Nitrate form of nitrogen does not appear to cause the actual toxicity. During digestion, the nitrate is reduced to nitrite, a more toxic form, 10 to 15 times more toxic than nitrates. In horses, conversion is in the cecum. When nitrate trouble is expected, contact veterinarian or county agent.
Select natural feeds that contain sufficient calcium and phosphorus. Feed a special mineral supplement. If the disease is far advanced, treatment will not be successful.	Feed balanced rations, and allow animals free access to suitable calcium and phosphorus supplement. Increase the calcium and phosphorus content of feeds through fertilizing the soils.	Calcium deficiencies are much more rare than phosphorus deficiencies in horses.
Antibiotics or corticosteriods administered promptly are helpful in some cases. Immediately (1) change to greener hay or grass, and (2) add riboflavin at the rate of 40 mg/day/animal.	Feed green grass, or well-cured green, leafy hay; or add riboflavin to the ration at the rate of 40 mg per horse per day.	This disease has been known to exist for at least 2,000 years.
If the disease has not advanced too far, treatment may be successful by supplying adequate amounts of vitamin D, calcium, and phosphorus, and/or adjusting the ratio o calcium to phosphorus.	Provide (1) sufficient calcium, phosphorus, and vitamin D, and (2) a correct ratio of the 2 minerals.	Rickets is characterized by a failure of growing bone to ossify or harden properly.
Salt starved animals should be gradually accustomed to salt; slowly increase the hand-fed allowance until the animals may be safely allowed free access to it.	Provide plenty of salt at all times, preferably by free-choice feeding.	Common salt is one of the most essential minerals for grass-eating animals and one of the easiest and cheapest to provide.
Provide large amounts of fresh water to affected animals. Those that cannot and do not drink should be given water via stomach tube, by a veterinarian. The veterinarian may also give (I.V. or intraperitoneally) calcium gluconate to severely affected animals.	If animals have not had salt for a long time, they should be hand fed salt, gradually increasing daily allowance until they leave a little in the mineral box, then self-feed.	Indians and pioneer handed down many legendary stories about huge numbers of wild animals that killed themselves by gorging at a newly found salt lick after having been salt starved for long periods of time.
The effect of chronic selenium toxicity may be reduced by feeding a high protein ration and by use of trace amounts of an arsenic compound. Pasture rotation and use of supplemental feeds from nonselenium areas are practical solutions to the problem. There is no known treatment for acute selenium poisoning.	Abandon areas where soils contain more than 0.5 ppm of selenium, because crops produced on such soils constitute a menace to both animals and humans.	Chronic cases of selenium poisoning occur when animals consume feeds containing 8.5 ppm of selenium over an extended period; acute cases occur on 500 to 1,000 ppm. The maximum level of selenium recommended by FDA is 2 ppm.
Once calculi develops, dietary treatment appears to be of little value. Smooth muscle relaxants may allow passage of calculi if used before rupture of bladder. In horses, bladder calculi must be surgically removed.	Good feed and management appear to lessen the incidence, but no sure preventive is known. Avoid high phosphorus and low calcium. Keep the Ca:P ratio between about 2:1 and about 1:1. Also, avoid high potassium. One to three percent salt in the concentrate ration may help (using the higher levels in the winter when water consumption is normally lower).	Calculi are stonelike concretions in the urinary tract which almost always originate in the kidneys. These stones block the passage of urine.

PARASITES

A ***parasite*** is a small, multicellular organism that lives on or in another animal (host) at the expense of the host. Parasites that attack the skin and body openings of the host are called ***external parasites***. Flies are often seen on the skin, around the eyes, and elsewhere on horses. They consume nutrients from the blood and tissue of the host. External parasites can transfer contagious diseases to other animals. Parasites that live in the internal organs, body cavities, and tissues are called ***internal parasites***. They can be found in the digestive system. The life cycle of internal parasites is directly related to the cleanliness and hygiene of the environment of the animal. Internal parasites are the major on-going problems for most horses.

All horse owners need to work in concert with their veterinarian to design and implement an effective parasite prevention and deworming program.

EXTERNAL PARASITES

Common external parasites include the following:

- blowflies—Blowflies live in decaying materials but may get into wounds on animals. They cause discomfort and lower growth and animal efficiency. Keeping areas clean around horse facilities eliminates breeding areas for blowflies. Approved insecticides can be used as well as traps and screens.
- biting flies—Biting flies include horse flies, stable flies, horn flies, biting midges, deer flies, and black flies. They suck blood from the horse and cause

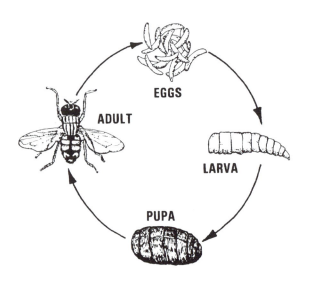

6-6. Disrupting the life cycle of flies is a good way to control them. (Removing breeding areas prevents the completion of their life cycle, which includes egg, larva, pupa, and adult.)

Health Management

discomfort. Horses may stamp their feet, switch their tails, and use other means to stop flies from bothering them. Pastures around low areas with stagnant water or near cattle have greater populations of biting flies. Some biting flies transmit diseases and parasites from one horse to another. Sanitation by destroying the breeding grounds is an effective prevention. An approved insecticide can be sprayed on horses to help control flies.

- mosquitoes—Mosquitoes bite and suck blood from horses. They cause discomfort and loss of blood. In some cases, diseases can be transmitted by the mosquito from a diseased horse to a well horse. Mosquitoes are most prevalent in warm areas near water. Control mosquitoes by doing away with breeding areas, such as pools of stagnant water.

- nonbiting flies—Common nonbiting flies include face flies and house flies. Face flies gather around the nose, eyes, and mouth. They take liquids secreted by the horse, resulting in increased tears from the eyes and more secretion from the nose and mouth. Approved insecticides can be used on horses to help control nonbiting flies. Some equestrians use face masks and nets. Sanitation helps reduce fly populations.

- lice—Lice are small, wingless insects that either bite or suck blood from a horse. Lice tend to be present on unthrifty horses. Nearly all horses have some lice, but the number must be kept low. Lice reduce the rate of growth and milk production. Horses may rub against posts, trees, or other structures to relieve itching. Lice can be controlled by spraying with approved insecticides.

- mites—Mites are very small animals related to ticks. Mites are not insects and do not fly. Mites produce a condition known as mange. Several species of mites attack animals,

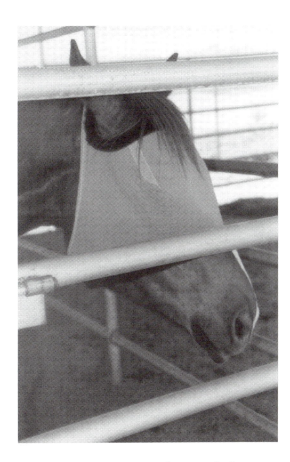

6-7. A face mask to protect the eyes of a horse from flies on a ranch in California. (Courtesy, Jasper S. Lee, Georgia)

94   EQUINE SCIENCE AND MANAGEMENT

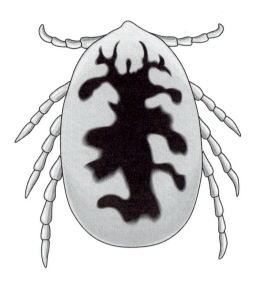

6-8. Enlarged drawing of a tick. (Ticks are not insects and are in the spider family!)

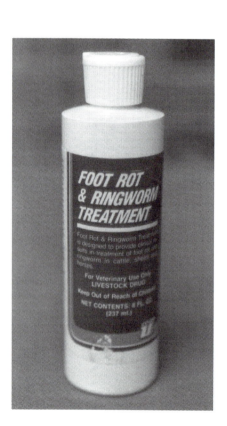

6-9. Various commercially-available materials may be used to control ringworm and other external parasites. (Courtesy, Jasper S. Lee, Georgia)

with three causing problems with horses. Scabs and other skin problems may be signs of mites. Mites feed by piercing the skin to feed on cells and tissue. Prevent mites by keeping infected animals away. Some materials are available for treating mites.

- ticks—Ticks are flightless parasites varying from microscopic size to the size of a pea. Ticks have eight legs and therefore are classified as arachnids, not insects. They attack horses, sucking blood and creating sores. High tick infestations reduce the vitality of horses. Some ticks transmit disease from one horse to another. Use an approved pesticide on horses to control ticks. Horses are sometimes dipped in water containing an approved chemical to remove ticks. Note: Ticks can easily crawl from a horse to its rider. Always check for the presence of ticks on your body if you find ticks on the horse you have ridden.
- ringworm—Ringworm is a contagious skin infection caused by some kinds of fungi. Round, scaly lesions occur on the skin. Crusts may form, and if ringworm

Health Management

is not controlled, they gradually increase in size. Contact of an infected animal with other animals spreads the disease. Indirect contact, such as with posts and gates that have been touched by an infected animal, may also spread the disease. Treatment consists of cleaning skin areas affected by ringworm and applying an approved medication.

INTERNAL PARASITES

Common internal parasites include worms and larvae of certain species of flies, known as bots. Losses to internal parasites can be quite large depending on the level of infestation. Tapeworms, stomach worms, and others compete with the animal for nutrition in the food that is consumed.

Details on internal parasites are shown in Table 6-2.

Table 6-2
Internal Parasites that Affect Horses

Parasite	Where Found	Damage	Signs
Ascarids (*Parascaris*), (Roundworms)	Small intestine.	Irritate intestinal wall, possible obstruction (impaction) and rupture of small intestine.	Digestive upsets (colic), diarrhea, weight loss, retarded growth, rough hair coat, pot bellied, death (ruptured intestine), more common in young horses.
Bots (*Gastrophilus*)	Larvae embedded in lining of mouth and tongue. Stomach.	Irritation and nervousness during the botfly egg laying season. Sore mouth and tongue. Inflammation, ulceration, perforation of stomach wall.	Excitement (caused by flies), evidence of pain when eating, digestive upsets (colic), retarded growth, poor condition, death (stomach rupture).
Pinworm (*Oxyuris*)	Large intestine. Rectum.	Irritation of anal region.	Rubbing of tail and anal regions, resulting in broken hairs and bare patches around tail and buttocks.
Stomach worm (*Habronema* adult), (*Habronema* larvae)	Stomach, attached to wall or free.	Stomach inflammation and colic. Larvae produce summer sores.	Gastritis, digestive disorders, and summer sores—which often heal spontaneously after first frost.
Strongyles, large (Bloodworms)	Adult strongyles are found in large intestine, attached to walls or free. Larvae migrate extensively to various organs and arteries.	Adults suck blood, cause anemia, and produce ulcers and mucosa. Larvae interfere with blood flow to the intestine, damage arteries, and cause aneurisms which may burst.	Anemia, rough hair coat, colic, loss of appetite, retarded growth, depression, soft feces with a foul odor. In large infestations, legs and abdomen swell.
Strongyles, small (*Triodotophorus, Poteriostomum, Trichonema,* and others)	Large intestine and cecum, attached to walls and free.	Injury to the large intestine.	Anemia, loss of appetite, retarded growth, dark or black manure, soft feces with a foul odor. In large infestations, legs and abdomen swell.
Tapeworm (*Anoplocephala*)	Varies according to species: A. magna and P. mamillana in small intestine and stomach. A. perfoliata mostly in cecum.	Ulceration of mucosa in area of attachment.	Unthriftiness, digestive disturbances, and anemia.
Threadworm (*Strongyloides*)	Small intestine.	Erosion of intestinal mucosa, enteritis.	Loss of appetite, loss of weight, diarrhea, worms disappear by time foals are 6 months old.

OTHER DISEASES

Horses are sometimes injured. This may be evident as cuts on the body, broken bones, and abrasions due to improper harness design or fit. Wounds should be properly treated to prevent infection and promote healing. Broken bones may need the attention of a veterinarian. In some cases, horses cannot recover from physical injury and should be humanely killed.

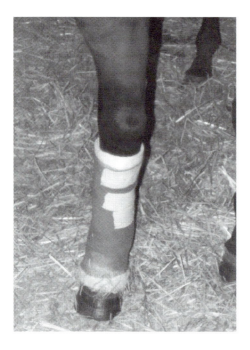

6-10. An injury to the leg of a horse has been treated by a veterinarian. (Courtesy, Jasper S. Lee, Georgia)

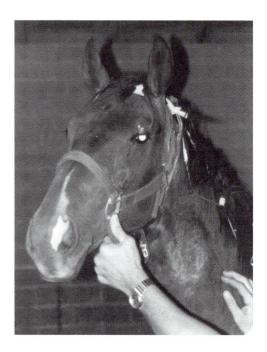

6-11. A diseased eye is undergoing treatment. (Courtesy, Jasper S. Lee, Georgia)

EXAMINATION PROCEDURES

Examination should take place daily to identify health problems. Here is what to look for:

1. Physical appearance
2. Daily eating habits
3. Daily bowel movements

Health Management

4. Daily urination
5. Behavior around you and other horses
6. Consumption of water, feed, and minerals

Keep records of your daily evaluations. Reviewing the records will help determine any changes in a horse's health.

If you suspect a problem:

1. Contact your veterinarian.
2. Conduct an examination of:
   a. Respiration
   b. Heart rate
   c. Temperature
   d. Reflexes
   e. Body Condition
   f. Behavior
3. Document all observations.
4. Once the problem is identified, correct the cause.

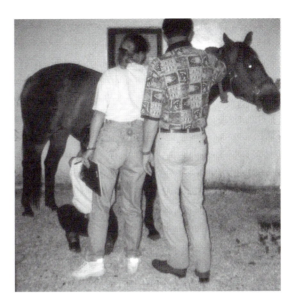

6-12. A horse examination should occur daily.

FOOT STRUCTURE AND CARE

The feet of horses are important in their mobility and in their ability to provide power. The foot of a horse is often referred to as a *hoof*. Proper foot

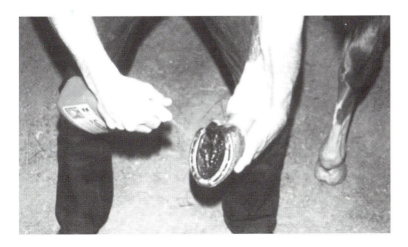

6-13. If the horse's feet become dry, apply an approved solution to prevent chipping and cracking.

EQUINE SCIENCE AND MANAGEMENT

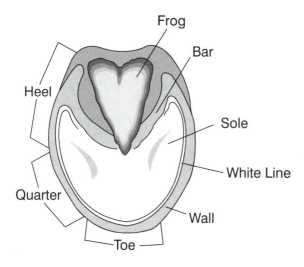

6-14. The structure of a horse hoof (bottom view).

care is essential. Nature provided horses with the kind of feet they needed in their natural environment roaming hills and meadows. Walking on hard surfaces and pulling heavy loads place increased demands on the feet.

The structure of a hoof is fairly complex. Fore (front) and hind hooves differ slightly but have a similar structure. Front feet tend to be rounder and wider than hind hooves. Bones, soft tissues, nerves, and blood vessels are protected by a reasonably hard outer material (sometimes known as horny material) similar to the fingernails of humans. This material grows downward and forward at the rate of no more than ¼ inch a month.

Foot care includes trimming, shoeing, and otherwise keeping the feet in good condition. Trimming helps the foot to retain proper shape. Nippers are used to trim the hard wall (horny material) of a hoof. Rasps may be used to file away horny material in shaping the hoof.

6-15. Shape of a ready-made horseshoe.

Shoeing protects the hoof from hard surfaces. A shoe is typically made of steel or aluminum. The metal shoe protects the foot from breaking and wearing away. Shoes are used to correct faults in the foot structure and stance of the horse. In some cases, rubber or other materials are used for shoes, depending on the use of the animal. For example, some special uses require horses to be on indoor hardwood or tile floors. Horses should be shod only by a qualified farrier. Improper shoeing can result in more problems than were solved by the shoes. Shoes should in no way interfere with the movement of a horse.

Health Management

6-16. A combination hoof pick and brush may be used to clean the foot. (The pick removes caked mud and other material stuck to the foot. The brush removes smaller particles.)

Shoes should be of the proper size and type. Some are ready-made and suited for most horses. Other shoes are heated and shaped prior to use. A shoe is attached by carefully nailing it in position. Nails should be only in the horny portion of the hoof. Nails that accidentally get into the soft parts or bone create serious foot injuries.

Daily inspection and care are needed. The feet of stabled horses are cleaned and checked for loose shoes. Feet are also inspected for thrush—a fungus disease that deteriorates the foot tissue, causing lameness. Cracked hooves result from dry conditions. Dry hooves can be prevented by having moist areas where horses go for water or using a commercial hoof dressing. With dry hooves, some equestrians spray the hooves with a mixture of 6 parts cod liver oil, 1 part pine tar oil, 1 part Creolin, and 2 parts glycerin. A few have tried feeding gelatin to horses, but research has not proven this to be effective. If a shoe is lost or must be removed because it is loose, a temporary barrier boot may be used over the entire hoof.

DISEASE PREVENTION

Disease prevention is keeping a horse healthy. It is an ongoing process and requires time and knowledge of horses. This can be done by the horse owner in cooperation with a veterinarian. Certain things must be done: make sure all vaccinations are current; practice good hygiene in the stables, paddocks, and pastures; remove debris from pastures or other areas around horses; provide clean, fresh water and clean, fresh feed; keep feeding facilities clean; restrict the contact of the horse to wild animals, rodents, and strange horses—if contact occurs, administer Coggins test. Isolate all newly pur-

6-17. A healthy horse if fun to own! (Dr. MeeCee Baker of Pennsylvania enjoys her recreational horses.) (Courtesy, Jasper S. Lee, Georgia)

chased animals for at least 30 days while you conduct a physical examination. Implement internal and external parasite control, and record and document daily activities and materials used, such as antibiotics, etc.

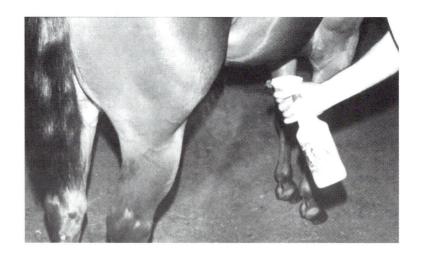

6-18. Spray your horse regularly with an approved insecticide to prevent fly problems.

REVIEWING

MAIN IDEAS

A horse's health is the responsibility of the horse owner. There are many ways to prevent problems from occurring, however, there must be a continu-

Health Management

ous effort. Every day many horses die and get sick from diseases. The horse owner can do many things, such as vaccinate, deworm, feed correctly, and provide a safe, clean environment.

Diseases vary. Bacteria, fungi, and viruses affect the health of a horse and are two organisms that humans can help control. Management procedures can protect your horse against these organisms.

Understanding the physiology of the horse is very important in managing the health of the animal. The horse is a very complex animal with many parts and systems. Knowing these parts and systems and how they work is important in keeping a horse healthy. The respiratory system, the circulatory system, the nervous system, the digestive system, and others keep the horse functioning. Many organs, such as the heart, liver, lungs, spleen, stomach, and intestines, play a major role.

Using the correct procedures for examinations is essential. Horse owners should know what to look for to diagnose a problem. This skill comes with experience, but can be learned on a daily basis.

QUESTIONS

Answer the following questions using correct spelling and complete sentences.

1. What is health? *The overall condition of an organism*
2. What is horse health management? *Management & prevention*
3. What is behavior? Name three categories of horse behavior. *action or response; contactual, ingestive, & elimination p.81*
4. What are the vital signs of horses? Name each and give acceptable ranges. *measurements of health p.83*
5. What is a disease? What is the distinction between contagious and noncontagious diseases? *abnormal condition p.84*
6. What are four diseases of horses? List the symptoms and treatment of each. *p.85*
7. What is a parasite? Distinguish between the two major types. *small org. p.92*
8. What are two examples of external parasites? For each, list the damage caused and how to control. *p.52*
9. What are two examples of internal parasites? For each, list the damage caused and signs of an infestation. *p.95*
10. What examination procedures are used with horses? *p.96-97*
11. Draw the structures of a hoof and label the major parts. *p.98*
12. What is included in foot care? *Shoeing*
13. Why are shoes used? *Protection*
14. How are diseases prevented? *protection*

EVALUATING

CHAPTER SELF-CHECK

Match the term with the correct definition. Place the letter by the term in the blank provided.

- a. disease
- b. bacteria
- c. veterinarian
- d. parasite
- e. contagious
- f. pathogen
- g. virus
- h. frog

___c___ 1. An animal health care professional.
___e___ 2. Spreading by direct or indirect contact.
___h___ 3. The triangular-shaped formation in the sole of the horse's hoof.
___b___ 4. One-celled organisms that enter the body and may cause disease.
___f___ 5. Any microorganism or virus that causes disease.
___a___ 6. An abnormal condition of an animal or organism.
___d___ 7. An organism that lives on or in another animal (host) at the expense of the host.
___g___ 8. A microscopic, contagious organism that enters the body through the air, the blood, water, or other conduits.

DISCOVERING

1. As a class project, take a field trip to visit a local veterinarian. Observe how the veterinarian conducts an examination of a horse. Prepare a short essay on your visit. Make an oral presentation to the class.

2. Collect information on the diseases of horses using the Internet and other references, such as *Horses and Horsemanship* by M. E. Ensminger, published by Interstate Publishers, Inc. List all contagious and noncontagious diseases. In addition, list the treatment and prevention of all the diseases.

3. Using horses designated for class, conduct a health examination under the supervision of a veterinarian or professional horse person.

4. Write an essay on the importance of horse health. Use several resources in collecting data, then deliver your essay to the class.

5. With the help of your veterinarian, develop a horse health care (disease and prevention control) calendar.

7
REPRODUCTION

It takes horses to make horses! ***Reproduction*** is the process by which an animal produces a new individual. In the wild, the stallion simply ran with a herd of mares and nature allowed for mating and reproduction of horses.

Throughout history, horse owners and breeders have worked to improve the process and have made much progress. Today, horse reproduction is controlled by the owner. Horses are reproduced to promote certain bloodlines. This enables owners to create horses with desired characteristics. Many new and innovative techniques are used to achieve this goal.

7-1. Mare with a healthy foal.

OBJECTIVES

This chapter focuses on the fundamentals of horse reproduction. The following objectives are included:

1. Explain the role of horse reproduction
2. Name and describe the reproductive functions of horses
3. Describe the phases of estrus in horses
4. Explain puberty
5. Describe factors in successful breeding
6. Explain technology used in horse breeding

TERMS

anestrus
artificial insemination (AI)
cervix
cloning
conception
ejaculation
embryo
embryo transfer (ET)
estrogen
estrous cycle
fertilization
fetus
genetic engineering
gestation
heat
insemination
metestrus
ovary
oviducts (fallopian tubes)
ovulation
parturition
puberty
reproduction
testicle

EQUINE KNOWLEDGE

The average gestation length for a mare is 336 days or a bit more than 11 months.

ROLE OF HORSE REPRODUCTION

Reproduction in horses is a scientific phenomena in which the genetic material of two horses is combined to produce an offspring. Traditionally, the stallion mated with the mare and produced a foal. Today, however, through many scientific breakthroughs, several different reproductive techniques can be used to produce an offspring.

The field of reproductive physiology includes the identification and function of reproductive organs. It also involves the knowledge of heat detection in mares and the breeding management of stallions. The study of the different phases of estrus (heat) is critical in successful horse breeding.

The different techniques used in today's horse breeding include hand breeding, pen breeding, and artificial insemination. The industry has dictated the techniques used because of the economics involved. For example, the semen from Triple Crown winner Secretariat would probably be worth millions of dollars; therefore, a semen sample using artificial insemination is critical. In addition, the collection and transportation of semen can link a stallion to many mares and foals. However, the Thoroughbred Breed does not permit the use of artificial insemination. Please check with specific breeds to determine their rules for breeding.

Other scientific breakthroughs, such as embryo transfer, have changed horse breeding. Eggs from a mare can be collected, fertilized, and placed into a recipient mare. This would be especially important in the horse racing industry or when dealing with expensive horses.

7-2. Selecting breeding stock is the first step in the reproduction process.

Breeding horses is important in the production of horses with desired traits. Various rules and regulations have been published by specific breed registries. Follow these regulations as appropriate.

The role of reproduction is to produce offspring. There are two very important components in the process—the stallion that will produce the sperm cells and the mare that will produce the ova or eggs and carry the fetus. With today's technology, embryo transfer makes it possible for a surrogate mare to carry the fetus. The selection process is the first step in reproduction. Horse owners must decide which sire or stallion is desired based on the characteristics of the bloodline. Then, the owner must choose which mare will carry the fetus. Once this is decided, then the technique can be determined to successfully achieve the goal of producing the desired foal.

REPRODUCTIVE FUNCTIONS

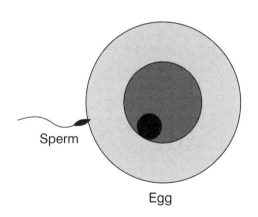

7-3. Fertilization of an egg. Drawing done to proportion.

Mating is the physical activity by which the male sex cell (sperm) is placed in the reproductive tract of the female. *Fertilization* is the union of a sperm and an egg. Whether fertilization takes place inside the reproduction tract or artificially in a test tube (in vitro), an embryo is produced. *Conception* is becoming pregnant. From this point, the female will carry the embryo to a fetus stage and deliver a foal in approximately 11 months. The period of pregnancy is known as gestation.

Insemination is the natural placing of semen in the vagina of a mare. *Artificial insemination* (AI) is the delivery of semen in the vagina through artificial means. AI is becoming more advanced and is a widely used method of insemination.

After insemination, the sperm cells travel up the reproductive tract into the oviduct to the site of fertilization. Once conception takes place, the embryo implants into the uterine wall until birth.

The reproductive organs of horses vary by the gender of the animal. Successful reproduction requires males and females with organs that can perform the necessary functions.

MALE ORGANS

The primary reproductive organ of the stallion is the testicle. The **testicle** produces the sperm cells necessary for reproduction. Stallions have two testicles. The scrotum provides a good environment for the testicles to produce sperm cells. Once produced, sperm are stored in tubes attached to the testicles. Males begin to produce sperm at puberty and will continue throughout life unless castrated or injured. The sperm cells are formed in the seminiferous tubules and are then carried through the epididymis to the vas deferens where they pick up semen fluid. **Ejaculation** is the expelling of semen. At ejaculation, semen passes through the vas deferens and the penis. The penis is protected by the sheath or folds of skin when not erect.

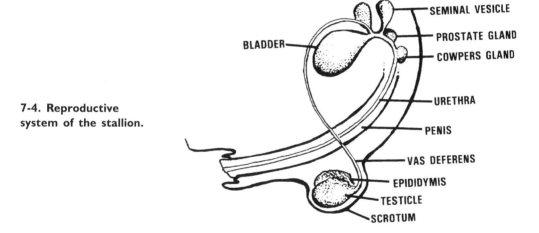

7-4. Reproductive system of the stallion.

FEMALE ORGANS

The primary reproductive organ in the mare is the **ovary**. The ovary produces an ovum or egg, which is a reproductive cell called a gamete. Mares have two ovaries, which produce several ova per cycle of ovulation. The ovarian follicles develop then release the ova monthly. This process is call **ovulation**. Ova are released from the ovaries, go down the bursa sack (cover over the ovaries), then down the oviducts or fallopian tubes. The **oviducts** are tubes through which ova travel to the uterus, the largest of the female reproductive organs. The uterus connects through the cervix to the vagina which

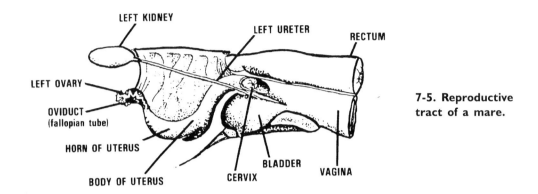

7-5. Reproductive tract of a mare.

extends to the external vulva. The *cervix* is the neck-like part of the female reproductive tract that separates the uterus from the vagina.

PHASES OF ESTRUS

The *estrous cycle* is the time from one heat cycle to the next. **Heat** or estrus is the period when the female is receptive to mating. The entire estrus cycle ranges from 21 to 22 days. It involves a complex body change that allows the mare to receive the stallion and for the release of eggs from the ovaries to meet the male sperm needed for fertilization.

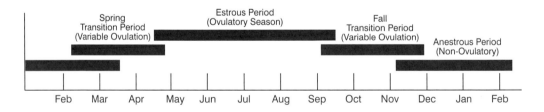

7-6. The estrus cycle in a mare.

ANESTRUS

Anestrus is an interval of sexual dormancy between two periods of estrus. During this phase, the ovaries are small and inactive. As the mare comes out of anestrus the ovaries will enlarge, soften, and follicles will begin to develop.

ESTRUS

Estrus is the "heat" period in which a mare will receive (mate with) a stallion without rejection and is physiologically able to conceive. The length of estrus (heat) for a mare is 1 to 6 days. The entire estrous cycle for a horse is 21 to 22 days. Heat is activated by estrogen. **Estrogen** is a hormone produced by the ovary and is responsible for estrus behavior. There are many behaviors and symptoms during this period, such as restlessness, liquid discharge from vulva, swollen vulva, and mounting other horses. Ovulation takes place near the end of estrus.

METESTRUS

The period following the estrus phase or heat is called **metestrus**. During this phase, ovulation occurs in which the ovaries release the eggs or ova through the bursa sac and down the oviducts. After ovulation, some bleeding may occur for a few hours to a few days. During ovulation, luteinizing hormone (LH) activates the corpus lutea (CL) to develop after the release of the eggs or ova. The CL is important in maintaining pregnancy and breaking the heat cycle.

DIESTRUS

The diestrus phase is the luteal phase of the cycle and begins with ovulation. During diestrus, the uterus is being prepared for pregnancy. A fully functional CL assists in the release of high levels of progesterone, the hormone that maintains pregnancy.

PROESTRUS

Proestrus begins with the regression of the corpus luteum and a drop in progesterone. Follicle stimulating hormone (FSH) causes growth of an ovum to full size in preparation for estrus and ovulation. You will begin to see a behavioral change as estrus approaches.

PUBERTY

Puberty is the age at which an animal can physically reproduce—sexual maturity. Puberty in the stallion is reached at 12 to 16 months of age, when

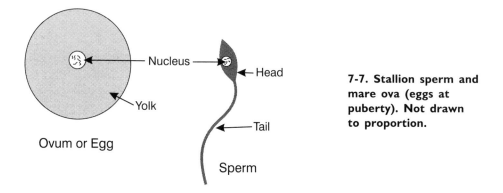

7-7. Stallion sperm and mare ova (eggs at puberty). **Not drawn to proportion.**

he can ejaculate with fertile sperm capable of fertilization. In the filly, puberty is reached at 12 to 15 months of age, when ovulation produces viable ova or eggs.

Puberty is a growing phase of both the stallion and mare and full reproductive performance and efficiency takes place over a period of time. There are several factors that affect the puberty of mares and stallions. The genetics of the breed, etc., along with the environment in which they are kept. It is very important to carefully introduce horses into a breeding schedule so they are not damaged or hurt.

AGE TO BREED

Horses must have sufficient body growth and development for breeding. The reproductive organs should be capable of completing the reproductive process. Horses are among the most difficult of all domestic animals to breed. Breeding practices vary with the breed of horse.

Usual practice is to begin using a stallion for breeding at two years of age. The number of breedings should be no more than 10 to 15 for a two-year-old. This can be increased as the horse matures. The number of times a stallion can be used depends on sperm production. Stallions are often used for breeding up to the age of 25 years or more.

With fillies, it is best to wait until age three, though some are bred at age two if they are well-developed. Breeding at age three results in foaling as a four-year-old. Best conception occurs if the mare is in good physical condition. The mare should be properly fed and exercised to avoid excess fat. Mares that run together in pastures usually get sufficient exercise. Only about 50 percent of mares bred produce live foals. A mare can be used for breeding purposes through age 15 or 20, depending on ability to conceive and overall health.

THE BREEDING PROCESS

The goal of breeding is to conceive and deliver a healthy foal. The breeding process involves:

1. Selecting the animals to breed.
2. Selecting the method of breeding (hand breeding or artificial insemination).
3. Obtaining the correct facilities and help.
4. Good record keeping (when mated, to whom, conditions, etc.).
5. Good heat detection of the mare.
6. Having an available stallion or semen for artificial insemination.
7. Using excellent hygiene practices with breeding animals.
8. Safety of handlers and horses.

Breeding may involve natural methods or newer technologies (which are covered later in the chapter). Most horse breeding is done by people who are trained in how to manage horses. Stallions and mares are not usually allowed to breed naturally in pastures. They are pastured separately and bred using a hand breeding process. Hand breeding involves natural service in a carefully controlled breeding environment. Injury to the mare or stallion may result if trained people are not involved in the breeding process.

FERTILIZATION AND GESTATION

In fertilization, the sperm unites with an ovum to create a zygote. Cell division will then take place to form an embryo. The **embryo** is the early stages of development of an unborn animal. The *fetus* is the more advanced stages of

7-8. Mare with a newly born foal.

development of the unborn animal. ***Gestation*** is the period when the mare carries the fetus before giving birth. In the horse, this is approximately 11 months from the time of conception. The average gestation period ranges from 335 days to 340 days. Mares typically have only one baby at a time. With good management, a mare will conceive and give birth to several foals in her lifetime. (Refer to Appendixes C and D for more details.)

PARTURITION

Parturition is the act of a mare giving birth to a foal. Many physiological changes take place during this time. Horse owners need to know the signs of parturition as many mares need assistance giving birth. The usual signs are:

1. Nesting behavior by the mare
2. Restlessness
3. Separation from other horses
4. Swollen vulva
5. Frequent urination
6. Milk drops from teats
7. Contractions visible
8. Water breakage and discharge

The first few hours after birth are critical for the foal and mare. The foal needs to be in a dry, warm, and clean environment. The mare should be observed to make sure she has passed the placenta and is nursing the foal. A health check should be given to both animals very soon after parturition.

LACTATION

Lactation is the process in which a mare produces milk for her foal. The foal needs to receive colostrum very soon after birth. Colostrum, the first milk, contains antibodies to fight off disease and other health risks. The nutrition also provided by milk is extremely important for the growth and development of the foal. Foals should nurse the mare for several weeks until other foods can be consumed.

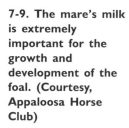

7-9. The mare's milk is extremely important for the growth and development of the foal. (Courtesy, Appaloosa Horse Club)

MODERN TECHNOLOGY

Modern technology is changing the way horses are bred. Today, artificial insemination, embryo transfer, genetic engineering, and cloning are being studied and performed. Some of these are in the early experimental stages while others are being used in the industry today.

ARTIFICIAL INSEMINATION

Artificial insemination (AI) has been used successfully in cattle for many years. The swine industry also uses AI. The horse industry has faced several breed organization policies and not all agree on the use of AI. However, it is being used in the horse industry and semen production and breeding is a growing and viable business. With AI, the semen is collected then placed artificially into the uterus of the mare without natural service. The semen is placed at the proper time in the heat cycle to enhance chances of conception.

The semen collection process is very critical. The stallion mounts an artificial animal and ejaculates into an artificial vagina. The semen is then taken to a lab and processed. Semen must be handled carefully not to harm the sperm cells. Semen can be divided and used soon after ejaculation or extended (diluted) with a solution and refrigerated. Semen can be mailed to horse owners to be used on mares worldwide. Because horse breeds associa-

Table 7-1. Breeding Data

Age	No. of Matings/Yr. Hand Mating	No. of Matings/Yr. Pasture Mating	Comments
2-year-old	10–15	Preferably no pasture mating unless the stallion is prepared for same and certain precautions are taken.	1. Limit the 2-year-old to 2–3 services/week; the 3-year-old to 1 service/day; and 4-year-old or over to 2–3 services/day.
3-year-old	20–40		
4-year-old	40–60		
Mature horse	50–70		2. A stallion should remain a vigorous and reliable breeder up to 20 to 25 years of age.
Over 18 yrs. old	20–40		

¹There are breed differences. Thus, when first entering stud duty, the average 3-year-old Thoroughbred should be limited to 20 to 25 mares per season, whereas a Standardbred of the same age may breed 25 to 30 mares; and the 4- or 5-year-old Thoroughbred should be limited to 30 or 40 mares, whereas a Standardbred of the same age may breed 40 to 50 mares. Mature stallions of the draft breeds may breed up to 70, or more, mares in a season.

tions have different regulations on artificial insemination, conduct a study to see what the criteria is for each major breed.

Conception rates are very important and the way semen is handled has a direct affect on conception rates. Some keys to good conception rates with AI are:

1. Collect enough good sperm cells.
2. Evaluate for motility (movement or swimming ability).
3. Divide adequately for each mare to be inseminated.
4. Transport and store properly.
5. Prepare the insemination dosage correctly.
6. Make sure the mare to be inseminated is in estrus or heat.
7. Practice good health hygiene.

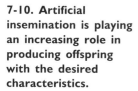

7-10. Artificial insemination is playing an increasing role in producing offspring with the desired characteristics.

NEW TECHNOLOGIES

Several new technologies are now being used or soon will be used. Three of these technologies are included here.

Embryo Transfer

Embryo transfer (ET) is the process of moving a developing embryo from a donor mare to the uterus of a recipient mare. Donor mares usually carry the specific genetic material needed, where the recipient mare is the animal that can carry the fetus to birth. Embryo transfer is widely used in the cattle industry but again, the horse industry has not fully approved this practice.

7-11. A facility for breeding which has a video system for monitoring behavior. (Courtesy, Harris Farms, California)

Cloning

Cloning is the duplication of genetic material or the production of an exact copy of an animal. To reproduce horses like Secretariat or Ruffian would be worth millions of dollars. However, the ethics of cloning are being hotly debated.

Genetic Engineering

Genetic engineering is the process of changing an animal's genetic material. Gene therapy could result in breakthrough techniques in the treatment of animals born with health problems or abnormalities. As with cloning, genetic engineering is surrounded in controversy.

REVIEWING

MAIN IDEAS

Reproduction is the process of producing a foal. The stallion produces sperm and the mare produces ova or eggs. The sperm and egg must unite for fertilization. With horses, this can be done through natural service or artificial insemination.

The stallion and mare have reproductive organs that are necessary for successful reproduction. The male must have functional testicles that produce sperm and fluids necessary for fertilization. The female must have functional ovaries that produce ova or eggs along with the fluids necessary for successful fertilization.

The reproductive cycle is a complex system that goes through several phases. The reproductive cycle in a horse is 21 to 22 days during which the mare comes into heat and releases eggs. The heat phase during which the mare will allow the stallion to breed or inseminate last for just a few days. This is important to ensure time for the sperm and egg to meet for fertilization.

Puberty is the age when an animal can physically reproduce. When this is reached the stallion produces sperm cells and the mare produces eggs. Caution should be taken with both sexes when entering into the breeding stage of life.

New technology is being used and introduced in the horse industry. The horse industry is controlled by the breed associations. Rules and regulations

Reproduction

are continuously evaluated for the best interest of the industry. All horse owners should know what developments are on the horizon and consider the ethics of each.

QUESTIONS

Answer the following questions using correct spelling and complete sentences.

1. Why is horse reproduction important?
2. What are the major reproductive functions?
3. What are the major reproductive organs of the male horse?
4. What is the male sex cell called? Female sex cell?
5. What are the major reproductive organs of the female horse?
6. What are the phases of the estrous cycle?
7. What is estrus? What hormone is responsible for estrus behavior?
8. What is puberty? How does puberty vary with male and female horses?
9. What is the breeding age for stallions and fillies?
10. What is the distinction between an embryo and a fetus?
11. What is parturition? What are the signs of approaching parturition?
12. What new technologies are now or soon will be used?

EVALUATING

CHAPTER SELF-CHECK

Match the term with the correct definition. Place the letter by the term in the blank provided.

a. testicle
b. cloning
c. ejaculation
d. ovary
e. fertilization
f. parturition
g. artificial insemination
h. gestation

____1. The male reproductive organ that produces sperm.
____2. A female reproductive gland.

_____3. The act of giving birth.

_____4. The period when the mare carries the fetus before giving birth.

_____5. The union of a sperm with an egg.

_____6. The duplication of genetic material; producing an exact copy of an animal.

_____7. The delivery of semen into the vagina through artificial means.

_____8. Expelling semen.

DISCOVERING

1. Draw a female horse's reproductive tract labeling all the reproductive organs and important parts. Collect your information from textbooks, the Internet, or other related sources.

2. Draw a male horse's reproductive tract labeling all the reproductive organs and important parts. Collect your information from textbooks, the Internet, or other related sources.

3. Tour a horse farm and observe the breeding process. Observe the male used in the mating process and the female. List the steps taken to prepare both for the breeding. If possible, observe one artificial insemination breeding and one natural breeding session.

4. Interview a horse breeder and discuss the usage of artificial insemination in the horse industry. Note the advantages and disadvantages and then prepare a written report to be delivered in class.

5. In groups, using the Internet, find the current status on artificial insemination for the American Quarter Horse Association, American Saddlebred Association, and the Walking Horse Association. Prepare a written report and deliver it in class.

6. Hold a debate in class on whether cloning should be used in the horse industry. Consider the pros and cons to this issue.

Having Fun with Horses

(Courtesy, Eastern Randolph High FFA Chapter)

(Courtesy, Madison High FFA Chapter)

(Courtesy, East Montgomery High FFA Chapter)

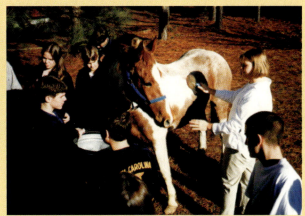

(Courtesy, East Montgomery High FFA Chapter)

Using horses to travel and camp in the mountains.

The Royal Canadian Mounted Police use horses in their work.

Equine Events

Showing

Parade dress

Rodeoing

Jumping

Horse racing

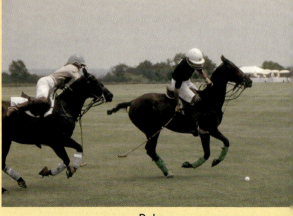
Polo

Recreational Horse Breeds

Standardbred
(Courtesy, U.S. Trotting Association, Columbus, OH)

The Buckskin
(Courtesy, International Buckskin Horse Association, Shelby, IN)

The Thoroughbred
(Courtesy, Harris Farms, Coalinga, CA)

The Tennessee Walking Horse
(Courtesy, Tennessee Walking Horse Breeders' and Exhibitors' Association, Lewisburg, TN)

The Connemara
(Courtesy, American Connemara Pony Society, Winchester, VA)

Recreational Horse Breeds

American Saddlebred and colt

Shetland Pony
(Courtesy, Kentucky Horse Park, Lexington, KY)

The Arabian
(Courtesy, Gainey Arabians, Santa Ynez, CA)

Hackney Hitch
(Courtesy, American Hackney Horse Society, Lexington, KY)

The Morgan
(Courtesy, American Morgan Horse Association, Shelburne, VT)

Paso Fino and colt
(Courtesy, Paso Fino Horse Association, Plant City, FL)

Recreational Horse Breeds

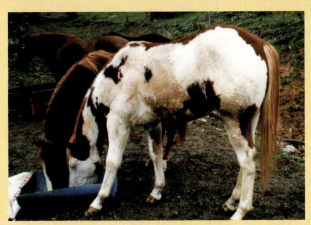

The Pinto
(Courtesy, Madison High FFA Chapter)

Spanish Mustang
(Courtesy, Southwest Spanish Mustang Association, Finley, OK)

Welsh Pony
(Courtesy, Welsh Pony and Cob Society of America, Winchester, VA)

The Appaloosa
(Courtesy, Madison High FFA Chapter)

The Quarter Horse
(Courtesy, American Quarter Horse Association, Amarillo, TX)

Specialty Horses and Related Species

The Mule
(Courtesy, Madison High FFA Chapter)

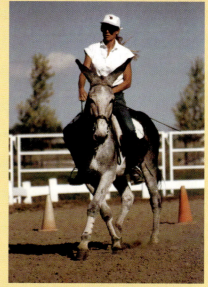

1st level dressage donkey doing
a leg yield on the diagonal.
(Courtesy, Lucky Three Ranch, Loveland, CO)

The Percheron
(Courtesy, Feed Corral Percherons, Springfield, IL)

The Clydesdale

The Miniature Horse
(Courtesy, American Miniature Horse Association)

The American Donkey
(Courtesy, American Donkey and Mule Society)

Equitation

Stock seat equitation requires a Western saddle.

In saddle seat equitation, the rider sits back in the saddle and remains vertical through all gaits.
(Courtesy, Melissa Hower-Moritz, University of Minnesota–Crookston)

Properly holding the reins in two hands English style.

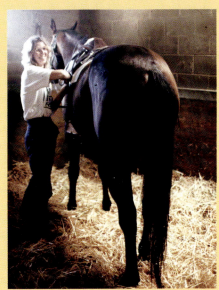

Horses must be properly prepared for riding and properly handled after riding.

Properly holding the reins Western style.
(Both or one hand can be used.)

The gait of a horse is how it moves.

Caring for Horses and Equipment

(Courtesy, American Quarter Horse Association)

(Courtesy, Brevard High FFA Chapter)

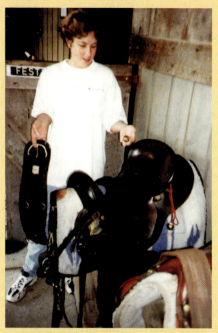

(Courtesy, Brevard High FFA Chapter)

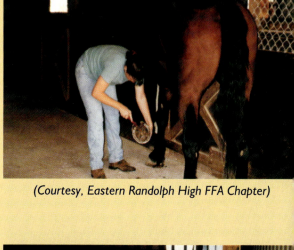

(Courtesy, Eastern Randolph High FFA Chapter)

(Courtesy, Eastern Randolph High FFA Chapter)

(Courtesy, Brevard High FFA Chapter)

8

FACILITIES AND EQUIPMENT

Horses like to live in a comfortable place! The facilities and equipment used in equine production and management are important for the safety and maximum performance of the horse. When designing any building, fence, or facility, keep in mind the basic nature of the horse. For example, fences and stalls that are adequate for cattle or other animals may be hazardous for horses. When designing facilities for horses, consider:

- Need—What facilities are needed?
- Cost—Can the facilities be paid for?
- Durability—Will the facilities last?
- Usefulness—Will the facilities be adequate for my needs?
- Flexibility—Can the facilities be used in a variety of ways?
- Zoning—Will the facilities meet land use, governmental, and other regulations?
- Waste handling—Will the facilities make easy waste management?
- Safety—Will the facilities promote safety of the horse and people?

8-1. Horse facilities are important to the horse, the owner, and the industry. This shows a Kentucky horse barn of great charm and beauty.

OBJECTIVES

This chapter examines the facilities and equipment associated with equine management. The objectives of the chapter are as follows:

1. Describe facility needs for horse management
2. Identify the basic tack and equipment needed with horses
3. Describe the proper environment needed for horses
4. Discuss the different types of barns and stables for small and large horse farms

TERMS

barn
bit
bridle
English saddle
foal creep
Hackamore
halter
hot walker
one ear bridle
Pelham
saddle
stable
stall
tack
Western saddle
Weymouth

EQUINE KNOWLEDGE

Did you know that a new foal's comfort zone is 75° to 80°F?

FACILITIES

Carefully select and plan facilities. One of the most important things to keep in mind when choosing horse facilities is safety for the horse and for you. Facilities must be designed to protect the horse during all kinds of activity. Many horses are hurt due to hazards, such as sharp edges or projections, bad fencing, and barb wire, that can be eliminated. In addition, many horse owners have been injured by these hazards. More injures are caused by human error or neglect than are caused by accidents. Most injuries can be prevented by correctly designing facilities and through a good understanding of horsemanship.

ENVIRONMENTAL NEEDS

Horses need the proper environment in which to live whether it is outside—pasture, paddock or holding lot—or inside—stable or barn.

Outside Environment

The outside environment is critical because horses face the elements of nature plus the elements that people have placed upon them. The factors are:

1. Ample space.
2. Clean hygiene.
3. Clean and proper eating area.
4. Clean and proper water.
5. Shelter or shaded area.
6. Correct fencing.
7. Debris free pasture or environment.

Inside Environment

Horses are sometimes kept in a barn. In very cold climates, warm barns protect horses from cold weather. The inside environment should consist of the following:

1. Clean surroundings.
2. Ample space.

122   **EQUINE SCIENCE AND MANAGEMENT**

8-2. This photograph shows clean, ample space providing a good environment for the horse.

3. Clean feeding and watering area.
4. Debris-free stalls or inside confinement area.

Horses need daily exercise. They like to run and play. They roll and enjoy sleep and rest.

COST

The cost of horse facilities varies greatly. Cost is a limiting factor in the construction of new horse facilities. Fancy, well-planned horse farms are a pleasure to visit, but many are far beyond the average horse owner's budget.

8-3. A modern horse facility. (Courtesy, Harris Farms, California)

Facilities and Equipment

There are many less-expensive, durable, and well-constructed facilities that will serve the animal and the owner for many years. Preparing an estimate of the cost of facilities is a part of planning.

LAND

After cost, land is the most limiting factor to the horse owner. Many people have horses on small lots and because of the grazing pressure the grass is either eaten or worn down by the hooves of horses. In addition to serving as pasture, land is important as the site for barns, holding lots or paddocks, exercise areas, and riding areas. If you are going to breed, board, or take care of other peoples' horses you will need much acreage. It is important to determine the goals and objectives of your horse operation before you buy or build any type of horse facility. Then, you can determine your land needs.

BARNS AND STABLES

A *barn* is a building that shelters harvested crops, livestock, and machinery. A *stable* is a structure in which horses or cattle are sheltered and fed. Barns and stables should be located on sites that are well drained and easily accessible in all types of weather. Barns and stables should be durable and made from materials that are not harmful to horses. Barns and stables should be surrounded by pasture or paddocks so a loose horse cannot get into roads, gardens, or yards. The facilities should be pleasant to everyone who

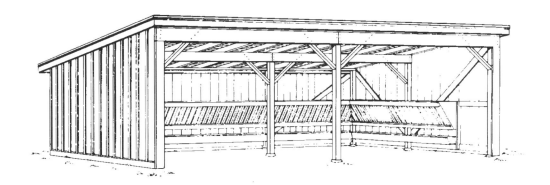

8-4. Open sheds are often used for horses on pasture or an exercise lot where the weather is not extremely cold.

visits or works there and should be designed for ease in feeding and cleaning. Construction considerations include:

1. Attractiveness of facilities
2. Ventilation inside barns and stables
3. Fire resistance
4. Safety
5. Durability
6. User friendly
7. Roofing that prevents dampness and controls water runoff
8. Drainage around the facility to properly divert excess precipitation

The type of barn depends on the goals of your horse operation. The type of barn needed for a breeding operation certainly differs from one of a pleasure operation. In addition, the cost factor will dictate your barn to a large degree. The type of barn is based on whether you have a small horse enterprise or a large horse enterprise.

Barns and stables are constructed to accommodate individual horses. A *stall* is a compartment within a facility that is designed for holding one horse.

Small horse enterprise:

1. Building is conveniently located and has a roadway to allow year-round access
2. Several stalls with a storage room for feed, tack, and other items
3. Storage room for feed, tack, and other items

8-5. A horse facility.

Facilities and Equipment **125**

Large horse enterprise:

1. Broodmare and foaling barn
2. Mare barn

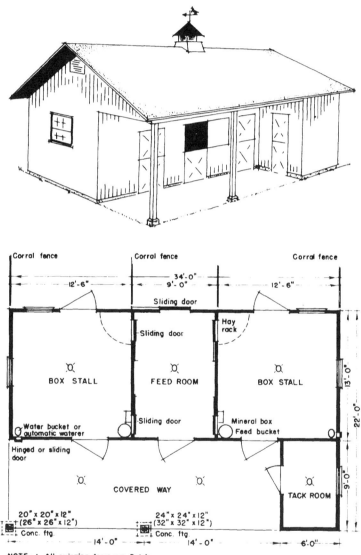

8-6. A riding horse barn layout with two box stalls, a feed room, and a tack room.

3. Stallion barn
4. Breeding shed and breeding arena
5. Weanling and yearling barn
6. Isolation barn
7. Riding and training barn
8. Office

The other components to consider are the open-front shelters, stalls, walls, windows, feeders, waterers, mangers, floors, tie stalls, foaling stalls, broodmare stalls, foal creeps, stallion facilities, breeding sheds, hay storage, feed room, tack room, office, wash rack, hot walker, and arena.

A *foal creep* is a feeder designed in such a manner that mature animals cannot access the feed. Such a feeder is needed to allow foals to access feed that supplements mare's milk and pasture. A *hot walker* is a mechanical device (in some cases, a person may perform this duty) that directs horses in a circle at a slow pace to cool them.

The major driving force in deciding whether these components are needed is the objective or type of operation you have.

BASIC TACK AND EQUIPMENT

Tack is the grooming equipment, the bridle, the saddle, and other equipment that may be needed. There are many types of specialty tack and equipment for different activities, such as racing, showing, and endurance.

GROOMING EQUIPMENT

The basic grooming equipment includes the following:

- hoof pick
- curry comb
- dandy brush
- body brush
- mane ad tail comb
- washer-groomer comb
- sponges
- sweat scraper
- rub rags
- hoof dressing brush

Facilities and Equipment **127**

- shears
- hard rubber curry comb
- clippers

These items should be used properly to get the desired results and prevent injury to the horse. Chapter 9 provides information on proper use.

SADDLES

A ***saddle*** is a leather seat that makes horseback riding safer and more comfortable. In addition, the saddle helps the rider control the horse. A saddle pad should always be used on the horse's back underneath a saddle.

The Western and the English are two basic types of saddles. The Western saddle was first developed by the Spanish in Old Mexico. The **Western saddle** has a curved, deep seat to provide all-day comfort while working livestock and a horn used to anchor a rope. It became famous when cowboys were portrayed in movies. The **English saddle** is generally light in construction and flat, without a horn. It was developed for training, racing, jumping, showing, and polo. It is much lighter and less bulky than the Western saddle.

Riding styles dictate the type of saddle used. Each saddle has its own characteristics. The Western saddle was developed for horse riders who spent hours in the saddle working cattle. The primary consideration with the Western saddle was and still is comfort. Of course, there are many types of Western saddles and many are used for shows or parades.

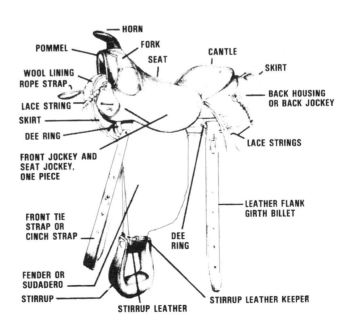

8-7. Parts of the Western saddle.

The English saddle is used for activities such as fox hunting, jumping, showing, and other events. Many people use English saddles for pleasure riding. There are three general types of English saddles.

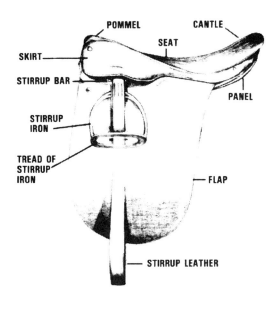

1. Flat or hacking — used for general purpose riding.
2. Forward seat — differs from the flat saddle in that the flats are cut in such a way that they are well forward and have padded knee rolls.
3. Show or cutback — used in saddle seat classes and for saddlebred and gaited horses. The pommel is cut back.

8-8. Parts of the English saddle.

Many variations of riding saddles, bridles, and bits are available.

BRIDLES

A *bridle* is the equipment placed on the head of a horse. It is used to guide and control the animal. A bridle consists of the headstall, bit, and reins. The bridle's purpose can be compared to the steering wheel in a car. Choosing the correct bridle is important to both the horse and the rider.

Four types of bridles are:

1. Weymouth—The **Weymouth** is a double-bitted, double-reined bridle used primarily for gaited horses.
2. Pelham—The **Pelham** is a single-bitted, double-reined bridle used on hunters, polo ponies, and pleasure horses.
3. One ear or split ear—The **one ear bridle** (or split ear) is often used on working stock horses. It is also used on pleasure horses.
4. Hackamore—The **Hackamore** is a bit-less bridle used on western ponies and on young horses when they are being broken. The Hackamore eliminates possible injury to the horse's mouth.

Facilities and Equipment

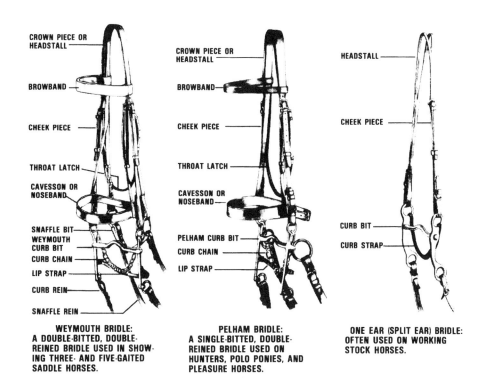

8-9. Three types of bridles. The Weymouth, the Pelham, and the split ear or one ear.

A *bit* is the metal mouthpiece on a bridle. It is the most important part of the bridle. There are three basic types of bits.

1. Hackamore bit—This is a bit used mostly on cow ponies.
2. Roper curved cheek bit—This is a bit used on many roping horses.
3. Snaffle bit—This is the most widely used of all bits and has a simple design.

A *halter* is a device used for either leading a horse or tying a horse. A halter fits over and around the head and does not have a bit. Types of halters include:

1. A rope halter is very strong and inexpensive. It will last longer than a leather halter if properly cared for.

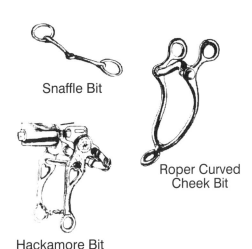

8-10. Three types of bits.

8-11. Split rail fences are easily seen by horses and are appealing to people in an attractive layout.

2. A nylon halter is very popular now and also inexpensive.

3. A leather halter can be very expensive and will not last long without the proper care.

4. A show halter is the most expensive halter. It is used mostly for shows, parades, and other special events. Show halters require much care.

It is a good idea to remove the halter from an unattended horse before it is turned into a pasture. The horse may be easier to catch with its halter on, but there are many dangers to the horse. Many horses have been injured and some deaths have occurred because halters were left on. Observing a horse several times each day will detect any problems.

8-12. Lunging ring for exercising horses on an Arizona ranch. (Courtesy, Jasper S. Lee, Georgia)

Facilities and Equipment

REVIEWING

MAIN IDEAS

Horse facilities and equipment are two of the main considerations of owning a horse. Horses must be controlled and confined to a given location whether in a 100-acre pasture or a stall. Correct facilities and equipment must be safe to both the horse and rider/owner.

Basic tack consists of the saddle, which can be Western style or English style, and the bridle, which has a function similar to the steering wheel of a car. There are several different types of bridles. The bit, which is the part of the bridle that goes into the horse's mouth, is available in several different styles and types. A horse's characteristics and the nature of its performance governs what type of bridle and bit to use.

The environmental needs of the horse should be the first consideration for all prospective horse owners. The correct shelter/barn and pasture or paddock is the beginning. Water, shade, and fencing should also be provided. Decisions should be made about these before obtaining a horse.

QUESTIONS

Answer the following questions using correct spelling and complete sentences.

1. What are the outside environmental needs of a horse? Inside needs?
2. What should be considered in constructing housing facilities for a horse?
3. Distinguish between housing for small and large horse enterprises.
4. What are the basic pieces of tack needed for horse owners?
5. Why is a foal creep useful?
6. What are the two major types of saddles? How do they differ?
7. What types of bridles are used?
8. What is a bit? What types are used?
9. What is a halter? What types of halters are used?
10. What grooming equipment may be needed?

EVALUATING

CHAPTER SELF-CHECK

Match the term with the correct definition. Place the letter by the term in the blank provided.

a. barn
b. hot walker
c. bit
d. stall
e. bridle
f. shelter
g. foal creep
h. stable

____ 1. A feeder designed in such a manner that mature animals cannot access the feed.

____ 2. A piece of equipment similar to the steering wheel on a car.

____ 3. Something that covers, protects, or defends.

____ 4. A mechanical device that directs horses in a circle at a slow pace to cool them.

____ 5. A building that shelters harvested crops, livestock, machines, etc.

____ 6. The metal mouthpiece on a bridle.

____ 7. A compartment for one animal in a barn.

____ 8. A building in which horses or cattle are sheltered and fed.

DISCOVERING

1. Tour a horse farm. Discuss the structures and buildings necessary to operate a horse farm with the owner or manager.

2. Visit a local tack store and conduct an inventory on the different kinds of equipment used in horse production. Prepare a display for the bulletin board at school with pictures of all the different types of horse equipment.

3. Conduct research on the different types of fences. List the pros and cons of each including costs. Consult with an expert (extension agent, farm supply dealer, horse owner, etc.) to gather his or her opinion. Prepare a written report and present an oral report to the class.

4. Conduct a survey as to the typical inside and outside environment of horses kept in your local community.

5. Participate in a class discussion about fire safety—prevention, alarms, and emergency assistance.

9

SAFE MANAGEMENT AND HANDLING

Horses can be hurt, and they can also hurt you! *Safety* is the prevention of accidents and being free from danger, injury, or damage. Safety of horses and owners is a critical issue. Every year people are hurt because of failure to respect the energy and "personality" of a horse. Who is to blame? Is it the horse or the owner?

Over 90 percent of all accidents with horses are the fault of the rider or owner. The reasons range from not being trained in handling horses to a basic lack of respect for horses. Regardless of the reason, accidents and safety problems can be prevented.

9-1. Handling horses correctly is important.

OBJECTIVES

Safety is important in raising and handling horses. This chapter covers the following objectives:

1. Explain safety with horses
2. Explain proper handling procedures with horses
3. Describe common horse equitation management techniques
4. Identify horse behavior as it relates to safety

TERMS

bridling
equitation
groom
haltering
leading
longe
longeing
monocular
mounting
restrain
saddling
safety
shy
weaning

EQUINE KNOWLEDGE

*Horses have **monocular** vision. Each eye is independent of the other and can see different pictures. Horses can also focus for binocular vision.*

SAFETY

The safety of individuals and horses is important. This cannot be stressed enough! When horse owners become overconfident or just let their guard down, someone can get hurt. Every year there are many accidents to people and horses because someone let their guard down. This is why a rigid safety program should be in place for all people that are around horses.

Every horse owner or rider should practice two things: follow safety procedures when working around horses and use the correct equipment and facilities.

The equipment used to handle a horse in any situation is a vital part of management. Riding, leading, moving, grooming, shoeing, administering health care, or working require good equipment. Facilities are essential to the everyday movement of horses regardless of whether they are in a pasture, in a stall, or being transported from one location to another. The National Horse Youth Council has done research on horse management and has written an excellent document that all horse owners should own. The Horse Industry Handbook has information regarding safety procedures, correct facilities, and the correct equipment to use with various styles of riding.

Owners should learn the proper handling procedures and techniques for leading, tying, mounting, loading, catching, haltering, and restraining a horse. In addition, owners should be able to identify horse behavior as it relates to safety. Know the basic safety associated with horses and know their field of vision. Many problems can be prevented and with the proper training,

9-2. Successfully hitching a horse to a carriage requires skill.

handling a horse can be fun. However, you should never underestimate the potential energy a horse possesses.

A horse's vision is limited to the front and rear, but its hearing is acute. Always speak to the horse when approaching it. Let the horse know where you are at all times. Always approach the horse at an angle—never directly from the front or rear. Touch the horse by placing a hand on its shoulder or neck. This will calm the horse and remove the unknown. Be sure to stay out of kicking range when walking around the horse. Use the correct equipment when working with horses. This pertains to leading, grooming, riding, hauling or other activities. Periodically, check and clean all equipment so breaks and other mishaps will not happen when you least expect them.

HANDLING

The way a person handles a horse directly influences its behavior. Experienced horse owners use specific techniques for successful behavioral outcomes. Many problem horses, accidents, and other unsuccessful outcomes arise from using the wrong handling procedures.

When working around a horse, stay close to the horse so if it kicks, the full impact is not received. Approach a horse from an angle, touch it on the shoulder, and move slowly. Know the horse's temperament and its reactions. Let the horse know what you intend to do and communicate this to the horse. Learn and use simple restraint methods. To **restrain** an animal is to limit or restrict movement. Never stand directly behind nor in front of a horse. Be calm and confident and let the horse know you are calm and confident. Horses can sense nervousness. Do not move quickly, do not drop things, or make sudden noises. Do not change your behavior and the way you respond to the horse's behavior. A horse is a creature of habit and will expect the same response everyday.

If a horse must be punished, do so only at the occurrence of the bad behavior. If you wait too long, the horse will not know why it is being punished. Never punish with anger and never be too severe. Also, never strike a horse around its head.

Do not unnecessarily leave halters and other equipment on horses. The equipment may catch on nails, boards, etc. Also, horse handlers should always wear correct clothing when working with horses. As an example, wear boots to help protect being stepped on or getting your feet caught in the stirrup. Remember, all horses can and will kick, shy, and run. As it pertains to horses, to **shy** is to suddenly jump or recoil.

Safe Management and Handling

MANAGEMENT TECHNIQUES

Equitation is being skilled in the riding, management, and care of horses. There are many techniques necessary to reach the full potential in caring for horses.

Handling horses is a management issue. Proper handling is critical to the well-being of both the horse and owner. Handling horses consists of :

1. Haltering
2. Leading
3. Longeing
4. Mounting
5. Restraining
6. Grooming
7. Saddling
8. Bridling
9. Hauling
10. Feeding and watering

Haltering is placing a halter on a horse. It is important in managing and handling a horse. The ability to approach and catch a horse without a strug-

9-3. Haltering is important in handling and managing a horse.

gle is important. Once the horse is caught, the halter can be installed and the horse can be led. A halter should never be permanently left on a horse whether the animal is in a stall or in a pasture. Haltered horses can be hurt by getting caught on fencing, nails, or other protrusions. Therefore, when turning a horse loose it is best to remove the halter.

Leading is the first step in training the horse. It involves getting a horse to move or walk upon command by pulling on the halter or reins. This part of training should occur before or just after weaning. **Weaning** is the gradual substituting of food for mother's milk. It is important to teach leading before the horse gets too big or too old. One of the most common ways to break a young horse to lead is to have someone lead the mare in front of the foal. The person leading the foal should use a lead to the halter and a butt rope. Older foals can be tied to a lead rope approximately 10 to 11 feet long. After the foal learns that it cannot free itself, it should be led around for a few minutes each day until it leads freely. It is very important not to push this training too fast or too hard and the horse needs constant positive feedback and rewards.

9-4. It is important to teach a horse to lead before it gets too old.

Longeing is a technique used to get the horse to circle you on the end of a longe line. A **longe** is a long rope fastened to a horse's head and held by the

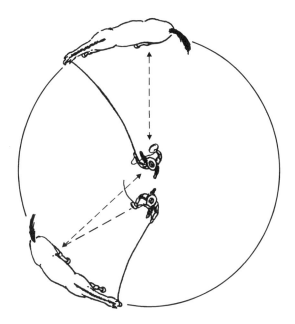

9-5. Longeing is one way of providing less active horses with exercise. (Note: Longeing is also spelled *lunging*.)

trainer, who causes the horse to move around in a circle. Owners should hold the lead shank in one hand while standing next to the horse's flank area and hold the longeing whip in the other hand. To get the horse to move, say "walk" and then cluck to it while tapping the horse from behind with a whip. To stop the horse, say "whoa" and give a quick jerk on the lead shank. Rather than the quick jerk on the lead, it may be better to step sideways toward the horse's head, which usually results in the horse responding to your body position. After the horse circles both ways, then trot and use faster gaits. Use your body position to move the horse. Start by moving back to the horse's flank to send it forward. Move to the horse's shoulder to block forward motion and to stop the horse.

Mounting (getting on) is the key to effective riding and performing. Always mount from the left side of the horse. Initially, it may be helpful to have someone hold the horse while the rider is mounting, but this should not become a habit. The rider should work with the horse so it can be mounted by an individual. Practice will help the horse learn. All tack should be fully functional and attached correctly. Teach the horse to stand and wait until it is asked to move. Use the reverse procedure when dismounting.

Restraining is tying a horse to a stationary object to keep it from moving so an activity can be performed. Properly tying a horse can prevent injury and escape. Horses that learn to escape can be very difficult to train. Many horse owners cross-tie a horse when working with it in the stable area. The two tie ropes should be firmly anchored at approximately shoulder height and snapped onto the halter. The ends of the anchors should be attached to the wall and have a slip knot. The horse does not need excessive length in rope, but should be comfortable and not threatened.

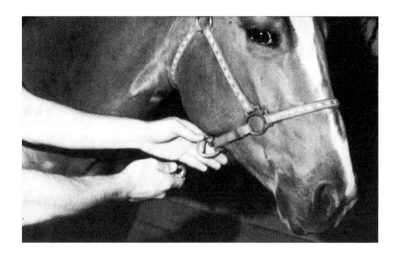

9-6. Tying a horse to a sturdy post is a convenient way of keeping it where it belongs.

Grooming should be done on a daily basis. To *groom* a horse includes washing, brushing, combing, and caring for the animal. Dirt and other debris

9-7. Equipment used to groom and care for horses.

Safe Management and Handling

ITEM	WHAT IT IS: HOW TO USE IT	WHAT IT IS USED FOR
Hoof Pick	A metal pick for cleaning the feet.	To clean out the feet.
Curry Comb	Use gently and in small circles, rather than with pressure and long strokes. Do not use the curry comb below the knees or hocks, about the head, over bony predominances, on horses that have been clipped recently, or that have a thin coat of hair.	To groom horses that have long, thick coats. To remove caked mud. To loosen matted scurf and dirt in the hair. To clean the brush.
Body Brush	The body brush is the principal tool used for grooming.	To brush the entire body of the horse.
Dandy Brush	The dandy brush is made of stiff fiber usually about two inches in length.	To remove light dirt from the skin. To brush the mane and tail.
Mane & Tail Comb	Gently pull through mane or tail to remove loose debris and straighten hair.	To comb out matted mane and tail.
Sweat Scraper	Metal or wood scraper for removing sweat or water.	To remove excess perspiration from heated, wet, or sweating animals.
Grooming Cloth	The grooming cloth can be made from old toweling or blankets. It should be about 18 to 24 inches square.	To remove dust or dirt from the coat. To wipe out the eyes, ears, nostrils, lips, and dock. To give the coat a final sheen or polish. To dry or ruffle the coat before brushing.

9-8. Basic horse grooming equipment.

9-9. This horse is protected with a waterproof blanket. (Courtesy, Jasper S. Lee, Georgia)

can cause health problems. Dirt can cause sores and infections on the horse's body, especially on the horse's back where the saddle makes contact with the skin. Proper grooming equipment should be used, such as the dandy brush, body brush, curry comb, hoof pick, and mane comb.

Saddling is properly placing a saddle on a horse. It should always begin with an examination of the horse's back. The withers and cinch areas should be clean. The two most common types of saddles are the Western and the English. Saddles should have the proper padding or a saddle blanket can be used to protect the horse's back. To saddle a horse for Western riding, the saddle pad is placed on the horse's back forward of the horse's withers. If a

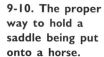

9-10. The proper way to hold a saddle being put onto a horse.

Safe Management and Handling 143

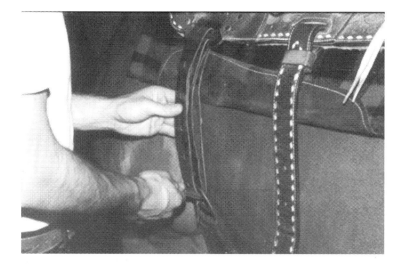

9-11. Pull the girth through the cinch ring twice before hooking it.

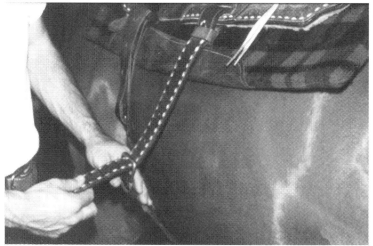

9-12. Fasten the back girth so that it is loose under the horse's stomach.

9-13. The breast collar can be fastened easily to the saddle rings using small straps.

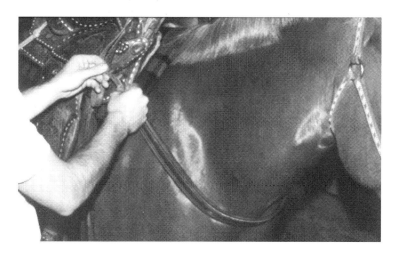

saddle blanket is used, the fold should be placed forward of the withers. Place the cinches and right stirrup across the seat of the saddle. The saddle is gripped by the pommel and cantle and placed gently on the horse's back and saddle pad just behind the shoulder blades. The saddle and pad are moved backward to a position where the bars will not rub the shoulder blades. If the saddle has front and back cinches, the front is tightened first to prevent the horse from bucking the saddle off. The back cinch should neither be too loose nor too tight. Loosen the back cinch first when removing a saddle. The saddle cinch should be properly tightened and checked on a regular basis for rider safety and the health of the horse.

Bridling is placing a bridle on a horse. It takes practice. When bridling a horse, approach the animal from the left side. The crown of the bridle is held in the right hand. As the right hand pulls the bridle upward, the left hand guides the bit into the horse's mouth. If the teeth are banged with the bit, the horse becomes shy and hard to bridle. Do not pin the ears or do anything might scare or hurt the horse.

Once the bridle is on the head and the bit is in the mouth, adjust the length of the bridle so there are one to two wrinkles at the corner of the horse's mouth. The throatlatch should be adjusted so three or four fingers can be inserted between it and the throat. When removing the bridle, the left hand is placed on the horse's face to keep its nose down. If the horse's head is held in this position, the bit will not hit the teeth and will come out without any trouble. Do not jerk the bit out of the mouth.

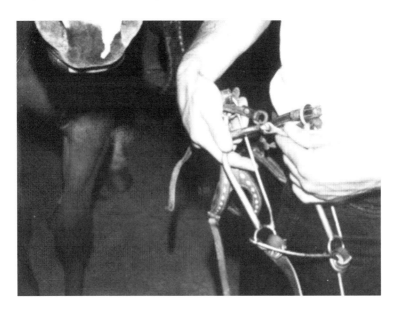

9-14. Check the bit to make sure it is clean.

Safe Management and Handling

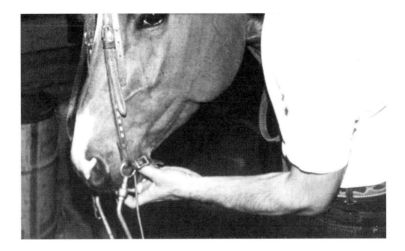

9-15. Putting your thumb in the corner of a horse's mouth will help make it open while bridling.

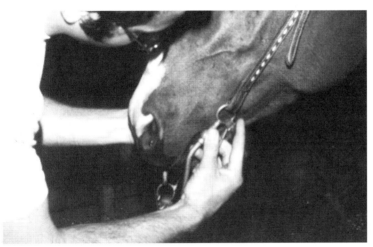

9-16. Check to make sure the bridle is adjusted for proper length.

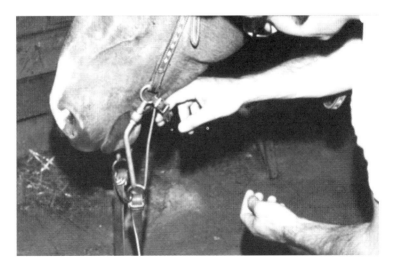

9-17. Check the tightness of the curb strap.

Feeding horses is involved in most behaviors and management techniques. Feed can be used as a positive reenforcement, but be careful not to develop bad habits or dependency on a certain food for certain behaviors. Also, it is very important to feed horses at the same time every day. Horses are creatures of habit and will expect the feeding. If they are not fed at the same time, bad habits, such as wood chewing, can develop.

Hauling horses is necessary and can be a challenging part of horse production. Horses, like other animals, need the proper training before being moved by modern transportation. Horses need to be taught that hauling is not threatening and is a safe activity. Horses will differ to degrees of difficulty. If transporting is properly introduced while the horse is young, it will load and haul without difficulty. Horses hauled by trailer or truck should first be taught to load. Take the animal on short trips and use positive reenforcement. It is important to be patient. Do not push too hard or too fast; be kind and consistent. If necessary, seek experienced horse trainers and owners to help train horses to haul.

9-18. Accidents are more likely to happen with improper equipment and operator error. (This shows an upside-down trailer on an interstate highway median in Arizona. Evidently, excessive speed going down a hill contributed to the crash.) (Courtesy, Jasper S. Lee, Georgia)

Safe Management and Handling 147

HORSE BEHAVIOR AND SAFETY

The importance of observing safety precautions when in the presence of horses is very important. Horse handlers can become overconfident around a horse. This may lead to an injury. A horse's behavior can be unpredictable regardless of how long and how well you know the animal. When in heat, a mare's behavior can change, bringing mature stallions together may result in aggressive behavior, and geldings can have behavior changes around unfamiliar horses. All horses, when startled, change behavior. It is imperative that handlers never let their guard down.

9-19. Correctly handling a five-month-old Belgian filly.

REVIEWING

MAIN IDEAS

Mastering the proper way to handle a horse is an important management skill. Unless you can perform this function, you will never become a quality horse handler. Without proper handling, someone or a horse can be hurt. The proper ways to lead, tie, mount, load, catch, halter, and restraint a horse are elements of effective equine management.

Lead from the left side of the horse. Always be in control and have a lead that is securely connected with just enough length. Never wrap the lead around your hand or other body part. If a horse is spooked and runs, it can pull you and hurt you. When tying a horse, always use a slip knot with appropriate materials. Tie close enough to restrain and to keep the horse from being caught by its legs, head, or neck. Training the horse to allow riders to mount should begin while the animal is young. This takes time, work, and requires much positive reenforcement. Always mount from the left side of the horse. Loading horses also should begin at a young age. Never force a horse to load. Be patient and use short trips to introduce a horse to this activity. When haltering a horse, the first step is catching the horse. Again, use positive reenforcement to make catching easier. Use halters to restrain horses and remove the halter when turning horses out.

A horse's behavior is predictable to a degree, but does change. Never let your guard down. When a horse is scared, its behavior changes. When a mare comes into heat, its behavior changes and a stallion is always unpredictable. The more time you spend with your horse the more accurately you can predict its behavior.

Always approach a horse on an angle, never directly. Speak to the horse as you approach. A horse's vision is limited and it relies on other senses to survive.

QUESTIONS

Answer the following questions using correct spelling and complete sentences.

1. What two things should a horse owner or rider practice?
2. What are the proper handling procedures with horses?
3. What is equitation?
4. How are young horses taught to lead?
5. What is longeing? Why is it important?
6. How do you get a horse to move and stop?
7. What is grooming?

Safe Management and Handling

8. How is a horse saddled?
9. How is a horse bridled?
10. Why should horses be fed at the same time each day?
11. How does the horse's field of vision affect behavior?
12. How are horses trained for hauling?

EVALUATING

CHAPTER SELF-CHECK

Match the term with the correct definition. Place the letter by the term in the blank provided.

a. safety
b. monocular
c. weaning
d. equitation
e. shy
f. grooming
g. restraining
h. longe

_____1. The act of limiting or restricting movement.

_____2. The prevention of accidents and the freedom from danger, injury, or damage.

_____3. Being skilled in the riding, management, and care of horses.

_____4. Each eye is independent of the other and can see different pictures.

_____5. A long rope fastened to a horse's head by the trainer, who causes the horse to move around in a circle.

_____6. To suddenly jump or recoil.

_____7. The gradual substituting of food for mother's milk.

_____8. To wash, brush, comb, and care for an animal.

DISCOVERING

1. As a class project, visit a horse farm. Examine the safety management for the entire farm including horses and people. Prepare a short essay on the information that you obtain from your observations. Deliver the written report to the class in the form of an oral presentation.

2. Using data from the visit to the horse farm, prepare a display or visual that can be used as a safety promotion.

3. Researching different resources, come up with a list of management techniques for handling horses. This should include leading, tying, mounting, loading, catching, and haltering horses.

4. Using a variety of resources, collect data on the most frequent accidents and mishaps on horse farms. This should focus on two elements: people and horses. Prepare a short essay on your findings and represent a report to the class.

5. Develop a horse safety management plan for a given horse farm.

6. Observe the proper loading, hauling, and unloading of horses.

7. Research and write a brief outline of common vices of the horse.

8. Demonstrate how to safely catch, halter, lead, tie, groom, clean the feet of, and work around a horse.

9. Examine and discuss safety helmets.

10. Observe horse safety, management, breeding, foaling techniques.

10

THE ECONOMICS OF HORSES

Horses involve dollars and cents! People who raise horses for marketing are well aware of the costs that are involved. They know that they must be able to sell horses for more than what they have invested in them.

On the other hand, people who keep horses for pleasure need to understand the costs involved. In addition to the cost of buying horses, feed, tack, health care, and other costs can mount up.

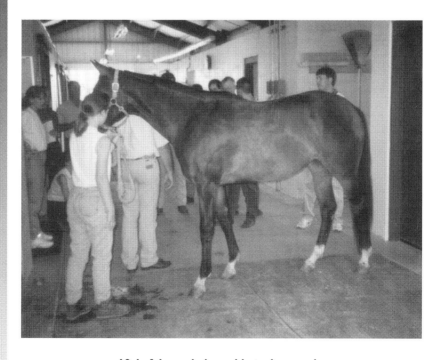

10-1. A horse being sold at a horse sale.

OBJECTIVES

This chapter examines the economics of horse production. Upon completion of this chapter you should be able to:

1. Explain the economic impact of horses in the United States
2. Describe entrepreneurship in horses and list available opportunities
3. Explain how horse production fits into the livestock industry
4. Explain consumers and the role of consumers in horse production
5. List and describe the ways to market and buy horses

TERMS

buying
consumer
demand
economics
economic impact
entrepreneur
selling
supply

EQUINE KNOWLEDGE

Horses were valuable assets during the Depression in the 1930s.

ECONOMIC IMPACT OF THE HORSE

Economics is the science of the production, distribution, and consumption of goods and services and the related problems of labor, finance, and taxation. The economics of horses is very important. It affects not only the buyer and seller of horses but the associated goods and services that support the industry.

Supply and demand drive the dollar value of the industry. The **supply** is the amount or quantity of a commodity available for purchase at a given price. The **demand** is the desire for a commodity together with the ability to pay for it. The demand for horses, feed, equipment, health products, etc. and the supply of these elements can either increase or decrease the costs. Whether you own a horse or not, you may be connected to the economics of horse production. Most, but not all, horse operations are generally expensive and not profitable. However, profit can be defined in many ways other than in dollars.

An *economic impact* is the change made by the introduction of a resource to the total industry. In the United States, the sale and production of horses and related items brings in millions of dollars. Most people do not realize the connection horse economics has to society. For example, the horse racing industry brings in millions of dollars to communities near a race track as well as federal, state, and local taxes. The horse industry also provides jobs for millions of people in all areas of horse production. Some of these areas include feed producers and dealers, health professionals and pharmaceutical companies, equipment manufacturers, the racing industry, and boarding and

10-2. Ranchers use horses in their work.

breeding facilities. The show circuit creates many jobs for the people that train and show horses.

Although horses are not seen as a meat-food animal in the United States, they contribute millions of dollars to our society and create jobs for many people. Can you identify how horses affect the economy in your community?

ENTREPRENEURIAL OPPORTUNITIES

An *entrepreneur* is a person who manages and assumes the risk of a business. With the horse industry, this may involve owning horse enterprises, providing services to horse owners, and providing supplies needed to keep horses. There are many entrepreneurial opportunities for young people in the horse industry. Identify these opportunities in your local community and learn how to prepare yourself to meet them. (Chapter 13 of this book will focus on these specific career opportunities.)

Some students have supervised experience that involves horse entrepreneurship. Get involved by exploring and learning. Set realistic goals to get started.

10-3. A student who owns a horse is an entrepreneur.

HORSE PRODUCTION AND THE LIVESTOCK INDUSTRY

How do horses fit into the livestock industry? The biggest difference in horses and other livestock is that in the United States we do not use horses

The Economics of Horses

10-4. If you look back in history, horses were important on farms as work animals. Today, horses are tied to the business arena and livestock industry.

for food. Therefore, many assume that horses are not a part of the livestock industry. But, if you look at the history of horses, they were important on farms and on the range as work animals. In addition, they provided transportation for everyone. Today, we use horses for many different purposes and every usage is tied to the business arena and to the livestock industry. Here are some ways horses have economic impact:

1. Horses consume feed produced by farmers.
2. Horses provide access to cattle and other animals in many locations.
3. Horses need equipment made from cattle and other animal skins.
4. Horses need trucks and trailers.
5. Horses need health care and products.
6. Horses provide income from breeding, showing, racing, etc.
7. Horses provide many jobs in all areas.
8. Horses are used for pleasure and recreation.
9. Horses provide millions of dollars to the economy.
10. Horses are used as human food in some countries.
11. Old horses are used in manufacturing pet food in the United States.

CONSUMERS AND HORSE PRODUCTION

Consumers are people that purchase and use products or services. Who are the consumers of horses? Where do these people live, what do they do, and why do they purchase horses? These questions are not easy to answer because people buy horses for many different reasons.

The consumers of horses are FFA and 4-H members, children, young adults, males, females, rich and poor, different ethnic backgrounds, and professionals. People purchase horses for pleasure, to show, for trail riding, for competitive events, to race, to work, for breeding, and "horse trading." The money involved can vary from small to large amounts. A person getting into the horse business can purchase a pleasure horse for several hundred dollars. A person in the show horse industry will spend from a thousand to several thousand dollars for an animal. Breeding professionals may spend several thousand dollars to have a mare bred. Race horses can cost millions of dollars.

This is why a consumer should first determine the goal of his or her horse enterprise. Seek unbiased information from qualified horse professionals in making your purchase. Your extension agent, breed associations, agriculture teacher, and university specialists are most helpful. Be very careful of people you do not know, especially around grade horse sales. "Horse traders" are

10-5. FFA members examining a horse.

very sharp when it comes to selling you a horse for their own gain. Many people have been cheated by traders. However, true horse owners and users are very helpful.

Attend workshops, read updated materials, and learn how to evaluate horses. There are many good resources for people interested in getting into horse production. Consumers should be knowledgeable about horses and people in the industry. Schools for riding and training are a good way to get started.

BUYING AND SELLING HORSES

Buying is paying money (or exchanging other valuables) to receive a product or service. *Selling* is receiving monetary resources to provide a product or service. There are many ways to buy and sell horses. Choose the one that best fits your needs.

PLACES AND WAYS TO BUY AND SELL

Horses are available in several ways. Here are a few examples:

1. One-on-one—buyer to seller directly from the farm
2. Special horse sales
    a. Breed sales—animals of known ancestry
    b. Grade sales—animals of unknown ancestry
    c. Farm sales—animals from a specific horse farm

10-6. Horses waiting to be sold.

3. Agent buying and selling for you
4. Computer buying and selling
5. Breeding contracts—payment for breeding fees with a foal or another animal
6. Syndication—more than one buyer or seller
7. Inheritance

BEING INFORMED

Buying and selling horses is a business regardless of how much money is involved or the method of the transaction. Remember, everyone is trying to make as much money as possible and is working in a business capacity. Therefore, it is very important to equip yourself with as much knowledge and skill as possible. If you are not confident with your buying and selling skills, get someone (an unbiased person) to help. Whether buying or selling, it is best to have a plan.

1. Assess your abilities, long-term goals and purpose, finances, and dedication. Horses are fun, but they involve work—a minimum of two times a day, everyday obligation.
2. Determine your method of buying or selling
3. Seek advice from unbiased professionals
4. Determine your level of negotiations
5. Put the plan into action

REVIEWING

MAIN IDEAS

Economics deals with the goods and services used by individuals. Factors to consider in the economics of horses are demands for specific horses or breeds, feed sources, health and health products, equipment, and jobs within the industry.

The sale and purchase of horses in the United States brings in millions of dollars. Additional income is generated from other areas related to the horse industry. The horse industry provides opportunities in racing, breeding, boarding, training, grooming, feeding, health care, equipment manufacture and sales, and many more areas.

There are many different opportunities for young people to be involved in the horse industry. It is important for young people to identify their areas of interest and get involved through high school agriculture education, FFA, SAE, 4-H, and other related areas. A student entering a high school agriculture education program has many different opportunities, such as using horse production in supervised agricultural experience. They can also participant in the FFA/4-H horse judging events, enter the horse FFA Proficiency award program, and get so much valuable knowledge and experience. This will be beneficial for employment and or college after high school.

Consumers buy and sell horses everyday. They use a wide variety of methods in this process. These consist of one-on-one purchase or sale, grade horse sales, specialty sales, computer agreements, agent buying and selling, and breeding contracts. Consumers range from rich to poor, urban to rural, different races, male to female and all walks of life. People buy and sell horses for many reasons therefore, it is critical that you become knowledgeable about this process.

QUESTIONS

Answer the following questions using correct spelling and complete sentences.

1. How does the horse industry impact economics in the United States?
2. What are the entrepreneur opportunities in horse production?
3. How do horses fit into the animal science arena?
4. What is the consumer's role in horse production?
5. What are the ways to buy and sell horses?
6. What may happen in buying from a "horse trader"?
7. Why is unbiased information needed to buy a horse?
8. Why do some people assume that the horse industry is not a part of the livestock industry?

EVALUATING

CHAPTER SELF-CHECK

Match the term with the correct definition. Place the letter by the term in the blank provided.

- a. economics
- b. consumer
- c. economic impact
- d. demand
- e. entrepreneur
- f. selling
- g. supply

____1. A person who manages and assumes the risks of a business.

____2. The desire for a commodity together with the ability to pay for it.

____3. The science of the production, distribution, and consumption of goods and services and the related problems of labor, finance, taxation, etc.

____4. The amount or quantity of a commodity available for purchase at a given price.

____5. The change made by the introduction of a resource to the total industry.

____6. A person who purchases and uses a product or service.

____7. Receiving monetary resources to provide a product or service.

DISCOVERING

1. Develop a plan to purchase a specific horse.

2. Develop a plan to sell a specific horse.

3. Schedule a visit to a local horse sale. Take notes on the procedures used. Highlight the pros and cons. Discuss in class each item on both lists.

4. Interview a horse owner and ask about ways to market horses. List the pros and cons of the ways discussed by the horse owner. Write a report indicating the findings and make an oral report in class.

5. Using the Internet, newspaper, or farm publication, find the current prices for horses in your area.

6. Attend a demonstration of a pre-purchase examination by a veterinarian.

11

RECREATIONAL HORSES

Horses are fun! Many people are now learning about horses and finding them enjoyable. This has resulted in demand for more horses.

The number of horses has been increasing at a strong rate for the past several years. Many people seek ways to relax and have fun from the normal stresses of work or school. Horses provide that relaxation. Approximately 75 percent of the horses in the United States are used for pleasure. Most horse owners live in rural areas or small towns. Many horse owners earn, or belong to families that earn, less than the average per capita income.

11-1. Horses are used for a variety of activities—from pleasure riding, to fox hunting, to parades, to rodeos.

OBJECTIVES

This chapter examines the recreational use of horses. Upon completion of this chapter you should be able to:

1. Describe the recreational uses of horses
2. Identify the breeds of recreational horses

TERMS

breed
dressage
gait
grade horse
gymkhana
hand
light horse
polo
pony
recreation
rodeo

EQUINE KNOWLEDGE

Ponies are small horses that stand under 14-2 hands and weigh 500 to 900 pounds.

Light horses stand 14-2 to 17 hands, weigh 900 to 1400 pounds, and are used for riding, driving, showing, racing, or pleasure.

Draft horses are large horses that stand 14-2 to 17-2 hands, weigh 1400 pounds or more, and are used for work.

A **hand** = A height measurement for a horse. The measurement is taken at the top of the wither to the ground. A hand=4 inches. Therefore, a horse measuring 62 inches is said to be 15-2 hands (15 hands and 2 inches) high.

RECREATIONAL USES OF HORSES

Using horses for recreation is increasing in the United States. *Recreation* means that a horse provides enjoyment and relaxation. Keeping horses as companion animals or for riding and showing is a popular form of recreation with some people. Other people go as spectators to races, rodeos, and sporting events that feature horses.

Here are some of the major recreational uses of horses:

1. Pleasure Riding
2. Horse Shows
3. Fox Hunting
4. Competitive Trail Riding
5. *Polo* (A game played by two teams of three or four players on horseback. Players are equipped with long-handled mallets for driving a small, wooden ball through the opponent's goal.)
6. *Rodeo* (An event that consists of bronc riding, roping, barrel racing, and other exciting activities.)
7. Horse Racing
8. Horse Breeding

11-2. Polo players are equipped with long-handled mallets for driving a small, wooden ball through the opponent's goal.

Horse showing is the process of competing in an arena against other riders and horses for awards. Originally founded in New York City in 1917 as the Association of American Horse Shows, Inc., the name has since been changed to the American Horse Show Association. The association sanctions shows; keeps records; licenses judges and stewards; handles disciplinary matters, awards, and prizes; and compiles the annual rule book for the show world. There are many small independent shows that operate under loose supervision and control.

Horse shows fall under the following divisions: Appaloosa, Arabian, Combined Training, *Dressage* (exhibition riding in which the horse is controlled by the slight movements of the rider), Equitation, **Gymkhana** (competing in various games while on horseback), Hackney and Harness Pony, Hunter and Jumper Pony, Jumper Junior Hunter and Jumper, Morgan, Palomino, Parade, Pinto, Paint, Pony of the Americas, Quarter Horse, Roadster, Saddle Horse, Shetland Pony, Tennessee Walking Horse, Welsh Pony, and Western. Each breed has specific classes. There are open shows where the horse can be of any breed or nonregistered. Some of the most popular classes are the equitation, hunter, jumper, Western, gaited, roadster, and halter.

DIFFERENT TYPES AND CLASSES OF HORSE

There are many different types of horses. Type is an ideal combination of characteristics that make an animal suitable for a specific purpose. The types of horses in today's society range from pleasure horses, work horses, race horses, breeding horses, miniature horses, and show horses. The value of a horse varies greatly based upon the type, the breeding, and the genetics of the animal.

Classes of horses also vary. Classes are based on the breed, the use, and the pedigree of the specific horse. A crossbred horse with no papers and no specifically desired characteristics could be of very low value. Whereas, a specific breed, which is the offspring of a proven genetic line, could be valued at millions of dollars. This range in value makes equine ownership available to everyone.

Horses range in type and class. The value of a horse depends on the breeding, genetics, and the pedigree. **Grade horses**, animals with no specific heritage, may have a low value. Whereas, a horse with a pedigree of a specific breed and heritage may have a high value. Training and performance also relate to value.

OWNING A RECREATIONAL HORSE

Purchasing and owning a recreational horse is a very serious thing. Horses need daily care from the owner or manager. Horses require a safe, clean environment; adequate feed; fresh, plentiful water; preventative medical care; daily exercise; and proper grooming. There are many horses in America that are neglected by irresponsible people. Before buying a horse, you should interview horse owners and conduct research about the time and effort horse ownership involves. If your attitude changes after purchasing a horse, the horse should be sold or sent to someone that will take proper care

Recreational Horses

11-3. Horse ownership is a big responsibility.

of the animal. There are many sources of help in conducting the research. Your local extension agent, agricultural teacher, university horse specialist, breed associations, and experienced horse owners. Remember, the horse is dependent upon people for its quality of life.

BREEDS OF RECREATIONAL HORSES

A *breed* is a group of animals descended from common ancestors and have similar characteristics. An example of a breed of horses is the Appaloosa. This horse has a set of color patterns determined by the genetic make-up and other physical characteristics, such as body size.

All breeds are traced to a particular origin. Breed registries depend on correct identification to ensure accuracy of ancestry and to establish standards for the fair exchange of horses between buyer and seller. Most of the major breeds of horses and ponies that maintain registries in the United States are discussed in this chapter.

AMERICAN QUARTER HORSE

Origin

The Quarter Horse originated in the colonies in the 1600s. The Thoroughbred had a lasting influence on the development of the Quarter Horse. These horses are bred for racing (the quarter mile) and as stock horses.

11-4. A Quarter Horse. (Courtesy, American Quarter Horse Association)

Characteristics

Well-muscled forearm and back; short, close-coupled and powerful across loin; deep girth and well-sprung ribs; broad, deep, heavy, well-muscled quarters that are full. The range of weight is 1100 to 1300 pounds and 14-3 to 16-0 hands high.

AMERICAN SADDLEBRED

Origin

The American Saddlebred was developed from Thoroughbreds, Canadian Pacers, American Trotters, Morgans, and Arabians. This breed was developed to fulfill the need for an easy-gaited saddle horse. A *gait* is a particular way the horse moves, either natural or artificial, which is characterized by a distinctive rhythmic action of the feet and legs.

Characteristics

The American Saddlebred emphasizes flashy and exaggerated, but controlled, gaits, high carriage head, and distinctive set of the tail. It has a well-shaped head, small alert ears, large eyes set well apart, good muzzle, and wide nostrils. The average height is 15 to 16 hands and weighs from 1000 to 1200 pounds.

Recreational Horses 167

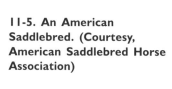

11-5. An American Saddlebred. (Courtesy, American Saddlebred Horse Association)

APPALOOSA

Origin

The name was developed from the slurring of " A Palouse," which later became Apaloosie and is now Appaloosa. The Palouse River Country of the

11-6. An Appaloosa horse.

northwestern United States has given its name to this breed of horse. It is believed that this breed was introduced to the United States by the Nez Perce Indians. Horses with the colorful characteristics of the Appaloosa appear in Chinese art dating from 500 B.C. and in Persian and European art of the fourteenth century. Horses brought to Mexico about 1600 A.D. apparently have formed the basis for the present day Appaloosa.

Characteristics

Three distinctive characteristics are required of all Appaloosas:

1. The eye is encircled with white, like the human eye.
2. The skin is mottled irregularly with black and white.
3. The hooves are narrowly striped vertically in black and white.

ARABIANS

Origin

The Arabian horse has had a great influence on most breeds of horses in today's society. Although the history and origin of the Arabian horse is not

11-7. An Arabian horse.

always agreed upon by experts, there is no question that Arabians have been bred and selected for improved horses for more than 2000 years. One example is the Thoroughbred, which was developed largely from the Arabian.

Characteristics

Small head, profile of head straight or preferably slightly concave below the eyes, small muzzle, large nostrils, 14-1 to 15-1 hands, colors include bay, brown, chestnut, gray, and black. One less vertebra in back. Known for endurance.

BUCKSKIN

Origin

Since 1963, two registries have developed for saddle horses with buckskin, dun, and grulla colors: the American Buckskin Registry Associate, Inc. and the International Buckskin Horse Association.

Characteristics

The body coat of the Buckskin is predominantly a shade of yellow, to nearly brown. Points (area from knees down) are black or dark brown. The true Buckskin has a dorsal stripe, shoulder stripe, and barring on the legs.

11-8. A Buckskin horse.

CONNEMARA

Origin

The Connemara originated in the Connemara region of County Galway, Ireland. The ancestry includes Spanish-Barbs, Jennets, and Andalusians. The first Connemaras were imported to the United States in 1951 for breeding purposes.

Characteristics

The Connemara stands at 13 to 14-2 hands. It ranges in color, but neither spotted nor blue-eyed cream ponies may be registered.

HACKNEY PONY

Origin

The Hackney Pony has been called the Prince of Ponies. They were derived from the same ancestors as their bigger brother, the Hackney horse. The ancestors were bred for riding and driving in England.

Characteristics

The Hackney Pony is classified as having height of 14-2 hands and under. The Hackney Pony is a horse in a small package.

11-9. A Hackney Pony.

MORGAN

Origin

The Morgan took its name from its owner. Justin Morgan was a Massachusetts school teacher in the later 1700s. Justin Morgan, the horse, could

11-10. A Morgan horse. (Courtesy, American Morgan Horse Association)

outrun, outpull, outwalk, and out trot most competitors. It is believed that the sire of the Morgan was a Thoroughbred and the dam was an Arabian.

Characteristics

The Morgan is strongly built and heavily muscled. The size ranges from 14-1 to 15-1 hands and 1000 to 1200 pounds. The Morgan is very versatile and used for all types of riding and driving.

PAINT

Origin

The American Paint Horse Association was formed in 1965. Paints originated in the United States. Paints may be double registered as Pinto and Paint.

Characteristics

These horses must be sired by a registered Paint, Quarter Horse, or Thoroughbred. Paints may be any horse color and have white in bold patches all over the body. They are viewed as a light breed and are variable in height.

11-11. A Paint Horse.

PASO FINO

Origin

Pasos were imported from Peru (the Peruvian Paso) and from Puerto Rico, Cuba, and Columbia (the Paso Fino).

11-12. A Paso Fino mare and foal.

Characteristics

Pasos are noted for the smoothness of their natural gait, called the paso gait. This gait has five forms, of which the most important are: the paso fino, a slow ring gait; the paso carto, a more relaxed form; and the paso largo, a speed gait that may exceed the speed of the canter. The same rhythm is maintained for all speeds of the gait.

PINTO

Origin

The Pinto Association was founded in 1956. Pintos are associated with Native Americans.

Characteristics

Pintos are any horse color and have white with bold patches all over the body. Their height is variable and they are considered light horses. Pintos originated in the United States.

11-13. A Pinto Horse.

SHETLAND PONY

Origin

These ponies were developed in the Shetland Islands north of Scotland. The name "Shetland" was derived from the old Norse word meaning "highland." The native pony of the Shetland Islands was a miniature draft horse.

Characteristics

These ponies are shaggy, furry coated and can withstand the rigors of winter and weather.

11-14. A Shetland Pony.

SPANISH MUSTANGS

Origin

Robert Brislawn, Sr. and his brother, Ferdinand Brislawn, organized the first and oldest Mustang registry in 1957 in Sundance, Wyoming. These horse are remnants of the naturally selected wild horses of the Spanish-Barb and Andalusian ancestry.

Characteristics

The typical mustang is approximately 13-2 hands, short backed and wiry, and weighs 800 to 900 pounds. They have many different color patterns.

Recreational Horses

11-15. A Spanish Mustang. (Courtesy, Southwest Spanish Mustang Association)

STANDARDBRED

Origin

This breed was developed from Thoroughbred, Norfolk Trotter, Barb, Morgan, and Canadian pacing ancestors. The name Standardbred comes

11-16. A Standardbred horse. (Courtesy, United States Trotting Association)

from the practice that began in the 1800s of registering horses that trotted or paced the mile in less than a "standard" time.

Characteristics

Standardbreds are similar to Thoroughbreds, but are generally smaller in size. They range in height from 14-2 to 16-2 hands and 850 to 1150 pounds. Standardbreds are "driven," rather than ridden, using a sulky.

TENNESSEE WALKING HORSE

Origin

This breed originated in the Middle Basin of Tennessee and can be traced to the Thoroughbred, Standardbred, American Saddlebred, Morgan, and Canadian Pacer. It was bred by plantation owners to provide a quick comfortable gait for riding to check on crops.

11-17. A Tennessee Walking Horse. (Courtesy, Tennessee Walking Horse Breeders' and Exhibitors' Association)

Characteristics

Tennessee Walkers are similar to the American Saddlebred but are heavier and more powerful. It is the only horse that is routinely capable of overstriding. When performing the running walk, it will place the back hoof ahead of the print of its fore hoof.

THOROUGHBRED

Origin

The history of the Thoroughbred as a breed began in England. Native horses had been crossed with light horse mares imported from Spain, Turkey, and Italy. The first recording of a Thoroughbred in England was in 1791 by James Weatherby, Jr.

11-18. A Thoroughbred horse. (Courtesy, The Jockey Club)

Characteristics

Thoroughbreds tend to have long forearms and gaskins and display length from the hip to the hock. They have long smooth muscles and are very powerful. They range in size from 15-1 to 16-2 hands and 900 to 1150 pounds. Bred to run distances of ½ to 1½ miles.

WELSH PONY

Origin

The ancestors of the Welsh Pony were native to the severe terrain of Wales. Most Welsh Ponies can be traced to importation from England after 1947.

11-19. A Welsh Pony.

Characteristics

The Welsh Pony is an intermediate mount, between a Shetland and most riding horses, and is useful for children who have outgrown a Shetland Pony. Children can use the Welsh Pony as a hunter.

REVIEWING

MAIN IDEAS

Recreational horses are used for fun and noncompetitive activities. There are many breeds of horses used for recreational purposes. Some of those breeds include: Arabians, Thoroughbreds, American Quarter Horses, Standardbreds, Appaloosas, Morgans, American Saddlebreds, Tennessee Walking Horses, Paso Finos, Galicenos, Gotlands, Paints, Pintos, Palominos,

Recreational Horses

Buckskins, Native Chickasaws, Spanish Mustangs, Shetland Ponies, Welsh Ponies, Hackney Ponies, and Connemaras.

Uses of recreational horses range from pleasure riding to showing. Horses are also used for western events like barrel racing, rodeos, gymkhana events, fox hunting, hunters and jumpers, and wagon trains. Regardless of your interest, horses are available for many purposes and offer everyone opportunities.

Owning a horse brings responsibility. Horses are dependent on the owner or caretaker. Feeding, watering, grooming, and exercise are critical daily obligations. Unfortunately, many horses are neglected and suffer because of irresponsible owners. Before buying a horse, make sure you can give the animal the best of care possible.

QUESTIONS

Answer the following questions using correct spelling and complete sentences.

1. What does recreation mean as related to horses?
2. What are four recreational uses of horses?
3. What is the role of the American Horse Show Association?
4. What is a grade horse?
5. What is the responsibility of a recreational horse owner?
6. What are the major breeds of horses and what are their characteristics?
7. What breed can be double registered?
8. How did the name, Appaloosa, develop?

EVALUATING

CHAPTER SELF-CHECK

Match the term with the correct definition. Place the letter by the term in the blank provided.

a. breed
b. grade animal
c. polo
d. hand
e. dressage
f. light horse
g. gymkhana
h. rodeo

_____ 1. Competing in various games on horseback.

_____ 2. Exhibition riding in which the horse is controlled by the slight movements of the rider.

_____ 3. An event that consists of bronc riding, roping, barrel racing, and other exciting activities.

_____ 4. A horse that has no specific heritage and is not registered to any breed registry.

_____ 5. A height measurement for a horse. The measurement is taken at the top of the wither to the ground. A hand equals 4 inches.

_____ 6. A group of animals or plants descended from common ancestors and having similar characteristics.

_____ 7. A horse used primarily for riding, driving, showing, racing, or pleasure.

_____ 8. A game played by two teams of three or four players on horseback. Players are equipped with long-handled mallets for driving a small wooden ball through the opponents goal.

DISCOVERY

1. As a class project, select a breed of horse, conduct a research study to determine the origin and characteristics of the breed. Write a report that includes a color picture of the breed. Popular horse magazines may be used.

2. Visit a local horse farm to view the different types of horses. Interview the owner to determine the value of the horses. Using the Internet, find the current price of grade horses for the department of agriculture commodity price listings.

3. Interview an experienced horse owner to determine the responsibilities that are associated with horse ownership. Write a report that outlines these responsibilities.

4. Using the Internet, find the current address and promotional materials for the major breed associations. The following Web site will be helpful. http://www.haynet.net/breeds.html.

5. View one or more breed association videos or visit their Web site.

12

SPECIALTY HORSES AND RELATED SPECIES

Horses come in all sizes and shapes! Each has special uses based on its unique characteristics. Some are quite large and powerful and are used to pull heavy equipment. Others are of small size and have gentle personalities, which make them good pets.

A few close relatives of horses are used much like horses—one is even part horse! These relatives are often known as the "long ears." You can probably guess why they are known as "long ears"—they have long ears!

All horses and their "long ear" relatives need specific care that tends to their well-being. Kindness, adequate food and water, good environment, and proper health care promote "having fun with horses." This chapter will give you more information.

12-1. Miniature horse. (Courtesy, American Miniature Horse Association)

OBJECTIVES

This chapter examines specialty horses. Upon completion of this chapter, you should be able to:

1. List the breeds and purposes of draft horses
2. List the purposes of miniature horses
3. Describe the uses of "long-ears"
4. Discuss the existence of wild (feral) horses in today's society
5. List ways specialty horses can be incorporated into the family

TERMS

ass
bray
burro
donkey
feral horse
hinny
jack
jennet
miniature horse
mule
specialty horses

EQUINE KNOWLEDGE

Mules are produced by breeding a jack to a mare.

SPECIALTY HORSES

Specialty horses are those horses that are not traditional in size or are not used for traditional purposes in today's society. An example is the **miniature horse**. A miniature horse is a horse that has a maximum height of 32 inches—not much larger than a dog.

The draft horse is another example of a specialty horse. At one time, it was used in a traditional way and provided much needed power for work in the fields and transportation. Today, the draft horse is primarily used for hobbies, shows, wagon trains, and other recreational activities. In some cultures, the draft horse is still used for work, such as with the Amish and other groups. You can see this horse in some areas of the United States working the land, but for the most part, machinery has taken its place.

12-2. Draft horses.

Another group recognized as specialty horses is the long-ears: asses, mules, and donkeys. These animals are not horses; however, they are in the same family based on scientific classification. Of course, the mule is a hybrid cross of the ass and the horse.

The long-ears are known for their strength and their independence. They have a long tradition of working the fields, working in the gold and coal mines, and providing transportation. Today, they are primarily used for hobbies.

12-3. Mules may be trained for competitive events. (Courtesy, Lucky Three Ranch, Loveland, CO)

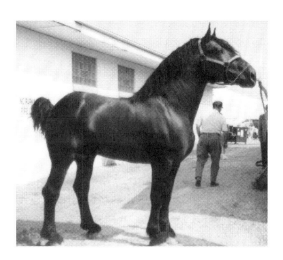

12-4. Grand Champion Percheron. (Courtesy, Feed Corral Percherons, Springfield, IL)

BREEDS OF DRAFT HORSES

Nearly all draft breeds are very large and have heavy muscles. They stand from 16 to 17 hands high and weigh from 1600 to 2200 pounds. The draft breeds were developed in northern Europe, Scotland, England, France, and Belgium. The breeds are named for their region of origin. The Percheron originated in La Perche; the Belgium is a descendent from the great horse of Flanders; the Clydesdale gets its name from the Clyde River area in Scotland; the Shire is named for the English areas of Lincolnshire and Cambridgeshire; and the Suffolk hails from the county of Suffolk, also in England.

PERCHERON

This horse was imported to the United States in 1839. After 1851, it was the most popular draft horse. The Percheron is known as the breed of blacks and grays.

THE BELGIAN

The predominant color of the Belgian is sorrel with a white mane and tail. The Belgian became very popular in the United States in the early 1900s. The characteristics of the Belgian were in very high demand by Americans and thus the stallions were sought for breeding purposes.

Specialty Horses and Related Species 185

12-5. The Belgian draft horse.

THE CLYDESDALE

The use of the Clydesdale in advertising has contributed to its recognition and popularity in America. The white face and legs and the "feathering" (long hair) on the legs gives the Clydesdale a distinct appearance.

12-6. The Clydesdale.

THE SHIRE

The Shire is a cousin to the Clydesdale and was developed from the English Great Horse. The Shire is known as the biggest of the draft horses, but there are very few in the United States in comparison to other breeds. Black is the dominant color of Shires, although the related color of bay and dark brown are known.

12-7. The Shire. (Courtesy, American Shire Association)

THE SUFFOLK

This breed of draft horse was developed primarily for farm use. The color of this breed is dusty chestnut or sorrel. The mane and tail are often lighter in color.

MINIATURE HORSE

Miniature horses (sometimes called "minni") are increasing in numbers, but still there is only a small population in the United States. The maximum height of a miniature horse is defined as 32 inches. They are used as pets and in certain types of entertainment. The true miniature is simply a small horse and is not a malformed dwarf. The standards state that a miniature horse must be proportioned like a horse and look like a horse. A miniature that looks like a pony is inferior. The American Shetland Pony Club maintains a registry called the American Miniature Horse Registry for horses under 34 inches.

LONG EARS: ASSES, MULES, AND DONKEYS

An *ass* is a close relative of the horse. The male ass is known as a *jack* and a female ass is known as a *jennet*. The most obvious differences between the ass and the horse is the size of the ear, a sparser mane and tail, and smaller hooves. The noise made by the animals is different also. The horse whinnies; whereas, the ass brays. A *bray* is the loud, harsh cry of an ass. The gestation period of the jennet is 30 days longer than the mare.

Mules are the offspring produced by breeding a jack to a mare. Mules were very popular when animals were used to provide power. The *hinny* is the reverse in breeding—a jennet to a stallion. The mule is more like the ass; whereas, the hinny is more like the horse. Like most hybrids, mules and hinnys are seldom fertile.

Donkeys are small asses. The name is from the English word "dun," which describes the color. *Burro* is the Spanish translation of donkey. The burro is small with a height of 40 to 50 inches. They are native to North and South America. The ancestors were most likely brought to the Americas with the Spanish expedition.

12-8. A mare mule. (Courtesy, American Donkey and Mule Society)

WILD HORSE (FERAL)

The presence of horses in the world goes back to drawings found in caves in southern France. The heavy draft horse, as well as the refined horse, was shown in these drawings. The bones of 40,000 horses that existed 25,000 years ago, found outside a rock shelter in France, provide evidence of the cave dweller's dependence on the horse.

The first horses to reach North America were the well-bred mounts of the Spanish conquistadors. It is believed that the wild (feral) herds that were later found roaming the Western United States were strays from this expedition. A *feral horse* is an animal, or its offspring, that was once domesticated but has escaped and become wild. It took about 200 years for the horse herds to adapt to the wild. The East Coast Indians were introduced to horses by the Spanish. The colonists brought horses with them from their native land.

12-9. Wild Chincoteague ponies of Virginia.

Wild horses exist today in certain locations in the United States. Herds are allowed to roam freely on islands off the coast of Virginia and North Carolina. These are in areas monitored by the National Park Service. With population growth in the East, wild horses are being pushed out of their natural habitat due to construction. In the West, wild herds also face tough issues. Round ups are conducted and the horses are sold to people across the country to maintain the ecosystem. A large population of wild horses exists in the Southwest. The United States government has developed an adoption program to manage the population.

SPECIALTY HORSES AND THE FAMILY

Specialty horses are popular in today's society. People find many ways to enjoy speciality horses. Draft horses are used in shows, wagon trains, and horse pulls at fairs. Some draft horses are still used to do work on farms. Miniature horses are enjoyed for their novel size—as pets, for breeding, and in shows. Miniature horses are very easy to handle, but their size and their inability to fight make them the prime target of dogs and other animals. Mules and donkeys are also becoming more popular. These animals are

12-10. These Belgians are being used to rake hay.

12-11. Champion mule at the South Carolina State Fair. (Courtesy, The American Donkey and Mule Society)

unique and people own them for many reasons, but the uniqueness plays a big part. It is fun to learn how to produce these animals and to study the genetics.

REVIEWING

MAIN IDEAS

Speciality horses have many of the same characteristics as other horses. However, speciality horses are different in a specific way that makes them unique to the industry. The draft horse was used for many years as the primary way to do farm work, transport goods and people, and to breed and trade for monetary gain. The draft horses were brought to America to serve a purpose. Today, these animals, for the most part, do not serve that same purpose. For example, the Clydesdale is part of a major marketing concept. You rarely see them plowing a field or pulling a hay-making machine.

Miniature horses are also unique to the horse industry. These are just "small horses." They are not dwarfs or mutations. They are used as pets and for shows and other related events. They are not big enough to pull large wagons or to plow the field.

Donkeys, burros, jacks, jennets, mules, and related animals have played a big part in our history. They have provided labor in the fields, mines, forest, and other places. These animals are different from a "normal" horse and have their own special characteristics. These animals provide a vast amount of opportunity to study the genetics and breeding of horses.

QUESTIONS

Answer the following questions using correct spelling and complete sentences.

1. What are specialty horses?
2. What is the maximum height of a miniature horse?
3. What animals are known as "long-ears"? What are they best known for?
4. What is the typical height of a draft horse? Weight?
5. What are the breeds of draft horses?

Specialty Horses and Related Species

6. What are the purposes of miniature horses?
7. What is a mule? Hinny?
8. Describe the purposes of donkeys and other long-eared animals.
9. How did the wild (feral) horse get to the Western United States?
10. Why are specialty horses important to families that keep them?

EVALUATING

CHAPTER SELF-CHECK

Match the term with the correct definition. Place the letter by the term in the blank provided.

a. jack
b. jennet
c. burro
d. feral
e. mule
f. hinny
g. Clydesdale
h. donkey

____1. A female ass bred to a stallion to produce a hinny.

____2. A domesticated animal that escaped and became wild.

____3. A small, domesticated ass.

____4. A hybrid animal produced from a jack and a mare.

____5. The male species of the ass.

____6. A popular breed of draft horse.

____7. The animal resulting from the breeding of a jennet and a stallion.

____8. The Spanish term for donkey.

DISCOVERING

1. As a class project, select a breed of draft horse; research the origin and characteristics. Write a narrative on your findings then prepare a class presentation and deliver it in class. Use visuals of the breed as part of the narrative and presentation.

2. Visit a miniature horse farm, or using the Internet, collect data on this industry. List the characteristics of these animals and how they are used in society.

3. As a group project, collect information on donkeys, jacks, jennets, mules, burros and other animals with long ears. In outline form, find the origin and characteristics of each. In addition, note any special breeding criteria for each. Then present the findings for each item from the outline. Divide the material among all group members.

4. Invite a specialty animal owner to class and discuss the management of the animals.

5. As a class, construct a display highlighting the breeds and history of these animals. Place the display in your school media center and enter the display in your local county fair.

6. Visit a draft horse show and/or pulling contest. Write a report on what you observe.

7. Ride in a horse or mule drawn vehicle.

8. Visit a horse show. Report on your visit.

13

CAREERS IN EQUINE SCIENCE

How about a job in the horse industry? Choosing a career is one of the most important decisions a person makes. Time and energy are needed to make the best decision. The field of equine science, or the horse industry, offers many opportunities. Just like any other career, not everyone will fit into this area. Always consider location of job opportunities, required training, personal interests, and the salary and benefits associated with the career.

If you think you are interested in a career in the horse industry, conduct a thorough study to identify the occupations and training needed. Find out a much as possible to see if the industry is right for you.

13-1. Horse trainers are closely involved with the animals they train. A trainer must understand the behavior of horses. (Courtesy, American Paint Horse Association)

OBJECTIVES

This chapter examines the careers in the horse industry. Upon completion of this chapter you should be able to:

1. Explain career success
2. Describe requirements for career advancement
3. List examples of careers in the horse industry
4. Explain why shadowing is important
5. Describe how to locate a job
6. Explain how to go for a job interview

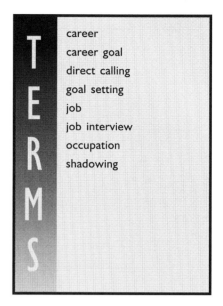

TERMS

career
career goal
direct calling
goal setting
job
job interview
occupation
shadowing

EQUINE KNOWLEDGE

The United States and China are the two countries with the most horses!

CHOOSING A CAREER IN EQUINE SCIENCE

A *career* is the general direction of your life's work. A career often involves several occupations and jobs. Choosing a career area is not easy. Many careers take much training and education; therefore, a decision needs to be made early in life to obtain the necessary skills, education, and experience.

The first thing a person should establish in choosing a career area in the equine field is the love for horses. Horses require attention day and night, weekends and holidays, and they cannot be left for another activity. Horses are completely dependent upon people for their existence. Many people are born with the love for horses; whereas, others acquire the love. However, there are those who do not like horses and should pursue other careers.

The second thing a person should be aware of is the education requirements for a specific job. Involvement in organizations such as FFA and 4-H, horse show organizations, and other related groups may be beneficial. If you are pursuing a career as a veterinarian, good grades in courses at school and hands-on work experience are necessary. If you would like to work in the agribusiness area of the industry, business and management courses may be needed.

Finally, your attitude regarding the industry is important. The horse industry is a multi-billion dollar industry. There are jobs in many areas, but the common denominator is the love of horses. In general, horse work is long and hard, albeit often rewarding. Job reality and dreams should be realistically analyzed. Dual preparations, top education, and career alternatives should be part of your plans.

13-2. Young people enjoy studying equine science.

OCCUPATIONS AND JOBS

An *occupation* is the specific work in a career that can be given a title. Occupations also have duties and required skills that tend to be consistent from one place to another. An example of an occupation in the horse industry is farrier.

People gain employment in their occupation with a job or position. A *job* is the specific work performed in an occupation for compensation (pay). Jobs have specific locations and demands. The same occupation can be performed as jobs for different employers. An individual could change jobs but continue the same occupation. Using the example of a farrier, a farrier could work for a horse farm in one location and change jobs to work for a horse farm in another place. The skills needed are consistent with both jobs.

BEING SUCCESSFUL

Being successful involves setting goals and going about achieving them. A *career goal* is the level of accomplishment you want to make in your work. The first step is to set goals by a process known as goal setting. *Goal setting* is describing what we want to achieve in life. In the process, people must consider their personal interests and what is realistic for them to achieve. As goals are set, steps to achieve each goal must be identified. Ways and means to accomplish the steps and deadlines for reaching each step are set.

13-3. Use the resources of your school counselor in setting career goals. (Courtesy, Jasper S. Lee, Georgia)

Goals can be changed. People sometimes gain more information and decide that goals they have set need to be modified. It is smart to regularly assess and modify goals. You want to be sure that you achieve what you are capable of doing.

Education and Training

Occupations often involve specific education and training. A part of goal setting is to identify what is needed. Determine the sources of the education and training as well as where they are offered, how much they cost, and how long it will take.

With some equine occupations, a high school education is adequate along with practical experience. Take agriculture or equine courses in high school. Get supervised experience under the direction of a qualified horse owner, trainer, or specialist.

Many occupations require education and training beyond the high school level. Community colleges may have programs that help you to qualify. College and university degrees may be needed in some occupations, particularly those that require a high level of knowledge.

Advancing in an Equine Career

Advancement requires the ability to perform the duties of an occupation well. This begins with the first job you take. Here are a few pointers on career advancement:

- Be prepared—Get the necessary training and education so you will be able to perform the work in a highly satisfactory manner for an employer.
- Get along with people—Good relationships with other people are essential. This includes co-workers as well as customers or people for who you might work. No one wants to work around a grouchy person who never says good morning, please, thank you, or excuse me.
- Dedication—Dedication means that your work is an important part of your life. You work hard to be productive and do the job right. You do not waste time while at work nor fail to be at work on time. You do not waste or abuse equipment and facilities of others. Certainly, loyalty and honesty are extremely important.
- Enthusiasm—People need to be excited about their work. This enthusiasm rubs off on other people and helps you enjoy what you are doing more.

13-4. The ability to get along with other people is essential for career success. (Courtesy, Jasper S. Lee, Georgia)

- Responsibility—Being able to assume responsibility is a key to success. In equine science, you are likely working with animals that depend on you. You also must demonstrate that you can assume responsibility to the owners of horses. The welfare of the horses is an owner's primary concern.
- Physically and mentally fit—Being fit is important. Go about life so that your mind and body are in good condition. Get plenty of rest. Do not use substances that harm your body. Eat properly and follow good health care practices.

OCCUPATIONS IN EQUINE SCIENCE

There are many opportunities for people who desire to work in the equine industry. Here are some occupational areas:

1. Farrier (a person who shoes horses and takes care of hooves)
2. Veterinarian
3. Horse trainer
4. Boarding stable manager
5. Breeding manager
6. Riding instructor
7. Feed dealer, producer, and sales
8. Public relations or marketing specialist
9. Equipment dealer, producer, and sales
10. Teacher of agriculture

13-5. Farrier preparing a horse's foot for a shoe.

11. Extension agent or specialist in equine
12. Horse magazine writer
13. Breed association professional
14. Pharmaceutical professional
15. Horse show professional
16. Horse judge
17. Horse racing professional
18. Jockey
19. Horse buyer and seller
20. Hunt club professional
21. Consultant in equine
22. Administrator, secretary, executive assistant of associations in the horse industry
23. Research technician in equine
24. Research scientist in equine
25. Semen and breeding professional
26. Race track manager
27. Transportation (moving horses, driving, etc.)
28. Equine disease specialist
29. Equine nutrition scientist
30. Financial advisor to horse owners

SHADOWING

Shadowing is the activity of following a person to observe exactly what is involved in an occupation. A student may even participate in limited activities to get a grasp of a career. An example may be when a student shadows a veterinarian and gets to "suit up" for a minor operation.

A shadowing experience is one of the most beneficial things a person can do in making a decision about a career. Sometimes, the job is exactly as perceived, but other times it is very different. Shadowing will help in evaluating the career decision.

13-6. Student shadowing a veterinarian.

EQUINE EDUCATION OCCUPATIONS

Teaching is one of the most rewarding jobs in America. Teaching allows a person to make an impact on people and to change their present and future. The horse industry has many careers in education. These include:

1. High school agriculture teacher
2. Two-year college equine instructor
3. College or university equine instructor
4. Extension agent
5. Extension equine specialist

13-7. High school agriculture teacher demonstrating how to use a bridle.

6. Youth organizations involved with equine
7. Horse breed association representative
8. State or federal government in agriculture/equine
9. Private equine trainer
10. Riding instructor

SCIENCE-RELATED EQUINE CAREERS

Science is the observation, identification, description, experimental investigation, and theoretical explanation of natural phenomena. In the field of

13-8. Testing a stream for water quality near a horse farm to determine if pollution is entering the water.

equine science, there are many jobs related to science, such as veterinary medicine, pharmaceutical sales and production, animal diagnostics, feed production and analysis, waste management, research, and environmental management. It is very important to identify which field of science is your choice in order to prepare yourself early and then follow a plan of study throughout your educational path.

COMMUNICATION, SALES, AND RELATED AREAS

Many occupations involve communicating information about horses or the supplies and services used in their production. People in these occupations need knowledge of horses in order to effectively carry out their work.

Here are a few examples of areas where equine knowledge is important:

- Advertising—Individuals who prepare advertisements for horses and horse supplies and services need to have some knowledge of equine science.

- Media—Individuals in the media who deal with topics involving horses need knowledge of equine science. These include agricultural or equine writers as well as television and radio broadcasters.

- Selling—Persons who sell feed, animal medicines, equipment, and other products used with horses need a knowledge of equine science.

13-9. Artists/illustrators dealing with horse projects need knowledge of equine science. (Courtesy, Jasper S. Lee, Georgia)

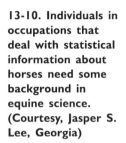
13-10. Individuals in occupations that deal with statistical information about horses need some background in equine science. (Courtesy, Jasper S. Lee, Georgia)

- Statistical reporting—Persons whose occupations involve collecting statistical information on horses need some knowledge of equine science.

GETTING A JOB

Once an individual has selected an occupation and received the necessary training, he or she is ready to get a job. This is not always an easy task. Of course, entrepreneurs make jobs for themselves rather than seeking a job from another person or business. Regardless, you must make the effort to get a job. Rarely do employers seek out an individual for a job. Just think, the employer may not know about you!

Getting a job involves a process of locating, applying for, and responding to a job offer.

LOCATING A JOB OPENING

A job opening must exist for an individual to get a job. Searching for a job begins shortly before a person completes the needed education and training program. Several sources of information can be used.

Here are a few sources of information on job openings:

- Teachers—Your agriculture or equine science teacher often hears about job openings. Ask your teacher for help.
- Counselors—Your school counselor may have information about job openings.

13-11. Direct calling involves contacting employers to see if jobs are available. (Courtesy, Jasper S. Lee, Georgia)

- Placement offices—Some schools and agencies have placement offices that can help you find a job opening. These offices may have lists of job openings posted on a bulletin board or a computer Web page.
- Media—Newspapers, magazines, radio, and television may have announcements of job openings. In the case of equine science, it is probably best to look at magazines especially for the horse industry.
- Friends and family—Your friends and family members may hear about job openings.
- Direct calling—*Direct calling* is the process of contacting a potential employer to ask if any job openings exist. Such contacts are made by telephone, e-mail, or in person.
- Internet—The Internet may have useful sites for locating jobs. These include sites of employment offices, as well as specific equine Web sites (refer to Appendix A).

APPLYING FOR A JOB

Once a job opening has been found, the next step is to apply for it. This may involve filling out an application form, writing a letter of application, preparing a personal data sheet, and going for an interview.

It is important to properly prepare written job application materials. Why? The written material you submit represents you. It is your ambassador. Good materials help "sell" you to the employer. Always spell words correctly, use correct grammar, give accurate information, and write legibly. Be neat!

Careers in Equine Science **205**

A part of applying for a job is going for an interview. A *job interview* is a personal appearance of the job applicant with the employer. The interview is two way: it provides information about you to the employer and provides you with information about the employer. Taking a job is an important step. Both you and the employer need to understand each other. Ask questions about the work. In most cases, the individuals interviewing you will provide most of the information you need without having to ask for it.

Here are a few tips in making job interview:

- Learn about the employer ahead of time—Read materials, use the Internet, or talk to other people about the employer. Learning about the employer will help you anticipate answers to questions ahead of time.
- Take needed things to the interview—It is always a good idea to have a note pad, pen, extra copies of your personal data sheet, and your Social Security number with you.
- Groom and dress appropriately—Appropriate dress depends on the nature of the job you are seeking. Your outward appearance communicates information about you to a prospective employer. Remove excess jewelry. In general, dress somewhat better than the typical person performing the job would dress.
- Be on time—Arrive on time for the interview. Never be late for a job interview.
- Have personality—Introduce yourself to people. Use good manners. Speak clearly and confidently. Use good grammar. Pronounce words correctly. Sit and stand with good posture. Look people in the eye. Smile and show enthusiasm for the job.

13-12. Good eye contact and communication are important in a job interview. (Courtesy, Jasper S. Lee, Georgia)

- Things not to take to a job interview—Never take chewing gum, tobacco products, alcohol, or illegal substances on an interview. Do not take friends or children with you. Go alone and demonstrate a competent, positive attitude. Never put-down other employers or people.

- Conclude—End the interview on time unless the individuals interviewing you wish for you to continue. Thank everyone who interviewed you for their time. After the interview, leave the employer's facilities. (In some cases, a follow-up thank you note for the interview would be appropriate.)

RESPONDING

The employer will likely indicate when a decision will be made about the job during your interview. Give the employer that amount of time. Do not call or visit the employer about the job.

When you hear from an interview, it will be to offer you the job or indicate that the job has been offered to another person. In either case, always appropriately thank the individual who contacts you.

If you get the job offer, ask when the work would begin and any other questions that you have. Indicate that you will provide a response within the time frame allowed. You may want to talk with trusted people before you make a decision. If you do not want the position, indicate to the employer that you have carefully considered the offer and feel that it is in your best interest not to accept it. If you want the job, indicate that you accept it. In either case, be most appreciative of the offer and the courtesy that you have received.

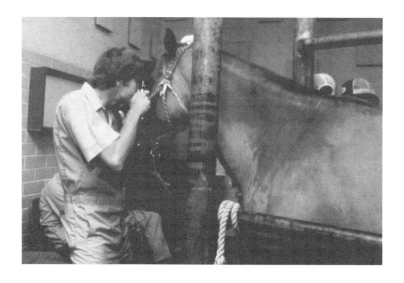

13-13. A veterinary medical student at Texas A&M University is learning how to examine the eye of a horse. (Courtesy, Veterinary Medical Center, Texas A&M University)

REVIEWING

MAIN IDEAS

There are many careers in the horse industry for those who prepare themselves early and stick to their plan. The main prerequisite is a love for horses and a dedication to the industry. Students should identify a specific area and make a plan to obtain the needed education and work experience. Shadowing is one of the best ways to investigate a career.

There are career opportunities in the horse industry as trainers, veterinarians, farriers, teachers, consultants, stable managers, researchers, marketers, horse magazine writers, breed registry professionals, horse show professionals, racing professionals, secretaries and office managers, equipment producers or sales representatives, feed producers or sales representatives, pharmaceutical researchers or sales representatives, and other related careers.

The field of education is very broad in the horse industry. High schools in most states have an equine science class. Extension agents work with horses and horse owners in many different capacities. A variety of college-level educational programs are available. Many companies and corporations have personnel to teach in different capacities.

The field of science is big in the horse industry. If you have a desire to work in science, equine could be the opportunity for you.

QUESTIONS

Answer the following questions using correct spelling and complete sentences.

1. What three major areas should be considered in choosing an equine career?
2. What is the distinction between an occupation and a job?
3. What is a career goal?
4. What are six requirements for career success and advancement?
5. List six career options in the field of equine science.
6. What is shadowing? Give an example of shadowing in an area of equine science.
7. List the educational career opportunities in the field of equine science.
8. Explain the science careers in the field of equine science.

9. What are four career areas in communication and sales?

10. How does a person locate a job opening?

11. What should be considered in making a job interview?

12. How does a person apply for a job?

EVALUATING

CHAPTER SELF-CHECK

Match the term with the correct definition. Place the letter by the term in the blank provided.

a. career
b. shadowing
c. career goal
d. direct calling
e. job interview

_____ 1. Personal appearance of job applicant with an employer.

_____ 2. General direction of a person's life related to work.

_____ 3. Contacting an employer to see if jobs are open.

_____ 4. The activity of following a person to observe exactly what is involved in a job or profession.

_____ 5. Desired level of accomplishment to make in work.

DISCOVERING

1. Interview someone with a career in the horse industry. What are his or her qualifications including, education, experience, etc. List the daily duties of the career, highlighting the highs and lows. List the salary scale from the beginning to the top of the scale. List the availability of jobs in this specific field and if relocating is necessary.

2. Review the career options in the horse industry. Select the one that most suits you. Seek a shadowing opportunity through your teacher. Conduct a one or two day shadowing experience. Keep a log on all activities observed and the one in which you participated.

3. Select five career options in the horse industry. Prepare a poster display showing each career along with a short narrative describing the career. Then present the display to the class.

14

THE HORSE RACING INDUSTRY

My horse is faster than your horse! Horse racing is a popular sport. It is the act of placing one horse against another for a given distance within certain parameters. Horse racing has been going on for centuries.

Horse racing involves different breeds chosen for a specific distance and speed. The Thoroughbred is designed for long distances. The Quarter Horse is built for short distances. If you evaluate each breed you will see that the physical build of each is suited for specific events.

14-1. Race horses in full stride.

OBJECTIVES

This chapter examines the race horse industry. Upon completion of this chapter, you should be able to:

1. Identify the different types of race horses
2. List the characteristics of Thoroughbred race horses
3. List the characteristics of Standardbred race horses
4. List the characteristics of Quarter Horses
5. Name the terms common in horse racing

TERMS

breakage
breeze
claiming race
driver
flat racing
furlong
handicapped race
harness racing
jockey
parimutuel
Quarter Horse
Standardbred
steeplechase
sulky
Thoroughbred
Triple Crown

EQUINE KNOWLEDGE

Horse racing ranks third in the United States as a spectator sport.

HORSE RACING

Horse racing is a big business. Horse tracks are in many towns and cities and provide many jobs and money to the local economy. The breeding industry is built around the racing industry. There are many breeding farms that raise horses for the racing industry. This is a very expensive and complex segment of the industry. The horse racing industry is a network made up of horses, riders, owners, breeders, trainers, track owners, and especially, the people that watch the horses race. Viable commercial racing relies on pari-mutuels (this can be a moral issue for many people).

TYPES OF RACING

The following are the different types of horse racing in the United States:

1. *Flat racing* — Racing on a flat, oval track as opposed to racing over obstacles. Several breeds are used in this type of racing including Thoroughbreds, Quarter Horses, Arabians, and Appaloosas.

2. *Harness racing* — A race in which trotters or pacers pull a driver riding on a sulky around a track. Standardbreds are most often used for harness racing.

3. *Steeplechase* — A cross-country race over obstacles, which consist of water, hurdles, and other jumps. Hunt clubs are organizations that conduct a combination of steeplechases and flat races.

14-2. A steeplechase is a cross-country race over obstacles.

14-3. Kentucky's historic Churchill Downs.

JOCKEYS

A *jockey* is a professional horse rider in races. Each state licenses jockeys for races within the state. Most jockeys are small people who weigh only about 110 pounds. Horses are assigned weights that they can carry in a race, including the weight of the jockey, the saddle, and any equipment the jockey takes.

Most jockeys use a whip, boots, and a safety helmet that is worn to protect them from injury in case of an accident. Jockeys wear special jackets and caps (known as silks). The colors of the jackets and caps vary with the owners of the horse.

THOROUGHBREDS

A *Thoroughbred* is a breed of horses that usually race on a flat track. No other breed can match the Thoroughbred racing distance of 6 furlongs or ¾ to 1½ miles. The ideal Thoroughbred has long forearms and gaskins and displays good length from the hip to the hock. The range in size at racing condition is 15-1 to 16-2 hands and weighs 900 to 1150 pounds. The world record mile was set in 1968 at a time of 1:32 1/5 seconds by Dr. Fager at Chicago's Arlington Park. The most notable Thoroughbreds are:

Swaps: World record in 1956 at 1:33 1/5 seconds at Hollywood Park

Secretariat: Triple Crown winner

Man-O-War: Winner in 21 of 22 starts

The ***Triple Crown*** is comprised of three annual races for three-year olds. Those races are the Kentucky Derby, the Preakness, and the Belmont Stakes. Refer to Table 14-1 for a list of Triple Crown winners.

Table 14-1. Triple Crown Winners

Year	Horse	Owner
1919	Sir Barton	J.K.L. Ross
1930	Gallant Fox	William Woodward
1935	Omaha	William Woodward
1937	War Admiral	Samuel D. Riddle
1941	Whirlaway	Warren Wright
1943	Count fleet	Mrs. John Hertz
1946	Assault	R.J. Kelberg, Jr.
1948	Citation	Warren Wright
1973	Secretariat	Mrs. Penny Tweedy
1977	Seattle Slew	Karen and Mickey Taylor Three Chimney Farm
1978	Affirmed	Louis Wolsson

STANDARDBREDS

A ***Standardbred*** is a breed of horses developed for trotting or pacing. The Standardbred is a mixture of the Thoroughbred, Norfolk Trotter, Barb, Morgan, and Canadian pacing ancestors. The name Standardbred came from the practice that began in the 1800s of registering horses that trotted or paced the mile in less than "standard" time. The first standards set were 2:30 for trotters and 2:25 for pacers. Standardbreds race on an oval track. The horse

14-4. Standardbred with his driver.

pulls a driver riding on a sulky. A *sulky* is a light-weight, two-wheeled cart with a seat for a driver. The Standardbred ranges from 15 to 16 hands in height. Bay, brown, chestnut, and black are the most common colors; but grays, roans, and duns are found. Some of the most famous Standardbreds are:

> Hambletonian 10: nearly all Standardbreds are traced to this stallion.
> Yankee: first trotted the mile under saddle in less than 3 minutes in 1806.
> Dan Patch: held the pacing record from 1903 until 1938.
> Greyhound: held the trotting crown from 1937 until 1969.
> Nevele Pride: broke the trotting record of Greyhound in 1969.
> Adios: had 50 offspring with less than 2 minute miles.
> Bret Hanover: held many records and whose bloodline has made a great impact on racing.
> Steady Star: broke Bret Hanovers pacing record by 2 seconds at 1:52.

QUARTER HORSES

A *Quarter Horse* is a powerfully built breed of horses that are adapted for tremendous speed at short distances. A well-muscled horse is desired. The

14-5. Racing Quarter Horses.

head is somewhat short and is distinct because of the small alert ear. The neck is well-developed, the back and loin short and heavily muscled, the forearms and rear quarters are well-muscled, and the legs relatively short. The most predominate colors of the breed are chestnut, sorrel, bay, and dun. Palominos, blacks, browns, roans, and copper-colored are not uncommon. Quarter Horse racing is measured with a stopwatch. This kind of horse racing is not as popular as Standardbreds and Thoroughbreds but is growing.

The most famous of all Quarter Horses, Steel Dust, made his debut in Texas around the middle of the 19th century.

HORSE RACING TERMS

Horse racing involves terms that have meanings related to racing. A few of these terms are listed below.

1. **Allowance Race**: A race where there are both allowances and penalties with regard to the condition of the race, monies won or races won, or the date the last races were won.
2. **Backstretch**: The stable area of a racetrack.
3. **Blow Out**: To work a horse fast over a short distance in order to put an "edge on him" for a race.
4. *Breakage*: In parimutual betting, the odd cents left over after paying the successful bettors to the nearest 10 cents.

5. **Breeder**: Owner of the dam at the time of service who was responsible for the selection of the sire to which she was mated.

6. *Breeze*: To exercise a horse at moderate speed.

7. **Chute**: Straight part of the racetrack behind the barrier.

8. **Claiming Price**: The predetermined price at which a horse in a claiming race must be sold, if it is claimed.

9. *Claiming Race*: The conditions for the race provide that each entry may be bought at a predetermined price by an owner who meets certain track qualifications: for example, one who has started a horse at the meeting.

10. **Condition Race**: A race in which certain conditions are specified. A calendar of races that includes the stipulations and provisions under which each race is to be run is published in the condition book.

11. **Coupled:** Two or more horses are grouped in the betting, and bets upon them are decided by the position of the foremost horse.

12. *Driver*: Individual who guides a harness horse from the seat of a sulky.

13. **Entry**: Two or more horses belonging to the same owner or trainer that compete in the same race. A bet on one is a bet on the other.

14. **Exerciser**: A jockey or other rider who gallops horses in workouts.

15. **Field**: When there are more horses entered in a race than there are positions on the odds board.

16. **Film Patrol**: Pictures of all races are taken immediately after each race and viewed by the stewards.

14-6. A Thoroughbred in full stride.

The Horse Racing Industry

17. **Flat Racing**: Racing on a flat, oval track as opposed to racing over obstacles.
18. *Furlong*: One-eighth of a mile or 220 yards.
19. *Futurity*: Nominations for a specific race made a long time before the race is run. Usually portions of the total nomination money are called for at specific times.
20. *Handicapped Race*: A race in which the competing horses are assigned weights to carry that will equalized their chances of winning.
21. **Handle**: In parimutuel betting, the total amount of money bet on a race, on the day's racing, on the races at a meeting, or during the entire racing season.
22. **Harness Racing**: Racing with Standardbred horses that either trot or pace in harness pulling a driver riding on a sulky.
23. **Hot Walker**: A groom (or an exercise device may be used) who walks horses after a race.
24. **Jockey**: A professional horse rider in races.
25. **Judge**: A stewart, placing judge, paddock judge, or patrol judge.
26. **Lapped:** To be one full length behind another horse during a race.
27. **Match Race**: A race between two horses owned by different parties.
28. **Nomination**: The naming of a horse for a stakes race on a specific date well in advance.
29. **Owner**: A person or stable that has property rights in a horse.
30. **Paddock Judge**: A racetrack official whose duty it is to get the jockeys or drivers and their horses on the racing strip on time.
31. *Parimutuel*: The system of racetrack betting that returns to successful bettors the precise amount of money wagered by unsuccessful bettors after deductions of commission and breakage.
32. **Patrol Judge**: A racing association official who watches a race.
33. **Penalties**: Extra weight a horse must carry in a given race due to winnings collected after a certain date.
34. **Placing Judge**: A racing association official who decides the placement of the horses in their order of finish.
35. **Pool**: Total money bet on horses in a race.
36. **Racing Chemist**: A chemist who analyzes saliva, urine, and blood to ensure the health of the horses and rules of racing.

37. **Racing Secretary**: The racetrack official whose duty it is to write the races, such as the handicaps.

38. **Route**: A distance race, usually $1^1/_8$ mile or longer.

39. **Stewart of the Race Meeting**: Person who insures the race is run by the rules (usually there are three).

40. **Trainer:** An individual who supervises and cares for the racehorses.

REVIEWING

MAIN IDEAS

Horse racing has a colorful history and is a very large, complex industry. The racing industry provides many jobs—from horse breeding to racetrack grounds keeper—and enhances the economy in those states that permit pari-mutuel betting. The decision to have horse racing in your state is a political, social, cultural, and personal issue. Regardless of whether racing is an organized activity in your state, some aspect of the industry may be—a breeding farm, transportation company, feed company, tack and equipment producer, etc.

In flat racing, horses race around an oval track. Thoroughbreds are the main breed of horses used with this type of racing. Quarter horses, Arabians, Appaloosas, and other breeds are popular in the West and Southwest for straightaway racing. Harness racing is another popular type of racing in which Standardbreds either trot or pace pulling a sulky with a driver aboard. Steeplechases are becoming more popular in today's society. In steeplechases, horses race over obstacles (hurdles, water jumps) either on dirt or grass. Hunt clubs organize many steeplechases. It is important to point out that the governing bodies that monitor and control horse racing in the United States are the state racing commissions, the National Association of State Racing Commission, The Jockey Club, The Thoroughbred Racing Association, The Thoroughbred Owners and Breeders Association, Horseman's Benevolent and Protective Association, The American Trainers Association, the Jockey's Guild, the Jockeys Association, and the Thoroughbred Racing Protective Bureau.

QUESTIONS

Answer the following questions using correct spelling and complete sentences.

1. What are the three types of horse racing in the United States? Explain each.
2. List the characteristics of the Thoroughbred race horse.
3. List the characteristics of the Standardbred race horse.
4. List the characteristics of the racing Quarter horse.
5. What is the meaning of the following terms as related to horse racing: exerciser, racing chemist, furlong, flat racing, harness racing, and trainer?

EVALUATING

CHAPTER SELF-CHECK

Match the term with the correct definition. Place the letter by the term in the blank provided.

a. parimutuel
b. furlong
c. sulky
d. jockey
e. harness racing
f. handicap race
g. backstretch
h. steward

_____ 1. A professional rider of racehorses.

_____ 2. One-eight of a mile or 220 yards.

_____ 3. The stable area of a racetrack.

_____ 4. A race in which trotters and pacers pull a driver riding on a sulky around a track.

_____ 5. A race in which the competing horses are assigned weights.

_____ 6. The system of racetrack betting.

_____ 7. Judge that conducts a race.

_____ 8. A light-weight, two-wheeled racing rig.

DISCOVERING

1. As a class project, list the record-breaking Thoroughbreds, and Standardbreds in the past 50 years. Use all available resources including the Internet, encyclopedias, and other related references. Highlight the unique thing about the record that was broken.

2. Using the Internet and other related sources, find all the statistics on this year's Kentucky Derby and select a "mock" placing. Use the knowledge learned in this class in making your decision. After the race, discuss the official placing and how you did.

15

EQUITATION

I love to ride horses! To do so requires skill and knowledge of equitation. Some people get involved in competitive equitation events.

Equitation is the art of being skilled in the riding, management, and care of a horse. It is the mastery of horsemanship. Equitation events are divided into three classes: Saddle Seat, Stock Seat, and Hunt Seat. Only the rider is judged in equitation classes. Therefore, any horse that is suitable for a particular style of riding is capable of performing the class routines.

15-1. Hunt Seat Equitation requires a forward, English saddle with knee rolls.

OBJECTIVES

This chapter examines equine equitation. Upon completion of this chapter you should be able to:

1. Define equitation
2. List the different types of horse equipment
3. Describe the different types of gaits
4. List the steps in preparing a horse for riding
5. List the steps in handling a horse after riding

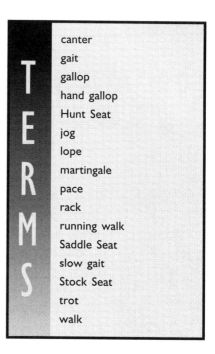

TERMS

canter
gait
gallop
hand gallop
Hunt Seat
jog
lope
martingale
pace
rack
running walk
Saddle Seat
slow gait
Stock Seat
trot
walk

EQUINE KNOWLEDGE

Foals are weaned from 4 to 6 months of age.

EQUITATION

In the *Saddle Seat,* the rider sits back in the saddle and remains vertical through all gaits. The stirrups are long and the hands are held high. Saddle

15-2. Parade before competition in Hunt Seat Equitation.

15-3. Stock Seat Equitation requires a Western saddle.

15-4. Standing close view in Saddle Seat Equitation. (Courtesy, Melissa Hower-Moritz, University of Minnesota–Crookston)

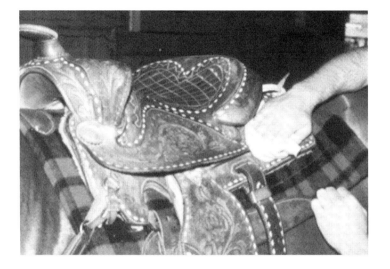

15-5. A Western Saddle has a curved, deep seat to provide all-day comfort while riding.

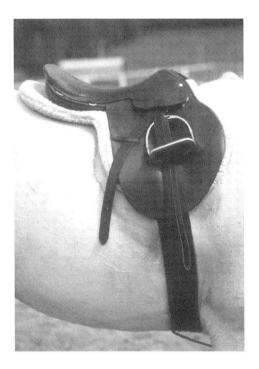

15-6. Forward saddle with knee rolls used in Hunt Seat Equitation.

Seat equitation requires an English saddle. The rider must demonstrate his or her ability to keep the prescribed seat and to manage the horse. The horse performs three gaits: the walk, the trot, and the canter.

In the **Stock Seat**, the rider's body position is straight and relaxed. The heel is lower than the toe in the stirrup and only one hand is used on the reins. Stock Seat equitation requires a Western saddle. A Western saddle has a curved, deep seat to provide all-day comfort while working livestock. The horse performs three gaits: the walk, the jog, and the lope. The *jog* is a slow, steady, jolting gait. The *lope* is the western adaptation of a very slow canter.

In the **Hunt Seat,** the stirrups are shorter and the rider sits erect and balanced (leaning forward with the faster gaits). The hands are held low. Hunt Seat equitation requires a forward seat English saddle with padded knee rolls. The classes may or may not be over obstacles. In non-jumping classes, the gaits performed are the walk, the trot,

Equitation

the canter, and the hand gallop. The **hand gallop** is an extended canter, but the horse remains collected, unlike the flat-out run when the horse's gait almost returns to a four-beat status.

GAITS

A *gait* is a particular way a horse moves, either natural or artificial, which is characterized by a distinctive rhythmic action of the feet and legs. There are different gaits performed by different breeds and types of horses. Gaits are classified as natural and artificial. The natural gaits include: the walk, trot, pace, canter, and the gallop. The artificial gaits are taught and they include: the running walk, slow rack, and slow pace.

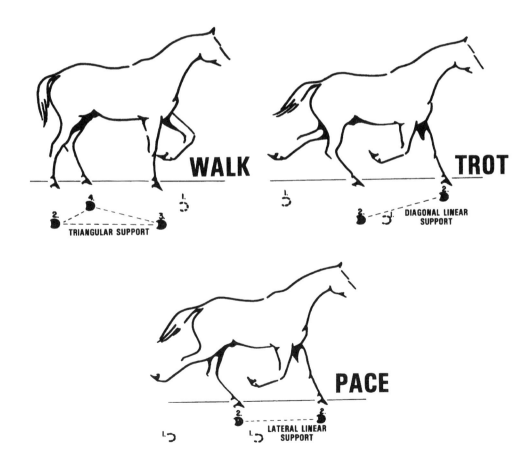

15-7. Walk, trot, and pace gaits.

NATURAL

The **walk**: A slow, flat-footed, four-beat gait. It is the most useful gait and is the basis for all other gaits.

The **trot**: A rapid, two-beat, diagonal gait in which the front foot and opposite hind foot take off at the same split second and strike the ground at the same time.

The **pace**: A rapid, two-beat gait in which the front and hind feet on the same side start and stop together.

The **canter**: A slow, three-beat gait in which the two diagonal legs are paired to make one beat, which falls between the beats of the other unpaired legs.

The **gallop**: A fast, four-beat gait. This gait is also called the *run* and is the fastest gait of the horse.

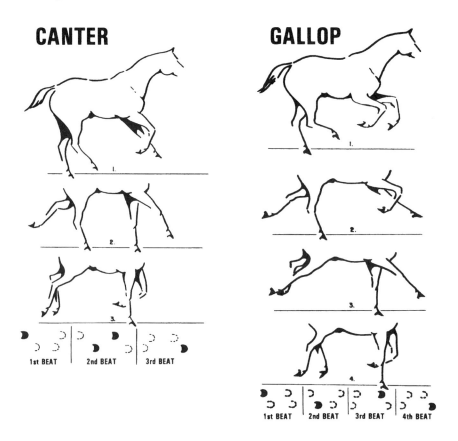

15-8. Canter and gallop gaits.

Equitation

ARTIFICIAL

The ***running walk***: The fast, four-beat, ground-covering walk characteristic of the Tennessee Walking Horse. The motion is smooth and fluid.

The ***slow gait*** or stepping pace: A four-beat gait with each of the four feet striking the ground separately.

The ***rack***: The fastest, most popular, four-beat gait.

TYPES OF EQUIPMENT/ TACK

The equipment or tack required depends upon the type or style of riding one plans to do. However, there are several general pieces of equipment:

1. Bridle
2. Halter
3. Lead line
4. Saddle
5. Saddle pad
6. Grooming equipment
7. Other tack

15-9. Several different styles of halters and bridles in a tack room.

BODY CONDITION SCORE

Body condition is the physical health of a horse. The condition of a horse is noticed most often by the appearance, but a horse can be in bad condition

15-10. Properly storing an English-style saddle promotes long life of the saddle. (Courtesy, Jasper S. Lee, Georgia)

and not show it on the outwardly. Body condition scores are the best way to detect whether a horse is in good or bad condition. Scoring is done by evaluating the horse from head to tail. Things to look for are:

1. Amount of fat on the horse
2. Degree of bones protruding, such as ribs, withers, backbone
3. Appearance of eyes, color of nostrils, etc.
4. Overall balance of horse with regards to condition
5. Energy level of the horse

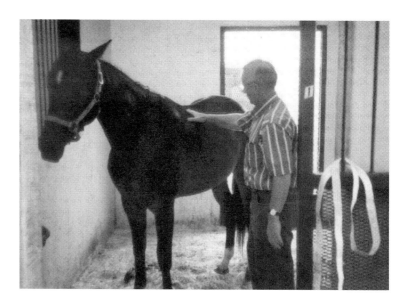

15-11. The condition of a horse is noticed most often by the appearance, but a horse can be in bad condition and not show it outwardly.

Equitation

The scale to measure the body condition of a horse is:

1	2	3	4	5	6	7	8	9
Extremely Thin				Ideal Body				Extremely Fat

The physical condition of a horse is very important.

RIDING

Horses must be properly prepared for riding and properly handled after riding. Good care promotes the well-being of the horse.

From the left, gather reins in left hand, and place left hand on or just in front of withers.

Turn stirrup iron one-quarter turn, steady stirrup with right hand and shove left foot into it.

Spring upward and lean on left arm, shift right hand from cantle to pommel of saddle; then swing extended right leg over horse's back and croup.

Ease down and sit easily, be alert and keep head up, and allow legs to hang comfortably with heels well down and toes turned out slightly.

15-12. How to mount a horse English style. (Dismounting is a reverse of the process shown here.)

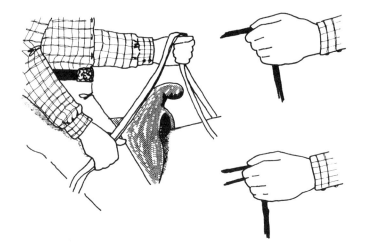

15-13. How to hold reins Western style. (Both or one hand can be used.)

PREPARING A HORSE FOR RIDING

When a horse is being prepared for a ride, several things must happen. First, the safety of both the horse and rider must be the priority. The steps involved in preparing a horse to ride include:

1. Catch and restrain the horse.
2. Brush and clean the horse, including hooves.
3. Observe the horse for any cuts, bruises, or other problems.
4. Check all equipment thoroughly.
5. Saddle the horse by placing a saddle pad or blanket on the horse's back. (Refer to Chapter 9 for details on saddling a horse.)
6. Set the saddle on the blanket and position it properly.
7. Tie the saddle cinch and tighten appropriately.
8. Attach any martingale, saddle bags, or other items. (A **martingale** is the strap of a horse's harness passing from the noseband to the girth between the forelegs, to keep the horse from rearing or throwing back the head.)
9. Place protective boots on the horse as necessary.
10. Place the bridle on the horse and properly adjust.

After you have properly "saddled" the horse, walk it around a minute to allow the horse to get used to the tack. Then, double check the saddle cinch and bridle. Lead the horse away from any structure before mounting. For safety, a novice should allow someone to hold the horse until mounted. A

Equitation 231

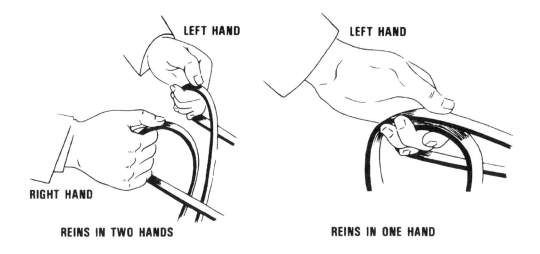

15-14. How to hold reins English style with a single-rein bridle.

novice should never mount an unknown or "green" mount. After you have ridden a few minutes, get off the horse and tighten your saddle as it probably has worked loose. Remember, safety is priority for both the horse and rider.

HANDLING A HORSE AFTER RIDING

Horses are just like any other animal regarding physical condition. Some horses are in good physical shape

15-15. A horse ready for riding.

and some are not. Some horses can go longer and do more and some need to work up to the task. Many horse owners will not exercise their horses during the winter. Therefore, horses need training and conditioning in the spring. When riding horses, whether on a trail ride, pleasure ride, show, or race, you should know the condition of your horse. All horses need to be exercised and prepared for riding.

232   EQUINE SCIENCE AND MANAGEMENT

15-16. A horse being cooled after a hard workout.

After riding is a very important time for the horse. If the horse has been worked hard and is sweating, it will require different treatment than a horse that has been walked and is not breathing hard. Horses that have been worked hard need to be walked and cooled down for 10 to 15 minutes. This will allow the horse's body temperature to cool as well as the muscles in the body to go through a chemical exchange. Horses can receive water in small amounts as they are walked-out. This promotes rehydration and reduces the chance of colic due to dehydration. Careful monitoring is needed to control water intake and prevent drinking too much too quickly. Customarily, cold water is not poured over a horse to cool it down. The sweat should be scraped off and a towel should be used to wipe the horse off as it is being walked. Remember, a horse is like an athlete—a ball player or a track runner—and needs special attention during this time. Research at the 1996 Olympics in Georgia found that pouring ice water on very hot horses resulted in no ill effects. Walking is important in all approaches to cooling horses. Of course, the condition of the horse is also a factor.

REVIEWING

MAIN IDEAS

Equitation is the ability of the rider to get a horse to perform. In equitation classes, only the rider is judged. There are three basic divisions of equi-

Equitation

tation: Saddle Seat, Hunt Seat, and Stock Seat. Each division is different and requires different tack.

The gait of a horse is how it moves. There are two kinds of gaits—natural and artificial. The natural gaits consist of the walk, trot, pace, canter, and gallop. The artificial gaits are taught to horses and consist of running walk, slow gait or stepping pace and the rack. The artificial gaits are all modifications of the walk.

Preparing a horse to ride is very important and the correct steps should be taken. Safety must be the top priority for both the horse and rider. The steps include catching the horse, grooming the horse, saddling the horse, attaching any special equipment, bridling the horse, and mounting. In addition, equipment checks need to made periodically after the initial mounting.

Cooling a horse down after a ride is extremely important. A horse's body condition may vary over the months and the rider should be aware of the ability of the horse. After riding, the horse should be walked for 10 to 15 minutes to allow the horse's body to cool. Some water may be given during this time. Water is usually not poured on a horse, however, sweat should be scraped off using a sweat scraper or towel. New approaches are being developed in cooling horses that include using ice water while being walked.

QUESTIONS

Answer the following questions using correct spelling and complete sentences.

1. Define equitation.
2. List the different types of horse equipment.
3. List the different types of gaits.
4. List the steps involved in preparing a horse to ride.
5. List the steps involved with cooling a horse.

EVALUATING

CHAPTER SELF-CHECK

Match the term with the correct definition. Place the letter by the term in the blank provided.

a. gait
b. artificial gaits
c. equitation
d. bridle
e. English saddle
f. Stock Seat
g. Weymouth
h. halter
i. walk
j. pace

_____ 1. The art of being skilled in the riding, management, and care of a horse.

_____ 2. A saddle developed for use in training, racing, jumping, showing, and polo.

_____ 3. A double-bitted, double-reined bridle used for gaited horses.

_____ 4. The control mechanism a rider uses to get a horse to perform certain commands.

_____ 5. A slow, flat-footed, four-beat gait. The most useful gait and the basis for all other gaits.

_____ 6. A piece of equipment used for leading or tying a horse.

_____ 7. Consist of the running walk, slow gait, and rack.

_____ 8. A rapid, two-beat gait in which the front and hind feet on the same side start and stop together.

_____ 9. A class of equitation in which a Western saddle is required.

_____ 10. The particular way a horse moves.

DISCOVERING

1. Visit a stable, or riding program, or invite an experienced horse person to bring a horse to school. Observe the steps involved in preparing a horse to be ridden. Make a written outline of these steps then perform them on a live horse. Present the teacher with a check list so your ability can be monitored.

2. List the different types of bridles, saddles, and grooming equipment. Construct a poster showing pictures of each with a definition of what it is used for on the horse.

3. List the different types of gaits and diagram the patter of each on paper.

4. Prepare a horse for riding with the appropriate equipment. Mount and ride a given course or pattern, then dismount and take the necessary steps in cooling the horse.

5. Using the proper grooming equipment, catch a horse, restrain the horse, and perform the correct grooming procedures including cleaning the feet.

6. Using the body condition scale, evaluate horses that are on all spectrums of the scale. Discuss your reasons why you placed the horses the way you did.

16

CITIZENSHIP, LEADERSHIP, AND ORGANIZATIONS

Are you a leader or a follower? The role one takes is important. People associated with the horse industry need to be good leaders.

There are many ways for horse owners to be active. Breed associations welcome new members. Service clubs, such as Rotary and Lions, may hold annual horse shows. Youth organizations, such as FFA, pony clubs, and 4-H Clubs, need volunteers to assist with horse events. Local government needs to hear from representatives about horse issues on a regular basis. A local horse club or organization should keep abreast of issues facing the horse industry. Good public relations from your farm to your neighbors is important. Horse owners need to be good citizens and active in their communities.

16-1. Participating in a local parade is one way to be a good citizen.

OBJECTIVES

This chapter examines leadership. Upon completion of the chapter you should be able to:

1. Identify leadership organizations related to the horse industry
2. List opportunities in FFA and 4-H leadership and competitive events
3. Identify and conduct a Supervised Agricultural Experience program in equine science
4. List major elements in an equine project record keeping system

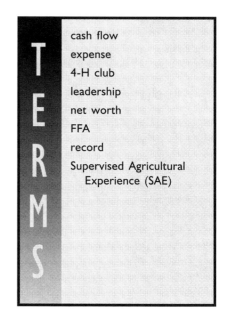

TERMS

cash flow
expense
4-H club
leadership
net worth
FFA
record
Supervised Agricultural Experience (SAE)

EQUINE KNOWLEDGE

State horse councils are groups that are very active in making decisions that affect the industry.

LEADERSHIP ORGANIZATIONS

Leadership is the position or guidance of a leader and the capacity or ability to lead. In all societies, there are a few people who make decisions that affect the entire population. Who are these people? Why are they influential? How can you get involved? Leaders get involved and spend time on issues that affect society. Many people wait until decisions are made before they express their concerns. By that time, it may be too late to do any good.

Leaders emerge and followers stay behind. Leadership organizations are the foundation of any cause, issue, or group. In the equine field, there are many issues that face horse owners and others. Who will make those decisions and how will they be made? The horse industry is no different than any other. Horse owners should be the ones that have a say in the decisions that affect them. This is possible, but horse owners must become involved.

Joining organizations, attending county commissioners' meetings, participating in PTA organizations, volunteering as a youth leader, and knowing the issues that face the horse industry is a start. Of course, you should be a member of the local horse council and saddle or hunt club. Volunteer to be member of your state horse council and get involved statewide.

The choice is yours to either accept what others decide for you or be a part of the decision-making process. For the student, the most beneficial organization is the FFA organization. You will learn leadership, citizenship, and teamwork. You will also learn parliamentary procedure and how to conduct a business meeting. These skills will help you in the future.

16-2. A business meeting being called to order by the chairperson.

EQUINE ORGANIZATIONS

Equine organizations can play a very important role in impacting decisions regarding many issues—from environmental laws and regulations to feed restrictions. Decisions are made daily at the local, state, and federal level that affect horse owners. Many of the decision makers have limited knowledge about horses and the horse industry. This is why it is important for horse owners to be involved with organizations and groups that keep up with what is going on and to have input in the decision being made. Who are these groups, where are they, and how can you get involved? Consider these opportunities for involvement:

1. Chamber of Commerce
2. Civic Clubs: Rotary, Lions, Kiwanis
3. Farm Bureau
4. Saddle Clubs
5. Hunt Clubs
6. Riding Clubs
7. Extension Advisory Committees
8. High School Agriculture Advisory Committees
9. 4-H and Youth Committees

16-3. 4-H Club members learning about horses on a field trip.

Organizations for students only:

1. FFA
2. 4-H Clubs
3. Student Government
4. Youth members of Civic Clubs
5. Riding Clubs
6. Saddle Clubs
7. Hunt Clubs
8. U.S. Pony Clubs

FFA AND 4-H ACTIVITIES

The *FFA* is an organization that offers students many opportunities while they are enrolled in agricultural education. The *4-H club* is a youth organization sponsored by the U.S. Department of Agriculture and open to young people from the ages of 5 to 19. These two organization are the building blocks for leadership in the equine field. The components that build character and skills in young people are:

1. Leadership through officer and committee work
2. Parliamentary procedures events
3. Public speaking events
4. Community service events

16-4. The new National FFA Center was dedicated on July 20, 1998, in Indianapolis, Indiana.

5. Projects and record keeping
6. Horse judging and other judging events
7. Appropriate dress
8. Appropriate manners and behavior
9. Teamwork
10. Individual growth and character development
11. Scientific and technical education

How can you become involved in these organizations? To become a member in the FFA you must be enrolled in agriculture in school. You can find out more by visiting with the agriculture teacher or counselor in your school. To become a member of 4-H, contact your county Extension office to find out more about the 4-H opportunities and clubs in your county. Express to each of these your personal interest so the sponsor can direct you in the right path.

SUPERVISED AGRICULTURAL EXPERIENCE

Supervised Agricultural Experience (SAE) is the ongoing agricultural project a student has throughout his or her high school career. In other organizations, it may be called by another name. The purpose is to learn about a certain subject and grow in knowledge and understanding with the assistance of other people. A horse project in agriculture education and 4-H is very broad and interesting. A horse project is a great way to learn about horses and the horse industry. It prepares people for jobs in this industry

16-5. FFA members participating in horse judging activities.

Citizenship, Leadership, and Organizations **241**

when they get out of school. Think of your goals and build your SAE around your interest. Specific horse projects include:

- Horse ownership/entrepreneur
- Horse placement—work on a horse farm or in a related area
- Horse experimental area
- Horse studies—independent study

Supporting areas:

- Horse judging
- Horse quiz bowls
- Horse workshops
- Horse showing

EQUINE RECORD KEEPING

Record keeping is an essential element of any business. A *record* is a permanent account to perpetuate a knowledge of acts or events. Regardless of whether you are keeping breeding records or expense records, they are important. An *expense* is a charge or cost associated with a business or property. What are the essential records for an equine project? Consider this list:

1. Beginning inventory of items (horse, tack, etc.) and their value
2. Expenses encountered in purchasing the items
3. Capital investments, such as barns, horse trailers, etc. Who provides these? Parent, friend?
4. Daily records of rations of feed, protein supplements, minerals, vitamins, etc.
5. Cost of daily rations
6. Health items

The major categories are:

16-6. An FFA member updating records.

16-7. Computers play a big role in record keeping.

1. Net worth statement—*Net worth* is the amount remaining after liabilities are subtracted from assets.
2. Cash flow—*Cash flow* is the amount of money coming in and going out in a given interval.
3. Daily activities records
4. Other, such as breeding records, health records, etc.

The youth organization in which you enroll will have a bonafide document to use in all these areas. Record keeping will be a part of your career and your personal life. Accuracy and efficiency are the keys to successful record keeping.

REVIEWING

MAIN IDEAS

Leadership is the capacity or ability to lead. Leaders who make decisions that affect people and specific industries need to be informed. The equine industry needs knowledgeable people in leadership positions. There are many ways to become involved and many organizations on the local, state, and federal level. Some local opportunities include saddle clubs, hunt clubs, pony clubs, Rotary, Lions, Kiwanis and other civic clubs, advisory councils, PTA, and other related groups. Equine councils, Extension councils, and animal groups are available on the state level. Regardless of the organization in which you become involved, you need to represent your interest and the equine interest. Do not wait until someone else makes decisions for your industry.

Youth organizations, such as FFA, 4-H, county councils, VICA, Beta Club, and student government are great places to learn leadership skills to help the horse industry. These organizations offer many opportunities to gain knowledge about horses and other fun things, such as public speaking, judging, and parliamentary procedures. Your agriculture teacher, counselor, Extension agent and others can guide you in the right direction. Get involved!

Horse projects are fun! There are many different kinds of horse projects in FFA and 4-H. You can judge horses, participate in quiz bowls, take field trips, ride in horse shows and parades, and just have fun with your horse.

Record keeping is important. FFA and 4-H organizations have bonafide record-keeping systems for a horse project. You will learn all aspects of record keeping—from daily feeding to cash flow. Begin today keeping your records.

QUESTIONS

Answer the following questions using correct spelling and complete sentences.

1. What are the leadership organizations that affect the horse industry?
2. What are the equine organizations in your local community?
3. What does FFA and 4-H offer regarding horses?
4. What is a Supervised Agricultural Experience project?
5. Why is record keeping important in the horse industry?

EVALUATING

CHAPTER SELF-CHECK

Match the term with the correct definition. Place the letter by the term in the blank provided.

a. leadership
b. SAE
c. FFA
d. 4-H
e. record
f. net worth
g. expense
h. cash flow

_____ 1. A youth organization for students enrolled in agriculture education.

_____ 2. The amount of money coming in and going out in a given interval.

_____ 3. A youth organization sponsored by the Department of Agriculture and open to young people from the ages of 5 to 19.

_____ 4. The amount remaining after liabilities are subtracted from assets.

_____ 5. Supervised Agricultural Experience.

_____ 6. The position or guidance of a leader and the capacity or ability to lead.

_____ 7. A cost associated with owning a business or property.

_____ 8. A permanent account to perpetuate a knowledge of an act or event.

DISCOVERING

1. Select a leadership organization in your community, interview the lead person for that organization. List the purpose of the organization, the structure of the organization, and how decisions are made.

2. Identify the equine-related organizations in your local community and your state. Use all available resources to identify these groups. Prepare a document to list and describe these organizations. Present your findings in class.

3. Choose the appropriate equine project book and begin to record your materials.

4. Attend one or more horse meetings or seminars at the county or state level.

5. Attend one or more meetings of your school board and/or your county board. Observe the roles, issues, and activities.

6. Attend one or more political meetings (of your choice).

7. Register to vote and vote.

APPENDIXES

APPENDIX A

USEFUL WEB SITES FOR HAVING FUN WITH HORSES

A list of Web sites that may be useful in learning more about equine science follows. The list is intended to list examples and is by no means comprehensive.

Agriculture Directory: www.handilinks.com/cat1Agriculture.htm

Agriculture Online (Successful Farming): www.agriculture.com/

American Connemara Pony Society: www.nas.com/acps/

American Quarter Horse Association: www.aqha.com/

American Miniature Horse Association: www.minihorses.com/amha/

American Warmblood Society: www.americanwarmblood.org/

Appaloosa Horses: www.appaloosa.com

Arabian Horse Interactive: www.arabian-horses.com/

Aztec Horse Registry of American, Inc.: www.equi-site.com/azteca/

Canadian Haflinger Association: www.rr3.com/associations/breed/haflinger/

Census of Agriculture: govinfo.kerr.orst.edu/ag-stateis.html

Clydesdales Breeders of the U.S.A.: members.aol.com/clydesusa/

Cyberhorse: www.cyberhorse.net.au/

Electronic Zoo (all animals): netvet.wustl.edu/

eQuest: equest.remus.com/

EquineOnLine: www.equineonline.com/

Equine Rescue League: members.ao.com/gerlwindee/

Equine Sports: www.planethorse.com/sports.html

Equine World: www.equine-world.com/

Farm Journal: www.FarmJournal.com

Feednet (Feed and Nutrition): www.feednet.com/

FFA (National Organization): www.ffa.org/

Haynet: www.haynet.net/

Horse Breed Associations: www.countrybarn.com/

HorseNet: www.horsenet.com/

Horses (breeds): www.ansi.okstate.edu/breeds/horses-w.htm

HorsesOnLine: www.horsesonline.net/

HorseWeb: www.horseweb.com/

International Arabian Horse Association: www.iaha.com/

International Museum of the Horse: www.imh.org/

Interstate Publishers, Inc.: www.IPPINC.com

Irrigation Association: www.irrigation.org

Jr. Riders Journal: www.horse-country.com/

Lipizzan Horses: www.lipizzan.com/uslr.html

Morab Registry: www.morab.org/

National Agricultural Education Headquarters: www.teamaged.org

New Rider: www.newrider.com/

NetVet: netvet.wustl.edu/horses.htm

Pacific Quarter Horse Association: www.pcqha.com/

Palomino Horse Breeders of America, Inc.: www.palominohba.com/

The Tennessee Walking Horse: www.twhbea.com/

U.S. Department of Agriculture: www.usda.gov/

U.S. Department of Education: www.ed.gov/

U.S. Equestrian Team: www.uset.com/

U.S. Trotting Association: www.ustrotting.com/

Western Haflinger Association: www.daylanns.com/wha/wha.htm

APPENDIX B

NAMES AND ADDRESSES OF SELECTED HORSE BREED ASSOCIATIONS AND OTHER ORGANIZATIONS

American Andulasian Horse Association
6990 Manning Road
Economy, IN 47339

American Buckskin Registry
P. O. Box 3850
Redding, CA 96049

American Connemara Pony Society
2630 Hunting Ridge
Winchester, VA 22603

American Hackney Horse Society
4059 A Iron Works Road
Lexington, KY 40511

American Indian Horse Registry
Route 3, Box 64
Lockhart, TX 78644

American Miniature Horse Registry
6748 North Frostwood Parkway
Peoria, IL 61615

American Morgan Horse Association
P. O. Box 960
Shelburne, VT 05482

American Mustang and Burro Association
P. O. Box 788
Yucaipa, CA 92399

American Paint Horse Association
P. O. Box 961023
Fort Worth, TX 76161

American Quarter Horse Association
P. O. Box 200
Amarillo, TX 79168

American Saddlebred Horse Association
4093 Iron Works Pike
Lexington, KY 40511

American Shetland Pony Club
P. O. Box 3415
Peoria, IL 61614

American Shire Horse Association
2354 Court
Adel, IA 50003

American Suffolk Horse Association
4240 Goehring Road
Ledbetter, TX 78946

Appaloosa Horse Club
P. O. Box 8403
Moscow, ID 83483

Arabian Horse Registry of America
12000 Zuni Street
Westminster, CO 80234

Belgian Draft Horse Corporation of America
P. O. Box 335
Wabash, IN 46992

Clydesdale Breeders of the U.S.A.
17378 Kelley Road
Pecatonia, IL 61063

Florida Cracker Horse Association
P. O. Box 186
Newberry, FL 32669

Golden American Saddlebred Horse Association
4237 30th Avenue
Oxford Junction, IA 52323

Haflinger Association of America
14570 Gratiot Road
Hemlock, MI 48626

International Morab Breeders Association
34628 Highway 99
Eagle, WI 53119

Jockey Club
821 Corporate Drive
Lexington, KY 40503

Lippizan Association of North American
P. O. Box 1133
Anderson, IN 46015

National Pinto Horse Registry
P. O. Box 486
Oxford, NY 12820

National Spotted Saddle Horse Association
P. O. Box 898
Murfreesboro, TN 37153

North American Mustang Association and Registry
P. O. Box 850906
Mesquite, TX 75185

Palomino Horse Breeders of America
15233 E. Skelly Drive
Tulsa, OK 74116

Paso Fino Horse Association
P. O. Box 600
Bowling Green, KY 33834

Pinto Horse Association of America
1900 Samuels Avenue
Fort Worth, TX 76102

Standardbred Pleasure Horse Organization
31930 Lambson Forest Road
Galena, MD 21653

Tennessee Walking Horse Breeder's and Exhibitors' Association
P. O. Box 286
Lewisburg, TN 37091

Thoroughbred Horses for Sport
P. O. Box 160
Great Falls, VA 22066

Welsh Pony and Cob Society of America
P. O. Box 2977
Winchester, VA 22604

APPENDIX C

CARE OF THE MARE AND FOAL

Successfully producing healthy foal that grow into strong horses requires attention to the needs of the mare and foal. This is especially true because of the poor reproductive performance of horses.

MARE AT BREEDING

Age of first breeding is important in successfully foaling. Some mares are bred the first time as two-year-olds for foaling as three-year-olds. In most cases, it is best to breed mares the first time as three-year-olds. This means that they foal as four-year-olds.

Mares should be in good condition at the time of breeding. Some exercise is needed before breeding. Mares in pastures will likely get sufficient exercise if they run and play with other mares. Mares should not be too fat nor lack sufficient finish. Prior to breeding, an examination of the reproductive system by a qualified veterinarian or equestrian is recommended. Estrus (heat) in mares varies with the season of the year. Longer days with more hours of light stimulate estrus. Late April through early September is the typical breeding season. Short days and long nights result in mares failing to come into heat. A few horse breeders try to use artificial but this often results in limited success. Estrous in a mare typically cycles every 15 to 19 days in the summer months. Estrus lasts 3 to 7 days, and is the time that the mare will be receptive to the stallion. Artificial and hand breeding require the ability to detect heat.

A mare that has recently foaled will have a foal heat. This is a heat that is 7 to 10 days after foaling. Mares can be bred at this time if the delivery of the foal was normal and there are no lacerations in the cervix or vagina or the appearance of infection. If not bred at foal heat, the mare will again come into heat 25 to 30 days after foaling.

CARE OF THE PREGNANT MARE

A mare that has been successfully bred is pregnant. The time of pregnancy is known as gestation. Gestation lasts approximately 336 days. Some mares may have a shorter gestation; others longer. Detecting if breeding has been successful is important. It the mare is not bred, arrangements need to be made for another breeding. Pregnancy is indicated by: failure to come back into heat, rectal palpation by a trained person, ultrasound, and blood testing.

Pregnant mares are best turned out to a good pasture. Grain and supplements should be used to assure adequate nutrition. Mares should be kept in good condition–not too fat nor too thin. Broodmares need nutrients to meet the needs of their body as well as the developing fetus and nutrients to prepare for lactation. Mares bred the first time are typically continuing to grow themselves and need additional protein, vitamins, and minerals (especially calcium and phosphorus). Greatest fetus growth is in the last 100 days or so of gestation. Additional grain and protein and vitamin supplement may be needed at this time. A good indicator is the condition of the mare.

Immediately prior to and after foaling, the amount fed is reduced. Good quality hay and light bran feed are used at this time. If a mare is in a dry lot and without pasture, feed a legume hay (lespedeza, alfalfa, or clover) each day in addition to grain and supplement. The amount of hay to feed varies with the weight of the mare. An 800 pound mare needs 12 to 16 pounds a day. A mare weighing 1,000 pounds needs 15 to 20 pounds a day. A mare weighing 1,200 pounds needs 18-24 pounds of hay a day. The hay should be free of dust and mold. In some cases, grass or mixed grass-legume hay will be used. Since grass hay is usually lower in protein and minerals than legume hay, additional grain and supplement may be needed. In some cases, silage may be used as feed. Depending on the quality of the hay or pasture, gestating mares need grain and mineral mix at a rate equivalent to 5 to 7 pounds a day for an animal weighing 1,100 pounds. Grains may be a mix of crimped or crushed oats and coarsely cracked corn.

With good pasture and hay, no grain mix may be needed the first months of gestation. Protein supplement is often from cottonseed meal, soybean meal, linseed meal, or a commercially-prepared protein supplement. Trace minerals may be provided through mineralized salt. For a person with a few horses, it is likely best to buy a commercially-prepared feed that has been formulated for a pregnant mare.

The signs of approaching foaling are distended udder (14 to 30 days before foaling), depression in the area at the top of the buttocks (7 to 10 days before foaling), and full and loose vulva (a few days before foaling). As foaling gets close, the mare will become restless and may have milk dropping from her teats. About a month before foaling it is a good idea to up-date the mare's vaccination program. This may include a four-way booster against tetanus, sleeping sickness, influenza, and strangles. Some effects of the booster shots are present in the colostrum, which offers protection for the foal. Feed is reduced at foaling, with grain being a bran mix rather than heavy grain.

CARE OF THE LACTATING MARE

Mares need proper nutrition to maintain their body weight and produce sufficient milk for the foal. In some cases, a mare may be bred and growing a developing fetus at the same time she is nursing a foal.

The first milk produced by a mare after foaling is known as colostrum. It is higher in proteins, vitamin A, and other substances than the milk will contain later. Colostrum also contains antibodies that help keep a foal healthy. Colostrum is also beneficial to digestive system of a young foal.

After some reduction in feed at the time of parturition, the mare should be back to full feed in a 10 days. Feeding too much just after foaling can cause digestive problems in the mare and result in too much milk for the foal. After 10 days, the mare should be back to full feed with a little additional grain and mineral supplement. Of course, the mare needs quality hay at about the same rate as during gestation. Some producers buy a commercial that has been formulated specifically for lactating mares.

CARE OF THE FOAL

New foals need special care. Nature has provided the mare with instincts to provide much of the needed care. In carefully managed situations and after the foal has arrived and is breathing properly, rub the foal dry with warm towels. Place it on clean straw in a corner of the stall. Protect the foal's eyes from bright light. Under natural conditions, the umbilical cord drys and falls off in a few days. It is a good idea, however, to treat the naval cord with a solution of iodine (7% tincture of iodine) and dust it with an antiseptic powder. Proper treatment of the umbilical cord helps prevent naval infections.

Typically, a foal will be standing on its feet in 30 minutes or so after its birth. Its first instinct is to nurse. This is the desired behavior because the foal begins taking in colostrum. Some foals may need to be coaxed toward the mare's nipples. Weak foals may have to be bottle fed with mare's milk. Sometimes a person can hold weak foals up and they will nurse. A foal may weigh more than you think and require two people to hold it up without injury. (Newborn foal weight varies with breed, stage of development, and other conditions. Weight of a newborn is 50 to 90 pounds, with a few weighing more.)

The bowels of a foal should move 4 to 12 hours after its birth. If not, the foal may need an enema. The services of an equine specialist or veterinarian are likely needed at this point. Foals can also have diarrhea (known as scours). Diarrhea is caused by an infectious disease associated with unclean conditions–something gets into the digestive system and causes irritation. Scours will need to be controlled or the foal may become dehydrated and die. Treatment for scours in a foal is sometimes difficult. Keep the area clean. Get help from a qualified person.

Milk gives a foal a good start but is deficient in iron, copper, and other minor nutrients. Over a period of weeks, foals that do not get sufficient iron become anemic. At three weeks of age, most foals will nibble hay or grain. A commercially-prepared feed prepared especially for foals is likely best and can be gradually started at this time. The feed should be provided so that the foal can gain access to it away from the mare. Many equestrians use a creep system or tie the mare while the foal is fed. Foals should need free-access to salt and mineral mix. Quality legume hay and pasture also help a foal begin supplementing the mare's milk. At about a month or six weeks of age, a foal will likely eat a half pound of grain a day for each 100 pounds of weight. The rate of feeding increases gradually in preparation for weaning. (Feeding rate for the mare decreases at weaning.)

In addition to nutrition, health care is needed. Vaccinations for equine encephalomyelitis (three types) are given at 2 to 3 months of age. At 3 months, vaccinations for influenza, rabies, strangles, and tetanus are given. Vaccinations for other diseases may be needed if the diseases are prevalent in the area. A local equine specialist or veterinarian should be consulted about the vaccination program. Recommendations vary. For example, some authorities recommend that the strangles vaccination be given at 6 months of age.

Some training is begun only a few days after birth. At about 10 days, a halter can be put on the foal. After the foal is accustomed to the halter, it can be tied to one side of the stall for 15 to 30 minutes a day. Early training develops better discipline and makes an animal more receptive to future training. Always be patient but firm. Grooming may be a part of being tied. After the foal adjusts to being tied, lead it around with mare for a few days. When the foal appears ready, begin leading it separately from the mare. Kindness and consistent behavior toward the foal will help train a good horse!

Another part of training is to begin young foals with foot care. Handle and clean the feet of a foal from its first day. In some cases, trimming or rasping may be needed. Any injuries or problems should be properly handled. Handling a foal's feet begins preparing it for shoeing as a yearling or older. Depending on the surface they walk on and other conditions, shoes may be put on two or three-year-olds. Since a horse's foot continues to grow until five or six years old, the shoes will need to be reset at intervals until the feet reach mature size. Careful observation of foot growth and shoe fit is needed to assess when attention is required.

CARE OF WEANLINGS AND YEARLINGS

Foals are weaned at 5 to 7 months of age. Developing a good appetite for feed prior to weaning helps make weaning go smoother. The few months following weaning is a critical time in the nutrition of a foal. At weaning, a foal is known as a weanling. Usually, weanlings should receive 1 to 1½ pounds of grain and 1½ to 2 pounds of hay each day for each 100 pounds of weight. Amounts will vary based on breed, pasture condition, and how the weanling will be used as an adult. Ample protein, vitamins, and minerals should be in a weanlings ration. A commercially-available feed is likely best for small producers.

A yearling is a colt that has grown beyond the weanling stage but is less than a two-year-old. Yearlings need pasture, grain, and mineral supplement. In the winter, hay is used when pasture is not available. The rate of feeding is ½ to 1 pound of grain and 1 to 1½ pounds of hay per 100 pounds of weight.

Two-year-olds and three-year-olds are fed to continue yearling nutrition. In addition, training, grooming, and other practices are much a part of the life of a young horse.

Training continues in the weanling and yearling stages. A colt should become accustomed to its name and learn the meanings of spoken terms such as "whoa." A saddle blanket can be placed on the back to begin preparing the young horse for a saddle. Later, a saddle can be gently placed on the back.

In most cases, it is best to get help from an experienced horse trainer. Training becomes more demanding when horses are taught specific moves, gaits, and other behaviors.

APPENDIX D

GESTATION TABLE

Date Bred	Date Due, 336 Days	Date Bred	Date Due, 336 Days	Date Bred	Date Due, 336 Days
Jan. 1	Dec. 3	May 6	June 6	Sept. 3	Aug. 5
Jan. 6	Dec. 8	May 11	June 11	Sept. 8	Aug. 10
Jan. 11	Dec. 13	May 16	June 16	Sept. 13	Aug. 15
Jan. 16	Dec. 18	May 21	June 21	Sept. 18	Aug. 20
Jan. 21	Dec. 23	May 26	June 26	Sept. 23	Aug. 25
Jan. 26	Dec. 28	May 31	July 1	Sept. 28	Aug. 30
Jan. 31	Jan. 2	June 5	July 6	Oct. 3	Sept. 4
Feb. 5	Jan. 7	June 10	July 11	Oct. 8	Sept. 9
Feb. 10	Jan. 12	June 15	July 16	Oct. 13	Sept. 14
Fe. 15	Jan. 17	June 20	July 21	Oct. 18	Sept. 19
Feb. 20	Jan. 22	June 25	July 26	Oct. 23	Sept. 24
Feb. 25	Jan. 27	June 30	July 31	Oct. 28	Sept. 29
Mar. 2	Feb. 1	July 5	April 7	Nov. 2	Oct. 4
Mar. 7	Feb. 6	July 10	April 12	Nov. 7	Oct. 9
Mar. 12	Feb. 11	July 15	April 17	Nov. 12	Oct. 14
Mar. 17	Feb. 16	July 20	April 22	Nov. 17	Oct. 19
Mar. 22	Feb. 21	July 25	April 27	Nov. 22	Oct. 24
Mar. 27	Feb. 26	July 30	May 2	Nov. 27	Oct. 29
April 1	Mar. 3	Aug. 4	May 7	Dec. 2	Nov. 3
April 6	Mar. 8	Aug. 9	May 12	Dec. 7	Nov. 8
April 11	Mar. 13	Aug. 14	May 17	Dec. 12	Nov. 13
April 16	Mar. 18	Aug. 19	May 22	Dec. 1	Nov. 18
April 21	Mar. 23	Aug. 24	May 27	Dec. 22	Nov. 23
April 26	Mar. 28	Aug. 29	June 1	Dec. 27	Nov. 28
May 1	April 2				

Source: M. E. Ensminger. *Horses and Horsemanship*. Danville, IL: Interstate Publishers, Inc., 1999.

APPENDIX E

USING BODY MEASUREMENTS TO ESTIMATE WEIGHT

It is easy to estimate the weight of a horse from body measurements. Studies have been revealed that the results obtained by the method herewith outlined are within three percent of the actual weight made on scales. The procedure is as follows:

1. Measure the heart girth in inches (C in Figure E-1)
2. Measure the length of body from point of shoulder to point of buttocks (A to B in Figure E-1)
3. Use the above two measurements to calculate the weight of the horse according to the following formula:

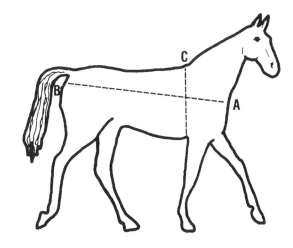

E-1. How and where to measure horses.

Heart girth × heart girth × length ÷ 300 + 50 lb = weight of horse

Example: A horse has a heart girth of 70 in. and a length of 65 in. What is its estimated weight?

Answer:

70 in. × 70 in. × 65 in. ÷ 300 + 50 lb = weight

4,900 × 65 = 318,500

318,500 ÷ 300 = 1,062 lb

1,062 + 50 = 1,112 lb body weight

Source: M. E. Ensminger. *Horses and Horsemanship.* Danville, IL: Interstate Publishers, Inc., 1999.

APPENDIX F

COMMON WEIGHT CONVERSIONS AND EQUIVALENTS USED IN EQUINE SCIENCE

Customary System

1 tablespoon (tbs)	= 3 teaspoons (tsp) or 0.5 fluid ounce (fl. oz)
1 cup	= 8 fl. oz
1 pint (pt)	= 2 cups or 16 fl. oz
1 quart (qt)	= 2 pt or 4 cups or 32 fl. oz
1 gallon (gal)	= 4 qt
1 bushel (bu)	= 8 gal or 32 qt

Metric System

1 milliliter (ml)	= 1 cubic centimeter (cc) or 1 gram (g)
1 centiliter (cl)	= 10 ml
1 deciliter (dl)	= 10 cl or 100 ml
1 liter (L)	= 10 dl or 1,000 ml or 1 kilogram (kg)
1 dekaliter (dal)	= 10 L
1 hectoliter (hl)	= 10 dal or 100 L
1 kiloliter (kl)	= 100 hl or 1,000 L or 1,000 kg

Equivalents

1 ounce	= 28.3495 grams
1 pound	= 453.59 grams or 0.45359 kilograms
1 kilogram	= 35.27 ounces or 2.2046 pounds
1 metric ton	= 2,204.6 pounds
1 hectare	= 2.47 acres
1 liter	= 1.057 quarts
1 liter	= 0.2642 gallons
1 gallon	= 3.79 liters
1 meter (m)	= 39.37 inches
1 acre	= 0.40468 hectares
1 inch	= 2.54 centimeters
1 centimeter (cm)	= 0.4 inch

Source: Jasper S. Lee and Diana L. Turner. *Introduction to World AgriScience and Technology.* Danville, IL: Interstate Publishers, Inc., 1997.

APPENDIX G

COMMON VOLUME MEASURES USED IN EQUINE SCIENCE

Customary Fluid Measures

4 gills (gi)	= 1 pint (pt)	= 28.88 cubic inches
2 pints (pts)	= 1 quart (qt)	= 57.75 cubic inches
4 quarts (qts)	= 1 gallon (gal)	= 231 cubic inches
31.5 gallons (gals)	= 1 barrel (bbl)	= 4.21 cubic feet
2 barrels (bbls)	= 1 hogshead (hhd)	= 8.42 cubic feet
7.5 gallons	= 1 cubic foot	= 1,728 cubic inches

Customary Dry Measures

2 pints	= 1 quart	= 67.2 cubic inches
8 quarts	= 1 peck (pk)	= 537.6 cubic inches
4 pecks (pks)	= 1 bushel (bu)	= 2,150.4 cubic inches or 1.244 cubic feet

Source: Jasper S. Lee and Diana L. Turner. *Introduction to World AgriScience and Technology.* Danville, IL: Interstate Publishers, Inc., 1997.

APPENDIX H

WEIGHT MEASURES COMMONLY USED IN EQUINE SCIENCE

Customary Weights	
Avoirdupois Weight:	
437.5 grains (gr)	= 1 ounce (oz)
16 ounces	= 1 pound (lb)
100 pounds	= 1 hundredweight (cwt)
2,000 pounds	= 1 ton (T)
2,240 pounds	= 1 long ton
Troy Weight:	
24 grains	= 1 pennyweight (pwt)
20 pennyweight	= 1 ounce
12 ounces	= 1 pound
Apothecaries Weight:	
20 grains	= 1 scruple (sc)
3 scruples	= 1 dram (dr)
8 drams	= 1 ounce
12 ounces	= 1 pound

Metric Weights	
1 centigram (cg)	= 10 milligrams (mg)
1 decigram (dg)	= 10 centigrams or 100 mg
1 gram (g)	= 10 dg, 100 cg, or 1,000 mg
1 kilogram (kg)	= 1,000 grams
1 metric ton (t)	= 1,000 kg

Source: Jasper S. Lee and Diana L. Turner. *Introduction to World AgriScience and Technology.* Danville, IL: Interstate Publishers, Inc., 1997.

GLOSSARY

A

Active immunity—Resistance to disease due to production of antibodies by the animal itself when antigens are present, either from disease or a vaccine.

Acute disease—A disease that is relatively severe but of short duration.

Aerobic—Living or occurring only in the presence of oxygen.

Aggressive behavior—conflict, submission, and fighting by horses.

Agribusiness—The business that surrounds agriculture.

Allergy—A hypersensitive or pathological reaction to environmental factors or substances.

Allowance race—A race in which there are both allowances and penalties with regard to the condition of the race, monies won or races won, or the date the last races were won.

Amino acid—Compound from which proteins are built.

Amniotic fluid—The fluid that surrounds the fetus inside the protective membranes.

Anaerobic—A bacteria or other organism that is capable of living without oxygen.

Anatomy—The science of the structure of a plant or an animal.

Anemia—A pathological deficiency in the oxygen-carrying materials of the blood.

Anestrus—An interval of sexual dormancy between two periods of estrus.

Animal agriculture—The production and marketing of animals.

Animal industry—The producing, buying, selling, and managing of animals and the products and services related to those activities.

Anthelmintic—The drugs used to treat internal parasites in horses.

Antibiotic—A chemical substance produced synthetically or by microorganisms that inhibits the growth of or destroys bacteria and other microorganisms.

Antibody—A specific substance produced within the body as a reaction to an invading antigen.

Antigen—Any substance that causes an immune response, the production of antibodies, when it is introduced into blood or tissues.

Archeohippus—An early ancestor of the modern day horse.

Artery—A blood vessel that carries blood away from the heart.

Artificial insemination—The delivery of semen into the vagina through artificial means.

Ascarid—A parasite commonly known as a roundworm.

Ass—A close relative of the horse.

Asset—A possession owned by an individual or business.

Atrophy—The degeneration of muscle tissue.

B

Backstretch—The stable area of a racetrack.

Bacteria—One-celled organisms that enter the body and may cause disease, such as mastitis.

Balanced ration—A feed that has all of the required nutrients for a specific animal.

Bald face—A white face that extends from the nostrils to the eyes.

Barn—A building that shelters harvested crops, livestock, machinery, etc.

Barren—Incapable of producing offspring.

Behavior—An action or response to stimulation.

Biology—The study of life.

Bit—The metal mouthpiece on a bridle. It is the most important part of the bridle.

Blacksmith—An individual who shoes horses and takes care of hooves.

Blaze—A broad white marking covering almost all of the forehead but not including the eyes or nostrils.

Blemish—Abnormality on a horse that does not affect the serviceability.

Blindness—Partial or complete loss of vision. It is characterized by cloudiness of the cornea.

Blow out—To work a horse fast over a short distance.

Bones—The separate parts of the hard tissue that form the skeleton of most full-grown animals.

Bone spavin—A bony enlargement located at the upper part of the hock on the inside and front of the hind leg.

Bowed tendon—A condition that affects a group of tendons and ligaments, but usually the superflexor tendon, the deep flexor tendon, and the suspensory ligament. It is located in the posterior space in the cannon region between the ankle and knee or between the hock and ankle.

Bray—The loud, harsh cry of an ass.

Breakage—In parimutuel betting, the odd cents left over after paying the successful bettors to the nearest 10 cents.

Breed—To produce an offspring; a group of animals or plants descended from common ancestors and having similar characteristics.

Breeder—Owner of the dam at the time of service who was responsible for selection of the sire to which she was mated.

Breed registry—An organization of breeders that record the lineage of their animals, protect the purity of the breed, encourage improvement of the breed, and promote interest in the breed.

Breeding horse—A horse used to produce offspring with certain genetics.

Breeze—To exercise a horse at moderate speed.

Bridle—A piece of equipment that is placed on the head of the horse and is used for guiding and control. It consists of the headstall, bit, and reins.

Glossary

Bridling—Placing a bridle on a horse.

Bronco—A wild, untamed horse.

Broodmare—A mare kept for breeding purposes.

Bucked kneed—A horse that displays its knees too far forward.

Burro—The Spanish translation of donkey.

Buying—The paying of money (or exchanging other valuables) to receive a product or service.

C

Calk—A substance on the outside of the front and heel of horseshoes designed to give the horse better footing and prevent slipping.

Cannon bone—The bone that extends from the knee or hock to the fetlock joint.

Canter—A slow, three-beat gait in which the two diagonal legs are paired to make one beat, which falls between the beats of the other unpaired legs.

Capillaries—Tiny, microscopic blood vessels that connect the arteries and veins.

Capital—Wealth in the form of money or property.

Carbohydrate—Any of a group of organic compounds, including sugars, starches, and cellulose, that aid in the use of proteins and fats and provide energy.

Career—The general direction of ones life work.

Career goal—The level of accomplishment one wants to make in his or her work.

Cartilage—A tough, white, fibrous, connective tissue attached to the articular surface of bone.

Cash flow—The amount of money coming in and going out in a given interval.

Cecum—The enlarged blind pouch forming the beginning of the large intestine.

Cell—The smallest structural unit of an organism.

Cervix—The neck-like part of the female reproductive tract that separates the uterus from the vagina.

Chestnut—The horny growth on the inside of the horse's legs above the knees and below the hocks.

Chromosome—The part of the nucleus of a cell that contains the genetic makeup that determines the transmission of hereditary characteristics.

Chronic disease—One of long duration or recurring often.

Chute—Straight part of the racetrack behind the barrier.

Circulation—Movement in a circle or circuit. Blood circulates throughout the entire body as a result of the heart's pumping action.

Claiming price—The predetermined price at which a horse in a claiming race must be sold, if it is claimed.

Claiming race—The conditions for the race provide that each entry may be bought at a predetermined price.

Cloning—The duplication of genetic material; producing an exact copy of an animal.

Club foot—The foot axis is too straight and the hoof is too upright.

Coffin bone—The bone of the foot of the horse, enclosed within the hoof.

Colic—A disease that causes abdominal pain in horses.

Color breed—A breed that does not breed true colors, such as Paints, Appaloosas, Buckskins, and others.

Colostrum—The first milk secreted by the mare's mammary glands for several days after birth that contains antibodies to protect the foal against diseases.

Colt—A young stallion up to three years of age (four years with Throughbreds).

Concentrate—A feedstuff that has a high energy value and low fiber (less than 18 percent).

Conception—Becoming pregnant.

Condition race—A race in which certain conditions are specified.

Condition score—A score given to a horse that is based on body fat.

Confinement—The restriction of space for an animal, such as a stall instead of pasture.

Conformation—The general body form and shape of a horse.

Congenital—A condition that exists at birth but was acquired during development in the uterus.

Consumer—A person who purchases and uses a product or service.

Contactual behavior—The result of seeking affection or protection.

Contagious disease—One spread by direct or indirect contact.

Contraction—The act of contracting; interaction of many parts of the nervous system and muscular system.

Coronary band—The area where the hoof meets the leg.

Coronet—The dividing line between the hoof and the leg of a horse.

Corpus hemorrhagicum—The eruption section of the ovary immediately after ovulation.

Corpus luteum—The follicle formed on the ovary at the site where an egg has been released.

Coupled—Two or more horses are grouped in the betting, and bets upon them are decided by the position of the foremost horse.

Creep feeding—Feeding system that prevents mature animals access from feed.

Cribbing—The grasping and gnawing of an object, such as a feeder or manger.

Croup—The rump of a horse.

Crude protein (CP)—The total amount of protein in a given feed.

Cryptorchid—A male horse in which one or both of the testicles are retained in the abdomen.

Curb—An enlargement at the rear of the leg just below the point of the hock.

Curb bit—A bit that utilizes a strap or chain to create leverage on the horse's tongue or jaw.

Curb chain—The portion of a curb bit that causes pressure against the chin groove.

D

Dam—The female parent of a horse.

Defecation—The process of moving fecal material from the bowels through the rectum and out the anus.

Dehydration—The removal of body fluids.

Demand—The desire for a commodity together with the ability to pay for it.

Dermatology—The study of skin and other body covers.

Diestrus—A period of sexual inactivity between two estrus cycles.

Digestible energy (DE)—That portion of the gross energy in a feed that is not excreted in the feces.

Digestion—The breakdown of foods by the digestive system to allow the nutrients to be utilized by the body.

Direct calling—The process of contacting a potential employer to ask if any job openings exist.

Disease—An abnormal condition of an animal or organism.

Disinfectant—A chemical that destroys microbes by breaking down cell proteins.

Dominance behavior—establishment of a hierarchy within a herd of horses.

Donkey—A small, domesticated ass.

Draft horse—A large horse that stands 14-2 to 17-2 hands, weighs 1400 pounds or more, and is used for work.

Dressage—The guiding of a horse through natural maneuvers by slight movements of the rider and without emphasis on the use of reins, hands, and feet.

Driver—Individual who guides a harness horse from the seat of a sulky or other vehicle.

Driving horse—A horse that is guided by a harness by a driver who is not mounted.

Dry-matter basis—The portion of feed that does not contain water.

Dun—Yellowish or gold body color with a black, brown, red, yellow, white, or mixed tail and mane.

Duodenum—The initial part of the small intestine.

E

Economic impact—The change made by the introduction of a resource to the total industry.

Economics—The science of the production, distribution, and consumption of goods and services and the related problems of labor, finance, and taxation.

Edema—An accumulation of fluids in tissue spaces.

Ejaculation—Process where semen is expelled from the body.

Elimination behavior—establishment by horses of an elimination area in a paddock or pasture.

Embryo—The early stages of development of an unborn organism.

Embryo transfer (ET)—The process of moving a developing embryo from a donor female to the uterus of a recipient female.

Employability—The potential for employment.

Encephalomyelitis—An inflammatory disease of the brain and spinal cord transmitted by mosquitoes.

Endocrinology—The study of the endocrine system.

Energy—Usable power.

English saddle—A saddle generally light in construction and flat, without a horn.

Entrepreneur—A person who manages and assumes the risk of a business.

Environmental behavior—relationship of horses to their surroundings.

Enzyme—A complex protein molecule that functions as a biochemical catalyst in living organisms without being used up itself.

Eohippus—A small, primitive, four-toed ancestor to the modern-day horse.

Equine—A horse.

Equitation—Being skilled in the riding, management, and care of a horse.

Equity—The value of a business or property minus the liabilities.

Equus—The genus of the contemporary horse family.

Esophagus—The opening or tube that extends down the pharynx through the thoracic cavity and diaphragm to the stomach.

Estrogen—A female hormone produced by the ovary and responsible for estrus behavior.

Estrous cycle—The time from one heat cycle to the next.

Estrus—(see Heat)

Evolution—The process of change over many years.

Expense—A charge or cost associated with a business or property.

Exerciser—A jockey or other rider who gallops horses in workouts.

External parasite—One that attacks the skin and body openings of the host.

F

Fallopian tubes—Ducts that connect the ovaries to the uterus and serve as a conduit for the eggs to travel after ovulation.

Farrier—A person who shoes horses and takes care of hooves.

Feed—A material an animal eats for growth, repair, energy, and the maintenance of life.

Feedstuff—A material or mixture of materials made into or used as food.

Fence—A barrier that limits the distance an animal can travel or move.

Feral horse—An animal, or its offspring, that was domesticated, but escaped and became wild.

Fertilization—The union of a sperm and an egg.

Fetlock—The joint above the hoof of a horse.

Fetus—The more advanced stages of development of the unborn animal.

FFA—An organization that offers students many opportunities while they are enrolled in agricultural education.

Fiber—The material left after food has been digested.

Field—When there are more horse entered in a race than there are positions on the odds board.

Filly—A female horse up to three years of age that has never been bred.

Fistulous withers—An inflammation or infection of the withers.

Flank—The fleshy part of the side between the ribs and the hip.

Flat racing—Racing on a flat, oval track as opposed to racing over obstacles.

Fluke—A flat, leaf-shaped parasite that affects horses.

Flushing—The process of removing embryos from a mare in preparation for embryo transfer.

Foal—A young unweaned horse of either gender.

Foal creep—A feeder designed in such a manner that mature animals cannot access the feed.

Foal heat—The heat that occurs after parturition.

Foaling—The act of a mare giving birth.

Follicle—A small sac which appears on the surface of the ovary and contains the developing ovum.

Follicle stimulating hormone (FSH)—A hormone secreted by the anterior pituitary gland which stimulates the development of one or more follicles in females.

Forage—Food primarily from the leaves of plants for domestic animals.

Forging—Striking the end of the branches or the undersurface of the shoe of the forefoot with the toe of the hind foot.

Founder (laminitis)—An inflammation of the sensitive tissue under the horny wall of the hoof. All the feet may be affected, but the front feet are most susceptible. This can be caused by too much carbohydrate intake.

4-H club—A youth organization sponsored by the U.S. Department of Agriculture and open to young people from the ages of 5 to 19.

Frog—The triangular-shaped formation in the sole of the horse's hoof.

Fungi—A unicellular organism that causes disease on the exterior of the body.

Furlong—A unit of measurement of 1/8 mile or 220 yards.

Futurity—Nominations for a specific race made a long time before the race is run.

G

Gait—A particular way the horse moves, either natural or artificial, which is

Glossary

characterized by a distinctive rhythmic action of the feet and legs.

Gallop—A fast, four-beat gait which is also called the run and is the fastest gait.

Gamete—A sex cell.

Gaskin—The area of the horse's rear leg just below the thigh and stifle.

Gastric juices—The digestive fluids in the stomach used to assist in breaking down food.

Gelding—A male horse castrated prior to sexual maturity.

Gene—A functional hereditary unit that occupies a fixed location on a chromosome.

Genetic engineering—The process of changing an organism's genetic makeup.

Genotype—The genetic make-up of an animal.

Gestation—The period when the mare carries the fetus before giving birth.

Girth—The distance around the barrel of the horse.

Glucose—A simple sugar; the ultimate source of energy for most cells.

Goal—The purpose toward which an endeavor is directed.

Goal setting—Describing what one wants to achieve in life.

Grade horse—An animal that has no specific heritage and is not registered to any breed registry; may have a low value.

Grain—A small, hard seed or fruit produced by a cereal plant, such as corn, wheat, oats, barley, etc.

Grass—Any of various plants having slender leaves.

Grazing pressure—The animal-to-forage ratio at a specific time.

Groom—To wash, brush, comb, and care for an animal; a person whose duties include tending, feeding, and currying horses.

Grullo—Body color that is smoky. Each hair is mouse colored. The mane and tail are black and usually the lower legs are black and often there is a dorsal stripe.

Gymkhana—Competing in various games while on horseback.

H

Hack—A horse used for riding on trails and roads; poor quality horse.

Hackamore—A bit-less bridle used on western horses and young horses when they are being broken.

Halter—A device used for leading and tying a horse.

Haltering—Placing a halter on a horse.

Hand—A height measurement for a horse. The measurement is taken at the top of the wither to the ground. A hand equals 4 inches.

Hand-feeding—Providing an animal with a given amount of feed each day.

Handicapped race—A race in which the competing horses are assigned weights to carry that will equalize their chances of winning.

Hand gallop—An extended canter, but the horse remains collected.

Hand mating—The process of breeding horses by handling their movements.

Harness racing—A race in which trotters or pacers pull a driver riding on a sulky around a track.

Health—The overall condition of an organism at a given time.

Heart girth—The circumference of the barrel of a horse just behind the withers and in front of the back.

Heat (estrus)—The period when the female is receptive to mating.

Heredity—The passage of traits from one generation to the next.

Heterozygous—Having different alleles for a single trait and therefore producing two or more different kinds of gametes.

Hinny—The offspring of a stallion and a jennet.

Hitch—To fasten.

Hobbles—A type of restraint used on horses to prevent movement of legs and feet.

Hock—The large joint halfway up the hind leg of a horse.

Homozygous—Having identical alleles and therefore producing identical gametes.

Hoof—The foot of a horse.

Hoof pick—An instrument used to clean hooves.

Hormone—A chemical that is essential for normal growth and development in the body.

Hot walker—A mechanical device or person that directs a horse in a circle at a slow pace to cool the animal.

Hunt Seat—A class of equitation in which the rider sits erect and balanced (leaning forward with faster gaits), the hands are held low, and a forward seat English saddle with knee rolls and short stirrups is used.

Hunter—A type of riding that involves a specific type of equipment and attire.

Hybrid—An offspring produced from breeding two different breeds.

I

Immunity—A resistance to a specific disease.

Imprinting—A learning mechanism in which a young animal is exposed to a specific stimuli in the thereby establishing an irreversible behavior pattern.

Infection—An invasion of the body by microorganisms.

Inflammation—A swelling, redness, and heating of an area of the body.

Influenza—A contagious viral disease characterized by respiratory problems.

Ingestive behavior—approach of horses in timing and procedure of taking in food and water.

Inherit—To receive genetic materials from parents.

Insemination—The natural placing of semen in the vagina of a mare.

Internal parasite—One that lives in the internal organs, body cavities, and tissues.

J

Jack—A male ass.

January 1 birth date—The month and day used in figuring the age of a horse regardless of the month in which the foal was born.

Jennet—A female ass.

Jockey—A professional horse rider in races.

Job—The specific work performed in an occupation for compensation.

Job interview—A personal appearance of the job applicant with the employer.

Jog—A slow, steady, jolting gait.

Jumper—A horse used to jump objects.

Juvenile—A horse that is two years old.

K

Kicking—The act of a horse striking at something with their legs.

Kinesiology—The study of muscles and their movement.

L

Lactation—The production of milk after parturition.

Laminitis—(see Founder)

Glossary

Large intestine—Includes the cecum where hay and other roughage is digested in horses.

Larynx—The area of the respiratory tract between the pharynx and the trachea.

Leadership—The position or guidance of a leader and the capacity or ability to lead.

Leading—Involves getting a horse to move or walk upon command by pulling on the halter or reins.

Legume—A plant, such as bean, peanut, and clover, with nitrogen-fixing nodules on the roots, which makes use of the atmospheric nitrogen possible.

Lesion—A wound or injury; a pathological alteration of tissue.

Libido—Sex drive.

Ligament—Tough, fibrous tissue that connects bone or cartilages to a joint.

Light horse—A horse that stands 14-2 to 17 hands, weighs 900 to 1400 pounds and is used primarily for riding, driving, showing, racing, or pleasure.

Liniment—A solution used to treat mild strains and irritations.

Longe—A long rope fastened to a horse's head and held by the trainer, who causes the horse to move around in a circle.

Longeing—The act of exercising a horse at the end of a rope; also called lunging.

Lope—The western adaption of a very slow canter.

Low ringbone—A bony enlargement on the pastern bones.

Luteal phase—The period of time during the estrus cycle when the corpus luteum is producing progesterone.

Lymph node—The gland-like bodies found in the lymphatic system that produces lymphocytes and monocytes.

M

Maiden mare—A female horse that has not been bred.

Maintenance—No loss or gain, to keep in a certain condition.

Mange—An external parasite that affects the skin.

Manger—A box or trough to hold hay.

Mare—A mature female horse after the age of four (five years with Throughbreds).

Marketing—The activity of buying or selling.

Martingale—The strap of a horse's harness passing from the noseband to the girth between the forelegs, to keep the horse from rearing or throwing back the head.

Mastication—The process of chewing and breaking down food.

Match race—A race between two horses owned by different parties.

Meiosis—Division process in sex cells.

Merychippus—The desert horse; an early ancestor of the modern day horse.

Mesentery—Membranes that encompass the small intestine and hold it in place.

Mesohippus—A three-toed ancestor of the modern day horse.

Metabolism—The chemical change in cells, tissues, and organs that provides energy for living organisms for growth, repair, and maintenance.

Metabolizable energy (ME)—Energy from the feed that is useful to the animal for growth, production, and reproduction.

Metestrus—The period following the estrus phase (heat) during which ovulation occurs in which the ovaries release the ova through the bursa sac and down two oviducts.

Mineral—An inorganic substance occurring naturally in the earth, such as calcium, phosphorus, etc.

Miniature horse—A small horse no more than 32 inches in height.

Mitosis—A type of cell division for growth and repair, a sequential process of cell division.

Monocular—Each eye is independent of the other and can see different pictures.

Motility—The ability to move or capability of movement.

Mounting—The act of getting on a horse.

Mucous—The viscous suspension of mucin, water, cells, and inorganic salts secreted as a protective, lubricant coating by glands in the mucous membrane.

Mule—The hybrid offspring of a jackass and a mare.

Muscle—Body tissue that contracts and expands to produce bodily movement.

Mustang—A horse native to the Western Plains of the U.S. and largely of Spanish breeding.

N

Nasal—A passage in the nose.

National Research Council (NRC)—A group that examines the literature and the current practices of animal nutrition.

Navicular bone—A small bone located in the horse's foot.

Nerves—Bundles of fibers interconnecting the central nervous system and the organs and parts of the body.

Nervous system—A complex set of nerves, organs, and sensory devices that cause different behaviors to occur.

Net energy (NE)—That energy fraction of the feed that is left after the fecal, urinary, gas and heat losses are subtracted from the gross energy.

Net worth—The amount remaining after liabilities are subtracted from assets.

Noncontagious disease—One caused by nutritional, physiological, environmental, or morphological problems; not spread by casual contact.

Nucleus—The control center of the cell.

Nutrient—A substance that provides nourishment to the body.

Nutrient deficiency—A shortage of any necessary substance that provides nourishment to the body.

Nutrition—The process of nourishing or being nourished.

O

Occupation—The specific work in a career that can be given a title.

Olfactory—The sense of smell.

One ear bridle—A bridle often used on working stock horses; split ear bridle.

Open mare—A mare that was not bred or did not settle in the previous season.

Organ—A collection of tissues that work together to perform certain functions.

Osteochondrosis—A metabolic disease of cartilage resulting in bone and joint defects.

Ovary—The female reproductive organ.

Oviduct—A tube through which ova travel from the ovary to the uterus.

Ovulation—The female reproduction process of developing and releasing eggs.

Ovum—The female reproductive cell or egg; called a gamete.

P

Pace—A rapid, two-beat gait in which the front and hind feet on the same side start and stop together.

Paddock—A small field or enclosure near a stable.

Pair—The term describing two horses ridden side-by-side or hitched together.

Palatability—Acceptable to taste.

Palpate—To examine by touch.

Parahippus—The upland horse; an ancestor to the modern horse.

Parasite—A small, multicellular organism that lives in or on another animal (host) at the expense of the host.

Parimutuel—The system of racetrack betting that returns to successful bettors the precise amount of money wagered by unsuccessful bettors after deductions of commission and breakage.

Parturition—The act of giving birth.

Pastern—The part of the horse's leg between the fetlock and the coronet.

Pasture—A grassy area designated for grazing.

Pasture renovation—The practice of reviving a pasture through chiseling, discing, or applying herbicide, lime, fertilizer, and reseeding.

Pathogen—Any microorganism or virus that can cause disease.

Pedigree—A record of the ancestry of a specific horse.

Pelham—A single-bitted, double-reined bridle used on hunters, polo ponies, and pleasure horses.

Penis—The stallion's reproductive organ that is used to deposit semen in the vagina of the mare.

Performance—The act of performing.

Phenotype—The physical or outward appearance of an animal.

Physiology—The study of the function of the body.

Pinto—A multi-colored spotted horse.

Placenta—An organ that develops in the female during pregnancy lining the uterus and holding the fetus. The placenta is expelled after birth.

Pleasure horse—A horse that is used for personal enjoyment.

Pliohippus—The first one-toed ancestor to the modern day horse.

Plug—A horse of poor conformation and common breeding; an old, worn-out horse.

Pneumonia—Any inflammatory disease of the lungs.

Poll—The head area.

Polo—A game played by two teams of three or four players on horseback. Players are equipped with long-handled mallets for driving a small, wooden ball through the opponent's goal.

Polyestrous—Having many heat cycles during the year.

Pony—A small horse that stands under 14-2 hands and weighs 500 to 900 pounds.

Post mortem—An examination to determine the cause of death or the extent of damage from disease.

Progeny—The offspring of one or both parents.

Progesterone—The hormone that is released by the ovary before the fertilized egg is implanted.

Protein—A chain of units called amino acids, which are essential for growth.

Puberty—The age when an animal can physically reproduce; sexual maturity.

Pulse—The contraction and expansion of the arteries.

Q

Quarter Horse—A powerfully built breed of horses that are adapted for tremendous speed at short distances.

Quittor—A festering of the foot anywhere along the border of the coronet.

R

Rack—The fastest, most popular, four-beat gait.

Ration—The amount of feed an animal is given.

Record—A permanent account to perpetuate a knowledge of acts or events.

Recreation—The use of a horse to provide enjoyment and relaxation.

Rectum—The terminal part of the intestine.

Registered—A horse whose name, along with the name and proper identification of its sire and dam, is recorded with a breed registry.

Reins—The control mechanism that connect the bridle to the rider.

Reproduction—The process by which an animal produces a new individual.

Respiration—The act of taking in oxygen and removing carbon dioxide; breathing.

Restrain—To limit or restrict movement.

Restraint—A device used to control and handle horses.

Roan—A uniform mix of white with black and red hairs on the body of a horse.

Rodeo—An event that consists of bronc riding, roping, barrel racing, and other exciting activities.

Rotational grazing—A system of heavy grazing followed by periods of no grazing.

Roughage—A coarse feed that is high in fiber.

Running walk—The fast, four-beat, ground-covering walk characteristic of the Tennessee Walking Horse.

S

Saddle—A leather seat that makes horseback riding safer and more comfortable.

Saddle Seat—A class of equitation in which the rider sits back in the saddle and remains vertical through all gaits.

Saddling—Properly placing a saddle on a horse.

Safety—The prevention of accidents and the freedom from danger, injury, or damage.

Saliva—A substance that moistens and lubricates food for swallowing.

Science—The observation, identification, description, experimental investigation, and theoretical explanation of natural phenomenon.

Self-feeding—Involves placing a large quantity of feed in a feeder and allowing the animal to eat as much and as frequently as it wishes.

Selling—The receiving of monetary resources to provide a product or service.

Semen—Sperm cells along with fluids from accessory glands.

Sexual behavior—courtship and mating process in horses.

Shadowing—The activity of following a person to observe exactly what is involved in an occupation.

Sheath—The double fold of skin that covers the penis.

Shelter—Something that covers, protects, or defends.

Shod—A horse with shoes on its feet.

Shoeing—The act of placing shoes on the feet of a horse.

Shy—To suddenly jump or recoil.

Silage—Fermented roughage.

Sire—The male parent of a horse.

Slow gait—A four-beat gait with each of the feet striking the ground separately.

Snaffle bit—A bit that works with direct action on the horse's mouth.

Specialty horse—A horse not traditional in size or not used for traditional purposes in today's society.

Sperm—Male sex cells.

Stable—A building in which horses or cattle are sheltered and fed.

Stag—A male horse castrated after reaching sexual maturity.

Glossary

Stall—A compartment within a facility for one animal.

Stallion—A male horse over four years of age (five years for Thoroughbreds).

Standardbred—A breed of horses developed for trotting or pacing.

Steeplechase—A cross-country race over obstacles, which consists of water, hurdles, and other jumps.

Sterile—Germ-free environment.

Stifle joint—The joint just behind the rear flank that is extremely important in the movement of the hind quarters.

Stillbirth—A foal that is born dead.

Stirrup—The part of the saddle used to mount and to position the rider's feet.

Stock Seat—A class of equitation in which the rider's body position is straight and relaxed, the heel is lower than the toe in the stirrup, and only one hand is used on the reins.

Strangles—An infectious disease of horses caused by bacterium and characterized by inflammation and abscesses in the mouth.

Stud—A stallion used for breeding purposes.

Sulky—A light-weight, two-wheeled cart with a seat for a driver.

Supervised Agricultural Experience (SAE)—A program where a student enrolled in agriculture education has an ongoing agricultural project throughout his or her high school career.

Supplement—A feed material that is high in a specific nutrient.

Supply—The amount or quantity of a commodity available for purchase at a given price.

T

Tack—Equipment used on a horse, such as a saddle and bridle and other equipment.

Testicles—The male reproductive glands that produce sperm necessary for reproduction.

Tetanus—An acute, often fatal infectious disease caused by a bacillus that enters the body through wounds. This disease is sometimes called "lock jaw."

Thoroughbred—A breed of horses that usually race on a flat track.

Throat latch—The part of the bridle under the throat that connects the bridle to the head.

Thrush—An inflammation of the frog of the foot caused by a fungus.

Tissue—A group of cells that are alike in activity and structure.

Total digestible nutrients (TDN)—The energy density of a feedstuff. It takes into account the fat, protein, and carbohydrates in the feed.

Toxic—Poisonous.

Trachea—The windpipe.

Trailer sour—A horse that is afraid of trailers.

Triple Crown—Comprised of three annual races for three-year olds—the Kentucky Derby, the Preakness, and the Belmont Stakes.

Trot—A rapid, two-beat, diagonal gait in which the front foot and the opposite hind foot take off at the same split second and strike the ground at the same time.

U

Unsoundness—Anything that prevents a horse from performing or functioning.

Ureter—The part of the urinary system that allows urine to move into the bladder.

Urethra—The channel through which urine, and semen in the male, is discharged.

Urine—A fluid that contains nitrogenous waste and other waste products.

Uterus—A part of the female reproductive tract. It houses fertilized eggs for development.

V

Vaccination—An inoculation with a vaccine to protect against disease.

Vaccine—Suspensions of bacteria or viruses that create an antibody when injected into an animal.

Vagina—The outer portion of the female reproductive tract that receives the penis and semen during mating.

Vein—A blood vessel that carries blood back to the heart.

Veterinarian—An animal health care professional.

Virus—A microscopic, contagious organism that enters the body through the air, the blood, water, or other conduits.

Vital signs—An indicator of an animal's health; consists of body temperature, pulse rate, and respiration.

Vitamin—A substance essential for an animal's growth and development.

Vulva—The external opening to the vagina.

W

Walk—A slow, flat-footed, four-beat gait.

Water—A clear, colorless, nearly odorless, and tasteless liquid that is essential for plants and animals.

Weaning—The gradual substituting of food for mother's milk.

Weanling—A foal that is weaned from its mother.

Weed—Any undesired, uncultivated plant.

Well-being—providing care so that basic needs are met without injury to health.

Western saddle—A curved, deep seat to provide all-day comfort while working livestock and a horn used to anchor a rope.

Wet mare—A mare that has foaled during the current breeding season and is nursing the foal.

Weymouth—A double-bitted, double-reined bridle used primarily for gaited horses.

Wind sucker (cribber, stump sucker)—A horse that bites or presses its upper front teeth against an object, while sucking air into its stomach. The condition is also referred to as cribbing, crib biting, wind sucking.

Wind-puff (windgall)—A soft enlargement at the ankle joint.

Withers—The highest part of the backbone.

Work horse—A strong animal used to plow, pull, and do many other physical activities.

Wound—A rupture or physical tear to the tissue.

Y

Yearling—A horse between one and two years of age.

Z

Zebra—An animal native to Africa with notable black and white stripes.

Zygote—The cell formed from the union of sperm and egg.

BIBLIOGRAPHY

American Youth Horse Council. *Horse Industry Handbook: A Guide to Equine Care and Management.* Lexington, KY: American Youth Horse Council, Inc., 1993.

Baker, MeeCee and Mikesell, Robert E. *Animal Science Biology and Technology.* Danville, IL: Interstate Publishers, Inc., 1996.

Barnes, Robert F.; Miller, Darrell A.; and Nelson, C. Jerry. *Forages.* 5th ed. Ames, IA: Iowa State University Press, 1995.

Cheeke, Peter R. *Natural Toxicants in Feeds, Forages, and Poisonous Plants.* Danville, IL: Interstate Publishers, Inc., 1998.

Davidson, B. and Foster, C. *The Complete Book of the Horse.* Lanham, MD: Barnes and Noble, 1994.

Drache, Hiram M. *History of U.S. Agriculture.* Danville, IL: Interstate Publishers, Inc., 1996.

English, J. E. *Complete Guide for Horse Business Success.* Grand Prairie, TX: Equine Research, Inc., 1995

Ensminger, M. E. *Animal Science.* Danville, IL: Interstate Publishers, Inc., 1991.

Ensminger, M. E. *Animal Science Digest.* Danville, IL: Interstate Publishers, Inc., 1991.

Ensminger, M. E. *Feeds and Nutrition Digest.* Clovis, CA: Ensminger Publishing Company, 1990.

Ensminger, M. E. *Horses and Horsemanship.* Danville, IL: Interstate Publishers, Inc., 1999.

Ensminger, M. E. The Stockman's Handbook. Danville, IL: Interstate Publishers, Inc., 1992.

Germer, Jerry. *Country Careers.* New York, NY: John Wiley and Sons, 1993.

Greer, William J. and Baker, James K. *Animal Health: A Layperson's Guide to Disease Control.* 2nd ed. Danville, IL: Interstate Publishers, Inc., 1992.

Harrington, Rodney B. *Animal Breeding: An Introduction.* Danville, IL: Interstate Publishers, Inc., 1995.

Herman, H.A.; Mitchell, Jere R.; and Doak, Gordon A. *The Artificial Insemination and Embryo Transfer of Dairy and Beef Cattle*. Danville, IL: Interstate Publishers, Inc., 1994.

Herren, Ray. *The Science of Animal Agriculture*. Albany, NY: Delmar Publishers, Inc., 1994.

Hunsley, Roger E. and Beeson, W. Malcolm. *Livestock Judging, Selection and Evaluation*. 4th ed. Danville, IL: Interstate Publishers, Inc., 1992.

Kreitler, B. *50 Careers with Horses—from Accountant to Wrangler*. Ossining, NY: Breakthrough Publications, 1995.

Lee, Jasper S.; Embry, Chris; Hutter, Jim; Pollock, Judy; Rudd, Rick; Westrom, Lyle; and Bull, Austin. *Introduction to Livestock and Poultry Production*. Danville, IL: Interstate Publishers, Inc., 1996.

Lee, Jasper S.; Leising, James G.; and Lawver, David E. *AgriMarketing Technology*. Danville, IL: Interstate Publishers, Inc., 1994.

Lewis, L. D. *Feeding and Care of the Horse*. 2nd ed. Baltimore, MD: Williams and Wilkins, 1996.

McKinnon, Angus and Voss, James. *Equine Reproduction*. Malvern, PA: Lea and Febiger, 1992.

Morgan, Elizabeth M.; Chelewski, Ray E.; Lee, Jasper S.; and Wilson, Elizabeth. *AgriScience Explorations*. Danville, IL: Interstate Publishers, Inc., 1998.

Mowrey, R. A. *Horse Judging Manual*. Raleigh, NC: North Carolina State University, Cooperative Extension Service, 1995.

Parker, Rick. *Equine Science*. Albany, NY: Delmar Publishers, 1997.

Phipps, Lloyd J. and Miller, Glen M. *AgriScience Mechanics*. Danville, IL: Interstate Publishers, Inc., 1998.

Spaulding, C. E. A Veterinary Guide for Animal Owners. Emmaus, PA: Rodale Press, Inc., 1996

Taylor, Robert E. *Scientific Farm Animal Production*. 5th ed. Englewood Cliffs, NH: Prentice Hall, 1995.

____. *Chronicle Agricultural Occupations Guidebook*. Moravia, NY: Chronicle Guidance Publications, Inc., 1997.

____. *The Horse Industry Handbook: A Guide to Equine Care and Management*. Lexington, KY: American Youth Horse Council, 1994.

INDEX

A

Age
    determination of, 42-43
    January 1 birthdate, 42
Amino Acids, 53
Anatomy, 28
Animal Health, 38, 79-100
Animal Welfare, 22
Artificial Insemination, 106, 113-115
Associations, Breed Registry, 247-250

B

Balancing Ration, 60-64
Barns and Stables, 123-126
Barrel Racing, 8, 161, 163
Behavior, 81-82
Biology, 25-37
Body Condition, 39, 227-229
Bones, 29-30
Breathing Rate of a Horse, 80, 84
Breed Associations and Organizations, 247-250
Breeding, 6, 110-116
Breeds, Draft Horses
    Belgian, 147, 184-185, 189
    Clydesdale, 185
    Percheron, 184
    Shire, 186
    Suffolk, 186
Breeds, Light Horses
    American Quarter Horse, 7, 165-166, 215
    American Saddlebred, 166-167
    Appaloosa, 167-168
    Arabian, 168-169
    Buckskin, 169
    Connemara, 169-170
    Hackney Pony, 170
    Miniature Horse, 7, 181, 186-187
    Morgan, 170-171
    Paint Horse, 8, 171-172, 193
    Paso Fino, 172-173
    Pinto Horse, 173
    Shetland Pony, 174
    Spanish Mustang, 174-175
    Standardbred, 175-176, 214
    Tennessee Walking Horse, 176-177
    Thoroughbred, 7, 177, 216
    Welsh Pony, 178
Breeds, Long-ears
    donkey, 27, 28, 187
    mule, 28, 184, 187, 189
Bridles, 128-129
Bridling the Horse, 144-145
Buildings and Equipment, 99, 119-130
Business Aspects, 151-158
Buying and Selling, 157-158

C

Canter, 225-226
Carbohydrates, 52-53
Careers in Equine Science, 193-206
Care of the Mare and Foal, 251-255
Circulatory System, 32-33
Cloning, 116
Colostrum, 38
Conformation, 41-42

D

Dermatological System, 37
Digestive System, 33-35
Diseases and Ailments, 84-96
Draft Horses, 5, 155, 183, 184-186
Dressage, 163-164

E

Economics, 151-158
Embryo Transfer, 115
Endocrine System, 37
Eohippus, 9
Equipment, 19, 99, 119-130
Equitation, 137-146, 221-232
Estrus, 108-109, 251
Examination Procedures, 96-97
External Parts of a Horse, 29

F

Facilities and Equipment, 99, 119-130
Fats, 53
Feed and Water Facilities, 51, 58-60
Feeding, 58-60, 252-253, 254, 255
Feeds, 16, 26, 49-51, 62, 252-253, 254

Fences, 70, 74-76
Feral, 10-11, 188
Fertilization, 106
FFA, 235, 237, 239-241
Foal, 38-39, 120, 222, 253-255
Foaling, 251-255
Foot, 97-99
Forage, 71-72
4-H Club, 235, 238-240

G
Gaits of the Horse, 225-227
Gallop, 225-226
Genetic Engineering, 116
Genotype, 27
Gestation, 111-112
Gestation Table, 256
Getting a Job, 203-206
Grain, 18, 49-50
Grazing Systems, 72-74
Grooming, 126-127, 140-142
Gymkhana, 164

H
Halter, 129-130
Hand, 43-44, 162
Hand Gallop, 225
Health, 19, 79-100
Heat, 108-109, 251
Height, Measurement of, 43-44, 162
History and Development of the Horse, 1-2, 8-11, 48
  early, in North America, 10-11
  origin, 9-10
Hoof, 40, 97-99
Horsemanship, 137-146, 221-232
Hunt Seat, 224-225

I
Industry, 15-20, 154-155
Internet Addresses, 245-246

J
Jog, 224

L
Lactation, 66, 112, 253
Light Horses, 162-177
Long-ears, 27, 28, 184, 187, 189
Longeing, 130, 138-139
Lope, 224

M
Measuring Horses, 43-44, 162, 257
Merychippus, 9
Mesohippus, 9
Metric Conversions, 258-260
Mineral Functions and Deficiencies, 54-57
Minerals, 54-58
Mounting, 142-144, 229
Muscles, 30-31

N
Nervous System, 35-37
Nutrients, 51-58, 60-62, 64-66
Nutrition, 47-66

O
Occupations, 198-199, 200-202
Organization, 235-240
Ownership, 20-21

P
Pace, 225-226
Parahippus, 9
Parasites, 92-95
  external, 92-95
  internal, 95
Parts of a Horse, 29
Parturition, 112
Pasture Management, 69-76
Pearson Square Method, 63-64
Phenotype, 27
Physiology, 28
Pleasure Horses, 5
Pliohippus, 9
Protein, 53, 62
Puberty, 109-110

R
Racehorses, 212-215
Racing, 209-218
Rack, 227
Ration, Balancing of, 60-64
Record Keeping, 241-242
Recreational Horses, 161-178
Reproduction, 37, 103-116
Reproductive Organs, 107-108
  mare, 107-108
  stallion, 107
Respiratory System, 32
Riding, 229-232
Roughage, 50

Running Walk, 227

S
Saddles, 127-128, 223-224
Saddle Seat, 223-224
Saddling Mount, 142-144, 229
Safety, 133, 135-136, 147
Scientific Classification, 27-28
Shadowing, 200
Showing, 221
Size, Determination of, 43-44, 257
Skeleton of a Horse, 30
Slow Gait, 227
Soundness, 41-42
Specialty Horses, 7, 183-190
Stock Seat, 224
Supervised Agricultural Experience (SAE), 240-241
Supplements, 51

T
Tack and Equipment, 99, 126-130, 140-142, 227
Teeth, 42-43
Temperature of a Horse, 80, 84
Total Digestible Nutrients (TDN), 60-62
Triple Crown, 213
Trot, 225-226
Types and Classes of Horses, 3-5

U
Unsoundness, 41
Uses of Horses, 1, 5, 7, 10-11

V
Vaccinations, 81
Vital Signs, 80, 83-84
Vitamins, 58

W
Walk, 225-226
Water, 51, 65
Weanling, 255
Weight, Determination of, 257
Weights and Measures, 258-260
Well-being, 22
Wild Horses, 10-11, 188
Work Horses, 5, 155, 183, 184-186

Y
Yearling, 255